Release 2.1

D0094572

Release 2.1

Release 2.1

Release 2.1

Release 2.1

@Release 2.1

A design for living in the digital age

Esther Dyson

Broadway Books * New York

BROADWAY

Broadway Books titles may be purchased for business or promotional use or for special sales. For information, please write to: Special Markets Department, Bantam Doubleday Dell Publishing Group, Inc., 1540 Broadway, New York, NY 10036.

BROADWAY BOOKS and its logo, a letter B bisected on the diagonal, are trademarks of Broadway Books, a division of Bantam Doubleday Dell Publishing Group, Inc.

Library of Congress Cataloging-in-Publication Data

Dyson, Esther, 1951–
Release 2.1 : a design for living in the digital age / Esther
Dyson.
p. cm.
Includes index.
ISBN 0-7679-0012-X (pbk.)
1. Computer networks—Social aspects.   2. Internet (Computer
network)—Social aspects.   I. Title.
ZA4150.D973   1998
303.48'33—dc21   98-34486
CIP

FIRST EDITION

Designed by Brian Mulligan

98 99 00 01 02 10 9 8 7 6 5 4 3 2

To the memory of Marek Car,
who used the Net as a tool to make
the world better for the next generation.

Contents

viii   Contents

Release 2.1

Welcome to Release 2.1

Welcome to *Release 2.1*! This is the paperback "up-grade" to the book I published a year ago, *Release 2.0*. Like any upgrade, it is designed to be complete in itself, but it also contains additions and enhancements that reflect feedback and progress since the previous version. Consider this preface the cover of the new version: Here I'll outline the "new and improved" features, but I have tried to integrate most of them seamlessly into the body of the book. The exceptions are a variety of e-mail comments, articles, and excerpts from postings to my Web site that you'll see throughout the book. Not surprisingly, I received more feedback about "consumer" issues—content control, privacy—than about the less day-to-day issues of copyright, security, and anonymity.

Considering that this book is about the Internet, which has seen its number of users approximately double over the last year, you might expect a lot of changes. Governments all over the world are trying to figure out what to do about the Internet, often as if it were some terrible epidemic. Companies and individuals are trying to figure out what's in it for them.

Indeed, a lot has happened, but little that's fundamental has changed. The companies and other entities I used to illustrate my points in *Release 2.0* have had eventful years, but the basic truths and conflicts they illustrate—privacy versus society's need for openness, freedom versus responsibility, security versus commitment—have not changed at all.

Likewise, the purpose of this book hasn't changed at all: It's to excite you about the potential of the Internet and to encourage you to help fulfill it for yourself and others, whether you're a new user or an old hand, a parent, teacher, or religious leader or a precocious child, a small-business person using the Web to sell goods, a temp or a salaried worker, a person collecting Social Security or a legislator defining the laws we live by. Each of us plays many different roles in life, even off the Internet, and the Internet offers us the opportunity and the freedom to play many more, often in communities we define for ourselves.

Over the past year I have seen many people use these opportunities responsibly, and a few abuse them. As more and more people come onto the Internet, they are discovering the promise it holds for changing their own lives in myriad ways. The impact of the Net may not seem immediate when it means more efficiency in business or new international trade agreements, but it hits home in other ways. Just recently, when I did a radio show about the book, I could hardly get a word in edgewise after the first ten minutes. The first caller complained about my excessive optimism. Then, one by one, the next eight to ten callers testified to their own or their friends' experiences: a woman who had quit her job to raise her children and do programming work from home, another whose disabled friend had constructed a social life on the Net, another using it to organize his neighborhood school . . . I don't remember all the details because I hear stories like this all the time.

Although I know it happens, I rarely hear from people who are victimized over the Web; perhaps, as in real life, people know that accidents happen—and that when victimization is not an accident, it's caused by people, not by technology. Perhaps that's an overly sunny view, but as I said, most people who actually use the Net are delighted by the power it gives them.

That doesn't mean that there's not a need for tools and services to make it less confusing: guides, easier-to-use software, computers that don't crash, and online services that don't time out or go offline. One of the changes over the past year has been the rapid growth in such tools and services, but it is barely enough to keep up with the masses of new people coming online.

The story so far . . .

The most visible changes since last year have been in business—the world of brand names and defined services, product roll-outs and marketing campaigns. Many of them have been implementations or extensions of ideas floated in *Release 2.0:* better tools for privacy and content control, anti-spam measures, and the like. As I hoped, the market has indeed responded with new ventures to some of the Net's problems. Several of the companies I mentioned last year no longer exist: Firefly (page 258) has been acquired by Microsoft, and Four11 (page 271) has been acquired by Yahoo! (in *Release 2.0,* they were just working together). A company called PowerAgent, aimed at helping individuals manage their personal data, spent $25 million in start-up funding and then disappeared. But its place has been taken by another start-up, ConsumerInfo.com (page 264), which unlike PowerAgent managed to launch its service *before* its publicity campaign.

Large mergers—MCI and WorldCom, Travelers Corp. and Citicorp, Compaq and Digital—attract most of the attention, but in the Internet world small acquisitions abound as well. Microsoft has bought HotMail

Release X.X

The very title of this book embodies the concept of flexibility and learning from errors: In the software business, "Release 1.0" is the first commercial version of a new product, following test versions usually called 0.5, 0.8, 0.9, 0.91, 0.92. . . . It's fresh and new, the realization of the hopes and dreams of its developers. It embodies new ideas and it is supposed to be perfect. Usually the vendor comes out with Release 1.1 a few months later, fixing unexpected bugs and tidying up loose ends, many of them pointed out by "helpful" users.

If the product succeeds, the vendor launches Release 2.0 a year or so later. Release 2.0 is supposed to be perfect, but usually Release 2.1 comes out a few months after that.

The book *Release 2.0* was indeed a new product for me, a follow-on to the *Release 1.0* newsletter I had been writing (each issue was its own Release 1.0) since the early '80s. It was a new product rather than a rewrite, putting into new form my years of research and feedback. But while *Release 1.0* was written for people in the computer *business, Release 2.0* was directed at a broader audience, one I felt needed an encouraging word rather than a marketing pitch. And *Release 2.1*, of course, is that same book, but with a year's worth of feedback and progress stirred in. Will there ever be a *Release 3.0?* I don't know, but if there is, it will be something else again. Right now, I think the message of *Release 2.0*—the Net's potential for personal empowerment combined with responsibility—still needs airing.

(10 million subscribers to a free e-mail service) and Mesa Group in addition to Firefly; Lycos has bought Tripod, an organizer of online communities; McAfee Associates acquired Network General, changed its name to Network Associates, and then proceeded to buy Trusted

Information and PGP, all companies selling various kinds of online security tools. All around them, however, new companies are springing up, and slightly less new ones are going public. ⟹ Chapter 7 on content control, you can find five new companies that weren't included in *Release 2.0.* Meanwhile, the original eight are still in business, although Cyber Patrol is now part of the Learning Company. As for spamming, in *Release 2.0* all I could offer was theory and a halfhearted attempt by one vendor to control the problem. In *Release 2.1* (⟹ Chapter 5), I describe four companies addressing the problem, and I know of several more who don't want to be mentioned yet. In Europe, Net-oriented start-ups are also becoming more common.

Government activities

Over on the government side, there has been a lot of activity, but with fewer concrete results—probably a good outcome, although government attention is spurring the private sector to action and fostering investment. The names and numbers of the bills in Congress about encryption technology have changed, but the essential conflict continues: Should individuals have access to encryption technology that they can use to secure their own privacy, but which can be used by criminals to cover up criminal activities? The Communications Decency Act, overturned just before the publication of *Release 2.0,* has spawned a number of progeny in state legislatures and even in Congress, all designed to be less broad so as to meet Constitutional requirements. Several have been slipped into unrelated legislation. So far, the presence of filtering tools has enabled free-speech advocates to hold them off. Meanwhile, however, the other side is fighting the mandatory use of filtering tools in schools, libraries, and other government-funded institutions. This is a conflict that won't be resolved because it is a fundamental human disagreement.

Overall, however, the U.S. government has been remarkably hands-off concerning the Internet. It made its intentions clear in July 1997 on a glorious day when Bill Clinton and Al Gore stood up and talked about the promise and potential of the Internet for the American people. They unveiled the Framework for Global Electronic Commerce, and

IBM's CEO Lou Gerstner said a few words. The Communciations Decency Act had recently been overturned, and the future looked bright. Government's first rule for the Internet, said Vice President Gore, should be "do no harm." There were mutterings about privacy, spamming, and the like, but the government, with strong guidance from White House Internet advisor Ira Magaziner, decided to let the industry see what it could come up with.

A year later, not much has happened on the privacy front, although e-commerce is booming. Privacy concerns may be a constraint on consumer acceptance of the Net as buying medium, but businesses aren't seeing the customers they're missing. There are numerous filtering tools and services available, but those who look—in order to enjoy or in order to call for censorship—can still find pornography and other questionable materials. And although the furor over spamming has died down somewhat, the problem hasn't. A number of private polls have convinced the government that it needs to do something, so in mid-1998 there are a record number of Net-related bills in Congress covering everything from unsolicited e-mail to copyright protection for databases.

Government's proper role

The question is how to focus the public's imagination on a better solution—not government regulation or even industry self-regulation, but an environment where consumers themselves can exercise their power and control their own information, the messages they receive, the content their children look at. So far, no one has been telling them that this is possible, and they look to the government as the most obvious source of answers.

The government does have several roles to play, but they are limited. Aside from enforcement of anti-fraud and child-abuse statutes, among others, one of the most important is to ensure that every child receives a proper education. (Support for the Net in schools is helpful, but a basic education is more important.) Another role, which the U.S. government has been exercising recently vis-à-vis Microsoft, Intel, and other companies, is to ensure that *companies* don't amass too much power. That's a fair fight, I think, and one I'm happy to see happen. The big hope for the Net is that it can stop anyone from having too much power, but that will happen only if we use our *own* powers and those of the institutions we create to make it happen.

On the individual front

Finally, I suspect there's a lot going on out there that I haven't seen, precisely because the Net is everywhere and its impact is everywhere. But I get reports—from friends and strangers via e-mail, from business colleagues, from people I meet as I travel around on business, from my own family. One of my favorite stories is that of my own literary agent, Andrew Wylie. Andrew was enthusiastic about my book partly because he thought he could learn from handling it. At the time we met in the summer of 1997, he had just signed up for an e-mail account. Now the Wylie Agency has its own domain name (not just a CompuServe account), and Andrew answers my e-mail the same day. When I give talks to U.S. business audiences, I no longer ask "Who has e-mail?" They all do—or those who don't are ashamed not to raise their hands.

But it's the non-business audiences, such as the National Democratic Women's Club or the American Library Association, that are often the most fun and the most stimulating. They ask the questions that the business types might dismiss as naïve: "Will the Net destroy our humanity?" "What if I don't *want* to go online?" "How can I control my children's Internet use?"

I love responding to those questions, even though there's no good answer. Perhaps just the sight of a friendly-looking woman, rather than the stereotypical nerdy hacker or gum-chewing online teenager, is comforting to people. And it's a good sign that people keep asking these questions. The basic answer, however I word it, is: "It's up to you. You control how you use the Net. You choose how to raise your children and what values to teach them." Sometimes I mention that I personally don't have a telephone at home—not as a statement, but as a personal choice.

Human nature on the Net

The point I keep trying to get across is the profundity of the changes that the Net will bring to human *institutions*—and its lack of impact on human *nature*. Everything that matters on the Net will happen to human beings—people who get hungry and tired, people who love and get jealous, people who need food every day to keep their minds sharp and their bodies alive, people who depend on chemistry, not electronics, for their very existence.

The Net is not going to push us into some antiseptic, digital landscape. It is a medium for us to extend our intellectual and emotional selves, but it will not change anyone's basic character. (Genetic engineering and biotech will, but that is not my subject here, thank goodness!) On the contrary, the Net will celebrate human nature and human diversity . . . *if* we do it right. Precisely because there will be so much information, so much multimedia, so many options, people will learn to value human connection more, and they will look for it on the Net as they do in other places.

Net, Net

Overall, I have been pleased with the reaction to the book, and encouraged to see it move into the even more accessible form of a paperback. Some reviews have called it overly optimistic; some are concerned that I expect too much of the private sector. It's not that I have boundless faith in individuals or companies; it's just that I have *less* faith in individuals when you give them the power and backing of large institutions.

Individuals have all kinds of motivations, ranging from greed and jealousy to love, hope, and kindness. But in the long run, organizations can really have only two motivations: self-perpetuation, and profits for their investors. That applies to everything from governments and corporations, to large-scale charities and trade associations. Interestingly, Microsoft is one of the few large-scale companies that are still driven more by an individual than by either management or a board of directors.

That means that in the end, in the fast-moving world the Net is creating, it's more than ever up to individuals to ensure their own happiness, and to worry about the future of their world. Organizations worry only about their own future, but people have to think ahead to their children's future.

Social entrepreneurs, commercial activists

One thing that intrigued me as I traveled around promoting *Release 2.0* was the lack of interest in my own business ventures. I don't know whether people thought it was impolite to ask, or whether they just didn't find me—a short, friendly woman—a credible figure in the world of Bill Gates. That's troubling: Business, and more particularly entrepreneurship, whether commercial or social, is not just the province of archetypal tycoons, kids in jeans and aging men in suits; it's something anyone can do, for profit or for satisfaction.

I don't want to promote the businesses I work with, but I certainly don't want to hide my involvement with a variety of profit-making ventures, many of them devoted to solving the very problems discussed in this book—spam, security, privacy, and the like. They include TrustWorks (a security company), Bright Light (anti-spam), Firefly (privacy), and of course the not-for-profit TRUSTe (privacy). There are many others (some mentioned here, others not) that I am not involved in directly but that I also support in principle, and publicly when I get the chance.

The solutions to most of the problems I discuss depend not on some global agreement or binding government legislation, but on the arbitrary, all-over-the-place actions of diverse individuals and organizations seeing opportunities and making up their own minds to do something about them. Our world depends not on general agreements, but on a robust fabric of locally motivated organizations. On occasion, they need a push from government, and bad actors need more than that. But there are a lot of other ways to change the world: by example, by commentary (such as this book), by incentives. Voluntary action is what it's all about. Go do your part!

Design rules for *Release 2.1*

In addition to revising, expanding, and updating the material in *Release 2.0,* I have incorporated some feedback from readers as discrete items, which you'll see throughout this book. They are lightly edited for spelling and punctuation, and excerpted for relevance. (I took out some personal comments, among other things!)

In the case of items from the Release 2.0 Web site, I simply copied what I found. All the other items are either press materials or e-mails to me used with express permission: When I asked for permission, I also asked people how to identify them. The items in brackets [ ] are based on their responses. When there's an exchange, like the one immediately below, my own replies are in italics.

I apologize to all the other people who wrote to me but are not included—especially those to whom I did not respond. (However, some of you had changed your e-mail addresses in the meantime, and my replies bounced!)

If you have comments on *Release 2.1,* please e-mail me at esther21@edventure.com. Let me know if they are for me only. We'll be posting updates to the book, occasional comments, and a list of active URLs at our site, www.edventure.com. Here's one, for example.

Your participation

Dear Ms. Dyson: First of all, your publisher needs to acquire a much, much larger pipeline to the internet if this website is going to be of much use to anyone. Response times and page loading times are very very long. Second, the statement: "Please note: Your participation in the discussions on this Website shall constitute permission to reprint your comments, in whole or in part, with or without attribution, in the revised paperback edition of Release 2.0, aptly titled Release 2.1 . . ." is extremely off-putting You appear to be claiming the right to take any idea expressed on this Website and repeat it as if it were your own. What would have been wrong, why didn't you say: ". . . permission to reprint . . . with appropriate attribution . . ."? As far as the ethics of discourse in the electronic age are concerned, you appear to have started off on the wrong foot. Sincerely yours, Bradford De Long delong@econ.berkeley.edu

>===============

Touché! That was the lawyers. Sorry! I have attributed what I used.

Why I wrote this book

You can find dozens of books on the digital world for consumers, and hundreds more on how to make a million bucks on the Net. I've even contributed to that literature myself, with my computer/software industry newsletter *Release 1.0.* But there's little out there to help us think about the Internet and our roles as citizens, rule-makers, and community members.

Like the American frontier of old, the Internet is being built by its members. Formally speaking, the Internet is a technical medium, a set of telecommunication lines and switches all linked by the so-called Internet protocol. In terms of design or architecture, call it a house. The Net, by contrast, is a potential home for all of us. It includes both the formal Internet and other networks and computers linked in through proprietary systems such as America Online, corporate intranets, and the free Juno e-mail service that my stepmother uses to communicate with relatives here and in Germany. More than that, the Net includes all the people, cultures, and communities that live in it. Like any home, it has rules, but it also has ways we *should* behave even if no one forces us to.

The Net offers us a chance to take charge of our own lives and to redefine our role as citizens of local communities and of a global society. It also hands us the *responsibility* to govern ourselves, to think for ourselves, to educate our children, to do business honestly, and to work with fellow citizens to design rules we want to live by. I won't presume to tell you precisely what all those rules should be. Some are local; some are global. Indeed, the Net is not a single home. Rather, it's an environment where thousands of small homes and communities can form and define and design *themselves.*

A design for living

My goal in this book is to pass on a little of my sense of the richness and potential of the Net. I want to take away the mystery and the technical mumbo jumbo, so that you can see the Net for what it is: a place where people meet, talk, do business, find out things, form committees, and pass on rumors. . . . Some of the capabilities are different from the so-called real world. Anyone can go online and publish something that can be read anywhere in the world; a child can write to a president; a Hungarian merchant can find a Chinese customer. Above all, the Net is a home for people.

Our common task is to do a better job with the Net than we have done so far in the physical world. The Net has some unique advantages. It takes away many of the logistical difficulties of space and time; information flows faster; markets are more efficient. The question is: How can we use these features to design a world that is more open, more accessible to everyone, and just a nicer place to live in?

What could be, what should be

Much of what I'm writing about is just starting to happen. Some of it is inevitable; some of it is not. Some of it could come true. But we need to do more than close our eyes and wish. To make it seem real, I've written a lot about what it will feel like to live on the Net and the kinds of communities and institutions we'll build: some real examples, and some only possible. The scenarios I describe are both predictions—if we do things right—and goals. (I've taken care to point out which is which.)

I'm describing how it could be if we do pay attention to the underlying rules: freedom of choice, freedom of speech, honesty, and disclosure. Markets will do a lot of the design if we let them, but we need a foundation of both traditional, or terrestrial, and Net-based rules to make the markets work properly. We also need habits of honesty and generosity.

In addition, we need the good guys—you—to be active in designing this new world. No system in the world is so well designed that it can't grow stale, rigid, or corrupted by those who benefit most from it. The only guarantee of continued freedom is the presence of pesky people who keep asking those in power to account for their actions. By its very nature, the system can't do that for itself. It's up to you.

You know more than you think you do

I do a lot on the Net. It's the medium I use to communicate with many of my friends and colleagues and arrange face-to-face meetings. I also depend on it professionally: It's the primary subject about which I write, talk, and consult, and the basis of most of the companies I invest in, both in the United States and in Eastern Europe. But I never studied it formally; I just started using it and discovered its capabilities as I needed them.

You will use the Net in your own way; maybe you already do. My goal is to help you interpret and shape this new world, rather than merely visit or live in it. You can join existing communities, or you can help to form new ones of your own.

As long as the world contains people, it will have conflicts. We need both vision and common sense to handle these conflicts: between one person's privacy and another's right to know, between cultures, between an employer's goals and an employee's priorities. But we can't resolve most conflicts with abstract principles in advance. That's why even now, with all our legal expertise and social experience, we need judges and juries, new laws and amendments to old laws, and free and open media to find out what's going on and to spread new ideas and opinions. We'll never get it quite right, but that's okay so long as we learn from our mistakes.

National interest

Today's Internet has a distinctly American flavor—one that will gradually diminish as more people in different countries get online. One central mystery is the delicate interplay of American culture and Internet culture. How much will the Net change the people who join it, and how much will the new people change the Net? Is the Net's free-spiritedness American, or is it inherent in the Net itself?

Whatever the answer, I'm trying to speak not as an American but as a member of multiple communities, many of them outside the United States—most notably the Russian computer marketplace. (One advantage of the Net is that it allows you to be a member of several different communities, not all of them geographical, at the same time.) So even though I'm American—and I have that typical American blend of pragmatism, idealism, goodwill, and bluntness—I hope my message will be intelligible to people worldwide. The Net belongs to no particular country or group. The Net is not a global village, but an environment in which many different villages will flourish.

Why the Net matters

The Net has no independent existence. It matters because people use it as a place to communicate, conduct business, and share ideas, not as a mystical entity in itself. It's a powerful tool for integrating local economies into the global economy and for establishing their presence in the world. Its impact—the widespread availability of two-way electronic communications—will change all of our lives. It will suck power away from central governments, mass media, and big business. Even now, the Net extends across and transcends traditional national borders and overcomes distance. It operates in real time, but lets people in different time zones communicate easily. It avoids the communications glitches that arise with missed or garbled phone messages, illegible or misdelivered faxes. But it must coexist with national regimes, cultural and language differences, and the realities of physical infrastructure that impinge on its theoretical spacelessness.

This digital world is a new terrain that can be a source of untold productivity—or a medium for terrorists, con artists, and untrammeled lies and viciousness. It is almost impossible for traditional governments to regulate, yet it does need to be governed from within—the cries of free-spirited Net citizens notwithstanding.

The Net gives awesome power to individuals—the ability to be heard across the world, the ability to find information about almost anything . . . along with the ability to spread lies worldwide, to discover secrets about friends or strangers, and to find potential victims of fraud, child abuse, or other harassment. With greater ability to exercise their rights or to abuse them, individuals will need to assume greater responsibility for their own actions and for the world they are creating.

Indeed, I believe individuals should be responsible for the basic rule of cyberspace, which is disclosure. Rather than having central authorities set global rules for disclosure, which could never fit all circumstances, we need to leave that up to individuals, too. The golden rule is not "Disclose yourself," but rather a two-way command: "Do ask. Don't lie."

The idea is to create a culture that *expects* disclosure, rather than a legal regime that requires it. People can decide how much they want to play, and others can decide whether to play with them. But for a healthy society, there has to be an overall high level of buy-in.

It drives the responsibility for requiring disclosure down to where it belongs—to those most likely to be affected by the disclosure. It decentralizes the requirement and the enforcement to everyone, instead of leaving it in the hands of a few at the top. (If that's an awkward use of "requirement," it's because we don't even have a word for "decentralized command.")

And note that "do ask" doesn't mean to ask only of the person disclosing; it can also mean asking third parties. "Is Juan trustworthy?" "Is Alice objective, or does she have some vested interest in the products she's recommending?"

As an individual, you are not commanded to answer; you may want to protect your own privacy or someone else's. But if you do answer, you must do so truthfully.

Then it's up to the people involved to decide whether to engage—in conversation, in a transaction, in whatever kind of interaction they might be contemplating. The magic of "do ask, don't lie" is that the parties to any particular interaction can make a specific, local decision about what level of disclosure is appropriate.

Not just for commerce

"The Internet is friction-free," Bill Gates has said, referring to the opportunities it presents for efficient markets. As he well knows, businesses such as Netscape can pop into view by distributing their products over the Net free of charge to customers and almost cost-free to their producer. But "friction-free" means more than just efficient markets and efficient business: It means the absence of the friction we're accustomed to in daily life. Friction keeps neighborhood gossip from following a person from one town to another. Friction keeps junk mail from overwhelming us, and it keeps most of the people we don't want to see out of our lives. It keeps cultures localized and it keeps people attached to their reputations. It provides texture to daily life and people's perceptions of one another. It separates the close and the distant with a fuzzy border that can be crossed, but only with effort.

The absence of friction online means that we can't rely on traditional means to resolve conflicts over the rights of individuals by simply damping them out. Once a person's privacy is breached, it may be breached worldwide. Anyone can check out what you said last week in the intimacy of the Provincetown PTA discussion group or the Friendly Felines chat room. "Free speech" is not restricted to a street corner audience, a locker room, or a limited-circulation publication, but travels the globe. A con artist can reach victims all over the world, finding people who may not have heard of each new trick and may not be familiar with scams or even direct mail. (I still get occasional personal notes from East Europeans in response to bulk-mailed invitations to my annual forums.)

Moreover, people can make the close seem distant by filtering out information. Those who have distorted views of the world can avoid evidence that might contradict their beliefs; they don't face the "friction" of running into reality every time they cross the street or open a newspaper.

Decentralization vs. fragmentation

The greatest structural impact of the Net is decentralization; things and people no longer depend on a center to be connected. People often confuse this with democracy, but democracy is where the majority rules (even if it elects a Communist president or a dictator), whereas decentralization is where the masses separate into small groups. In some of these smaller groups, the majority may rule; in others, consensus may reign; and in still others, a commercial provider or a dictator may set the rules. On the Net at least, people who don't like the rules can leave.

It's worth stressing that although the Net can be used for good and bad (like most powerful tools), it is asymmetrical in the way it gives personal power to the powerless. That is, it undermines central authorities whether they are good or bad, and it helps dispersed forces to act together, whether *they* are good or bad. In other words, it's a feeble tool for propaganda, but it's perfect for conspiracy.

Indeed, decentralization is a profound and destabilizing force. It affects not just governments, but businesses, media, health care, organized religion, and all other establishments. It changes the balance of power between large/rich and small/poor countries, in part by offering their citizens and companies a level playing field without regard to traditional borders.

Likewise, the Net changes the balance of power among companies by removing many economies of scale and valuing diversity over uniformity. Analysts and investors wonder who will replace Microsoft the way Microsoft replaced IBM as the information industry's standard-setter. The answer is that no one will: The model of an industry revolving around a central leader will give way to a new, decentralized market.

The Net also changes the balance of power between employers and employees, who are better able to find new jobs in a fluid market, and between mass media and their audiences, who can now not only talk back, but talk among themselves. It changes the balance of power between merchants and customers. It even gives individuals the tools to become small-scale producers themselves.

Yet the belief common among Net citizens (and increasingly in business) that decentralized systems automatically self-organize is not always valid. It's true only if the local rules are good and the individual agents/players honest. Many systems composed of smaller independent agents do not self-organize; they fall into chaos and die. The components need an environment where they can interact effectively and there's enough nourishment to keep them going; otherwise, you get a dead-end market/community that fails. Just compare the three stock markets in the Czech Republic (none of which has enough openness or critical mass to attract healthy commercial activity) with the Warsaw Stock Exchange, a model of openness and disclosure that is flourishing and attracting new investors for its listed companies. A more familiar example is a party where the star guest who knows everyone doesn't show up, and everyone stands around awkwardly. Communities are subtle things; they depend on people and atmosphere, not technical tools, to flourish. (The good news is that dying online communities don't leave behind dead neighborhoods and people who can't get out.)

The challenge

Global yet decentralized, the Net is inherently transnational. It needs a few basic principles honored worldwide in order for commerce and society to flourish and for criminals to not escape justice by changing jurisdictions. And it needs a culture of honesty, openness, accountability, and persistent reputations.

On the other hand, the Net allows for a profusion of self-defined communities with their own laws and policies, so long as they do not harm people or things outside their (virtual) jurisdiction. These communities' laws actually have higher moral authority than those of countries or most other governments, since their members join voluntarily and are free to go. (It is a challenge to such communities to find ways to make their members commit enough so that they don't leave at the first disappointment or sign of trouble.) Some of these communities will be commercial, with membership fees; others will be held together by common interests or goals. Many "government" functions will be partly privatized, from policing fraud and providing education to adjudicating disputes and registering businesses.

The challenge for all of us is to build a critical mass of healthy communities on the Net and to design good basic rules for its public spaces so that larger systems do self-organize and work effectively. Rule-making is not the job of legislatures and governments alone. You can make your own rules by designing an online service—or by setting up procedures in your workplace. Anyone who offers a service or product, anyone who votes in a PTA or discusses corporate policy with her boss, is a rule-maker. What will make the world a better place for you and your children (or friends) to live in? It's up to you to figure it out and to make it happen.

Chapter 1

How I got the story and learned to love markets

Because so much of this book concerns the value of openness and disclosure—of origins, of biases, of vested interests—I owe it to you to explain who I am and how I have come to the perceptions and opinions I hold.

First of all, I never expected to be a "techie." My parents were both scientists, so I wasn't afraid of technology. But I always assumed I'd end up being a novelist. I liked reading; I liked writing. I even founded the *Dyson Gazette* at the age of eight. The technology was ballpoint pen and carbon paper; the coverage was very local!

I was a child of my generation, with the single exception that we didn't have television at home. Because I was raised in the academic hothouse around Princeton's Institute for Advanced Study, with Nobel laureates as dinner guests, I grew up scorning the commercial world. My first regular job wasn't commercial either: I worked as a page in the local public library. I was fourteen when I discovered that most people did not get ten weeks of vacation in the summer. (Of course, I knew that the mailman kept coming; I assumed there were substitute mailmen just as there were substitute teachers.)

How I met Juan and Alice

When I reached Harvard, not much closer to reality in the late '60s, I spent most of my time not in class but at the *Harvard Crimson,* the university's daily newspaper. I tried out for it my freshman year and wrote for it ever after for love; I also proofread for money. Much as I love the digital world, I also love the old world of movable lead type, the building that shook every night after midnight as the presses rolled, the gruff professional linotypists who scorned us elite college kids. Our archenemies at the *Crimson* were at the *Harvard Lampoon,* the college humor magazine that didn't (at the time) take girls, but didn't mind them hanging around if they were pleasant and not too uppity. I liked spending time at the *Lampoon;* its members were funnier than the serious-minded would-be journalists at the *Crimson.*

There was one couple there that it took me a long time to figure out: Juan and Alice. People were always leaving notes for them: "Juan & Alice—Please don't leave your Tommy's Lunch in the refrigerator." "Juan & Alice—Please wash your dishes." It was college; a lot of our lives revolved around food, especially Tommy's Lunch, the local greasy spoon. Finally I figured out that Juan and Alice were a Spanish-English-German pun meaning "one and all" (one and Alles). I have used them ever since when I need some archetypal figures to make a point; you'll be seeing them throughout the book. Thank you, Lampy!

How I learned about markets

Like my friends on the *Crimson* (the *Lampoon* was somewhat more elit-ist), I was a good liberal. I thought the government was heartless be-cause it didn't simply take care of all the poor people; wasn't that what taxes were for? But somehow, I sensed that if I wanted to change the world, my best hope was to study economics, not politics. So I majored in economics at Harvard and learned about supply and demand and market equilibrium: If you allow a free market, prices will adjust so that demand will meet supply. If that produces unfairness, then the government should step in to fix things. But none of that explained how things really worked, or how markets could produce growth and progress instead of just equilibrium.

All that I learned later, first as a fact-checker and then as a reporter for *Forbes* magazine. Known as a magazine for investors, *Forbes* is fanat-ical about disclosure and investors' rights to know what is going on at their companies. But its articles also illustrate how numbers and the laws of economics that make markets work aren't the whole story; the men and women running companies by and large determine their fates within the broader market. It was real-life business school: Instead of sitting in the library I got to go out and interview the principals who made everything happen.

By 1977 I got tired of watching and reporting. I went to Wall Street as a securities analyst, following high-tech stocks and trying to tell in-vestors which companies would grow and prosper. That was where I switched from the electric typewriter I had used at *Forbes* to a word-processor and eventually a PC (a Tandy, for what it's worth). As it turned out, understanding companies was a lot easier than predicting stock prices. I discovered that I had less interest in the stock market than in the inner workings and the products of the high-tech compa-nies themselves—especially since their products were beginning to change how businesses operated.

But my financial experience taught me a few things. Apart from high-tech, I covered one other company, Federal Express. There I met Jim Barksdale, then chief information officer of FedEx, and now CEO of Netscape. The lessons we both learned about creating a market, not just a company, have proved relevant ever since.

In the end, I left Wall Street to get closer to the computer industry, joining venture capitalist Ben Rosen and taking over his *Rosen Electronics Letter,* a newsletter targeted to the industry itself rather than to investors in it. Rosen, also a former analyst, was finding the newsletter a burden as he became increasingly involved in venture capital. It also turned into a conflict of interest as two of his investments took off and it was impossible to write about the industry without mentioning them—Compaq and Lotus. I first met Lotus founder Mitch Kapor in Ben's office when Mitch was looking for funding for his new product, 1-2-3, a spreadsheet pitched as "VisiCalc for the PC."

In short order, Ben became chairman of Compaq and a director of Lotus. I assumed his burden entirely by buying the company and the newsletter, which I renamed *Release 1.0* (R E L—get it?). One of my first newsletter articles was based on a trip to Bellevue, Washington, to write about yet another start-up, Microsoft. I said that it needed to "lose some of its charm" to succeed in the cutthroat software business.

As a result of this career path I grew up intellectually regarding Federal Express, Apple, Compaq, Lotus, and Microsoft as typical start-ups—fairly high standards. Most of what happened in any of these companies had little to do with economics; it had much more to do with people, strategy, implementation. Nor did they look to government for any help. Left to their own, they could produce miracles.

And they did. They created not just hot new products but hot new markets. It all worked in a wonderful manner: Competing firms got stronger and stronger in the furnace of the market, while the weaker ones dropped out. That magical market worked for people, too: While troubled firms died or were swallowed up, the people within them found new jobs elsewhere, honing their skills as they went.

The industry flourished away from the spotlight, away from government interference, away from social responsibility. Personal computers were still largely novelties for hobbyists; serious mainframe computer folk considered PCs basically toys. While many people of this generation were reformed college activists settling down to reality, the PC

What is a market?

What *is* a market? And what does it have to do with the Internet? The fashion right now, one I follow, is to think of the Internet as a living environment, a place for societies, communities, and institutions to *grow*—rather than as something constructed, a superhighway, for example. That leads to appropriate metaphors, looking at the Net as something to be cultivated and nurtured rather than built or engineered. (Only its rules need to be designed so that it can grow in good health.) The structure has to emerge from individual actions rather than from some central authority or government. The guiding metaphor is evolution. Evolution is natural, the thinking goes. And markets are just a faster form of evolution.

But I'd like to disagree—or take the metaphor a step further. First, markets are not just a form of evolution, commonly considered survival of the fittest. Markets have rules and enforcement mechanisms agreed on (more or less) by all the players. And second, what does the survival rule apply to: Is it people? Is it firms? Is it the products or concepts the firms sell or operate on? And is it really the fittest? Or the best nurtured?

For starters, evolution is blind. Call it self-unaware. Its processes operate without visibility. Animals and plants live or die as a whole, eventually resulting in the evolution—creation or modification or dying out—of entire species. "Good" genes live on, fostering the survival of good features—whether wings or eyes or intelligence. An industrial analogy to such surviving features is the technology that runs motors—V-8 or diesel, for example. The technology lives on and spreads even as the individual cars and the brands and models that contain the engines disappear.

Markets are different. They are self-aware. We can see what is successful and what is not. What is the same is the decentralized approach, and tolerance for the destruction of bad ideas.

Businesses and communities can adopt good ideas (or "memes") that they weren't born with. "Memes" act like viruses and move across hosts. Whole firms do not need to live or die for the best memes to spread and the worst to die off. The market is more Lamarckian than Darwinian. In business, one example is how the concept of having a single fast-moving line feed several teller stations replaced the concept of several lines moving at different, unpredictable speeds spread through the bank lobbies of America in a matter of months. Likewise, the hub-and-spokes idea has "infected" the airline industry. Analogies for the Net will be rules in a community, business models, and the like. Some Net businesses and communities will come and go, but others will be able to learn and acquire memes from those around them.

"Memes" is the concept of ideas as objects that can evolve and adapt just as other "living" things do, courtesy of biologist Richard Dawkins. The best ones adapt and flourish; the foolish ones die off. Or so the theory goes. Darwin is the acknowledged founder of evolution theory, which needs no explanation; Jean-Baptiste Lamarck was the nineteenth-century French scientist who kept trying to prove, with little success, that the effects of behavior could be inherited—specifically, that giraffes that stretched their necks more had babies with longer necks. But given what we now know about genes (and markets!), some of Lamarck's ideas are beginning to make sense again.

industry remained a haven for freewheeling, free-market thinking. Its people couldn't understand why everyone couldn't be as successful as they were.

Personally, I was having a lot of fun covering Silicon Valley, the home of untrammeled commercialism, economic freedom, and technical innovation. I kept finding new stuff to learn as the industry kept changing. I took *Release 1.0* and changed its focus from PCs to software as the PC business grew mature and organized; there wasn't much new to say about PC hardware in the mid-'80s—just market-size forecasts and new product releases.

But suddenly software, which had been interesting as an emerging business, became even more interesting because of the nature of what it sold: Groupware, and networking in general, fostered social as well as technical change. Companies installing groupware systems (the precursors to today's intranets) had to deal with problems of personal interaction, workflow, sharing of credit, and people's tendency to hoard information as power. The new software involved classification of knowledge, not just manipulation of dry data. I had enjoyed the mathematical and logical challenges of figuring out how databases work, but this was more complex and somehow more real. It affected people's daily lives.

PC Forum

All along there was another facet of the business—the one that actually supported the company and allowed me to educate myself through the newsletter. That was my annual computer conference, PC Forum. When it started in the late '70s, it had been a little afternoon session at Ben Rosen's Semiconductor Forum. I took it over in 1983, when it had achieved its own identity but was still mainly a showcase for PC companies preening in front of investors. Its heart and soul was as a meeting ground for the industry itself. We had trade shows, where everyone kowtowed to customers and promoted products, but PC Forum was where we talked about our problems as an industry. This was where Mitch Kapor clashed with Bill Gates and with French-born Philippe Kahn, founder of Borland International (a pioneering software company), where people met by the pool to do deals, where Software Arts served a subpoena on its erstwhile partner VisiCorp. People came to argue and to catch up, to find new jobs, new partners, new technology.

PC Forum was and still is conceived as a commercial enterprise, but it also has the flavor of an annual high school reunion. Many of us know one another from before we became who we became. But by

1989, even that had become a little dull. I needed to find something new for commercial reasons, too; I now had ample competition writing about these topics. As I had learned by then, a market is not just the interaction of buyers and sellers; it involves competition between sellers. Rather than compete only on price, sellers compete on differentiation—the equivalent of the forces that produce new species in nature. Differentiation is a lot easier when you know what your competition is doing, which is why disclosure is good for markets as a whole as well as for investors and customers.

The trick is to find a niche that's unoccupied. As the only writer for my newsletter (and uninterested in finding and managing others), I couldn't hope to compete with other publications on depth of coverage or research. What I could do best was stake out and map new territory.

Next step: Moscow

So, naturally enough, I went to Russia—something I had wanted to do since learning the language in high school. There was a lot of new territory there in 1989—both for me and for the Russians themselves. I brought along five books, including James Gleick's *Chaos* (Viking Penguin, 1987), which is a layperson's explanation of the science of complexity, including evolution, markets, and learning. Two were books by my father (Freeman Dyson) that I had never had the time to read: *Infinite in All Directions* (Harper & Row, 1988), about evolution, life, and implicitly about markets; and *Disturbing the Universe* (Basic Books, 1981), his own intellectual autobiography, in which he explained his distrust of big organizations—as opposed to his trust and tolerance of individuals. (His distrust came from his experience as a mathematician working for the Bomber Command of the British Royal Air Force during World War II. The pitifully small survival rate of shot-down crewmen indicated their bombers' escape hatches were too small; crewmen couldn't climb out fast enough to open their parachutes in time. The Air Force and the aircraft manufacturers ignored Freeman's calculations about the problem and let the boys keep dying.)

Here I was with new intellectual eyes and a new world to look at. I could finally see what a market was—by seeing what the lack of one had done to Russia. No feedback loops. No competition. No differentiation. No growth. No progress. The Soviets had constructed a complex industrial machine after World War II, but for all its moving parts, it was static. It had no way to adjust to the unexpected, to allow for progress or for human nature. This giant edifice had gradually rusted beyond repair. As its parts broke down, they could not repair themselves, and the Soviet system could not fix them either. It could only vainly exhort its troops to work harder.

But all this was changing. The Congress of People's Deputies had just been elected, and all over the nation people were sitting at work and watching the Congress's deliberations on television instead of working. "Our government is going to set free-market prices just like yours," one exuberant Russian told me. It was clear that within a year or two Russia would be on its way to prosperity as a free state. Already the market was starting to work. Following the lead of small entrepreneurs opening restaurants and taxi services, the programmers I knew were beginning to leave their state jobs to form programmers' cooperatives and, they hoped, to get rich.

My self-appointed mission was to help them understand the market. "How are you different from the competition?" I would ask. "We have no competition," would come the answer.

"But what about Ivan and Volodya?"

"Oh, them. They're no good! We're much better!" But they could never tell me how they were better. In fact, no one knew much about anyone. Customers would simply buy from people they knew. Afraid of being bothered by the government or the growing mafia for being too successful, the entrepreneurs did not advertise.

Information is more useful than money

Why not just be better in something specific, I would ask, rather than defame the competition? Why not meet them and find out what they

were doing? Then I would glibly talk about differentiation and specia-
tion. Since it sounded scientific, they liked the idea. And indeed, in
Russia's computer market, several years later things are working quite
well. Vendors are advertising and explaining themselves clearly. There
are industry associations and trade shows where people gather to talk
about common problems, pick up competitive information, check out
new trends. Their customers are installing computers and accounting
systems to manage real businesses; they can't afford to pick suppliers
on the basis of bribes or connections.

I knew all about markets, I thought, but I had never realized how
important *information* was until I saw a market without it—not just pricing, but everything else. Who's doing what? Who's winning? Who is
failing, and why? I could see what it took to make a market precisely
because it was not there.

Although a market might follow the laws of nature, it is not a totally
natural thing. It works far better with information. Instead of firms
living and dying aimlessly, ideas and concepts can take shape. People
can learn from others' mistakes as well as from their own.

But another thing is lacking in Russia—another thing I never missed
until I saw what happens without it: a solid legal infrastructure, one
that enforces contracts and requires honest advertising and disclosure.
A market doesn't need a lot of complex regulations if those two are in
place: a culture of truth, and recourse for broken promises.

In other words, there are global rules that make the market work,
and then local players who push the market to improve, depending on
their own particular desires. Without those global rules, the specific
preferences of the players never get expressed.

Not by markets alone

Outside the computer business, the market in Russia is like evolution.
It is blind. Customers often don't know whom they're dealing with, so
they can't believe promises. Everything is short-term. There's not
much point in trying to develop a reputation in a market that doesn't
trust you to be who you say you are.

Consequences multiply. Employees don't trust their employers or one another, so they don't work as a team. They don't regard stealing from an employer (particularly if it is state-owned) as wrong. There's an old Soviet saying: "If you don't steal from the State, you are stealing from your family." People don't understand the role of investment in building companies for the long term, so they regard profit as evidence of exploitation.

Return from Russia

I returned from Russia with the scales gone from my eyes. Over the next couple of years I adopted the region as my territory. The U.S. market was doing fine on its own, but Central and Eastern Europe needed me. My knowledge of markets and specific contacts in the PC market made me uniquely able to be helpful. And it was fun to watch how each country's market developed differently.

Hungary, which had liberalized first, was the leader, but its new private companies were still run like state organizations, more for the immediate benefit of the top guys than for long-term profitability to shareholders. That eventually caught up with them, and a number of Hungarian computer companies went bankrupt. A major exception, Graphisoft, is still flourishing as a worldwide leader in design software for architects. (I joined its board in the spring of 1998.) In the Czech Republic, the market ruled supreme, but the government gave way too much power and too little oversight to the banks. The results are starting to show as the banks get into trouble and the companies they own turn out never to have gone through the management restructuring they needed. Poland is probably the greatest success story of all. It got a wholly new government and already had a tradition of small businesses.

But Russia! Russia is the country whose language I speak, which I love as one loves a self-destructive child. In power for more than seventy years, the Soviets had left no bourgeois culture to revive. Here the computer market is a little oasis in a huge, dysfunctional economy where people strike for back wages, not for pay hikes.

But all these insights weren't of great interest to the regular readers of *Release 1.0,* at least not when presented in terms of Eastern Europe. I started another newsletter, *Rel-EAST,* and another conference, East-West High-Tech Forum, to focus on Eastern Europe.*

The Internet

Once I returned from Russia in 1989 (and kept going back), I started to keep in touch with my new friends there by e-mail. I got myself an MCI Mail account—horrible to look at, difficult to use, but the best way of reaching people in Russia. I rarely used it for people in the United States, because other methods were easier. Ironically, the people I knew in Russia were quicker to use e-mail than those in Central Europe, where the alternatives of fax and phone already worked somewhat better.

One of the strongest promoters of e-mail was Borland International, the software company, not out of "vision" but because it wanted to keep in touch with its distributors cheaply and effectively. It made each of them get an MCI Mail account—and of course they ended up being among the Central and East Europeans with whom it was easiest to keep in touch.

At this point, the Internet was a specific technical network, the preserve of scientists and researchers using technical workstations based on UNIX. Those of us with PCs had our choice of a number of proprietary e-mail/online services, including MCI Mail, CompuServe, and Prodigy, but it was complicated and expensive to send mail from one to another.

---

*My dream was to merge them back: to see the Central and East Europeans be part of the world computer market, not a separate, charity-case venture. To a large extent, this has happened at PC Forum, where in recent years Poles, Czechs, Slovenians, Russians, Hungarians, and Slovaks have participated as regular attendees or as speakers. The kind of personal, physical contact the Forum allows strengthens the bonds you can build and maintain over e-mail. Meanwhile, *Rel-EAST* is gone since I started investing in the region, and the East-West High-Tech Forum has become the EDventure High-Tech Forum covering all of Europe.

One by one, they established better connections to the Internet. And meanwhile, Tim Berners-Lee developed the technology for the World Wide Web at the European Center for Nuclear Research (CERN) in Geneva. Over time the Internet, a formal research network, coalesced with a new crowd of less technically inclined users and commercial services. Together, they would blossom into the Net we know today.

But as the '90s began all this was still new to me. What I knew was that more and more people were sending me e-mail, even from the United States. Somehow I got the sense that something was happening. All over the United States and even worldwide, all those single-user PCs that (allegedly) improved individuals' productivity were becoming much more powerful—a medium for communication. The people who used e-mail had a secret smile, as if they knew some new kind of pleasure denied the rest of us. Maybe life was about to get interesting back in the United States, too.

Mitch Kapor, who had now left Lotus and sold all his stock, was one of the Net's biggest fans. But all I knew about Mitch's new life was that he had gotten involved—using some of his now considerable fortune—in supporting Steve Jackson, owner of a company that published books about games. Jackson had suffered business losses caused by overaggressive Secret Service agents who seized his computers and data when they suspected one of his employees of "cracking"—breaking into other people's computers over the Net. Jackson sued and was eventually vindicated in court in 1993. In 1991 Mitch called—or e-mailed, I can't recall—to invite me to join the board of his new venture, the Electronic Frontier Foundation, an online civil liberties organization.

Initially, I was dubious about joining the EFF board. "I'm not sure I'd agree with everything you're doing," I told Mitch.

He passed my test perfectly. "That's exactly why we want you on the board," he said.

Somehow, just as I had magically gravitated to the PC at the end of the '70s, I was magically gravitating to the Internet at the beginning of the '90s. I knew that joining the board would force me to learn more about it and since I liked Mitch, I signed up.

As time passed, I found more and more use for e-mail. The Electronic Frontier Foundation was run by e-mail, of course, and other friends began asking me for my e-mail address—and using it.

The lure of the Net

This was the time that Vice President Al Gore was discovering the Information Superhighway. Ironically, for all its free-market libertarianism, the Internet was a creation of the U.S. government. The government still owned most of it in the early '90s, although an increasing proportion of the equipment over which it ran sat in computer centers in universities, research organizations, and private companies. The Internet, after all, runs over existing phone lines as well as over its own high-speed, high-bandwidth telecommunications "backbones." Although it appears to be free to its users, most of its operating costs were borne first by the government and then increasingly by private computer centers, whose computers were being used to hold the content of the Internet—newsgroups, Web sites, e-mail archives, and the like—and to forward messages from one node to another.

Among the high-tech community, lively arguments raged over whether commercial imperatives should be allowed to intrude on this pristine environment. Mitch Kapor cast his vote by becoming chairman of the Commercial Internet Exchange, a group of commercial Internet service providers considered social outcasts by the anticommercial Net community of the time.

As one of the most visible entrepreneurs of the '80s, Mitch had good contacts in Washington, and the government (as opposed to the law-enforcement community) was interested in our views. If Big Government wanted our advice, we were happy to give it. The first question was how to foster the development of the Internet.

Mitch's advice was: "Let the market do it." We had both seen the wonders the PC market had accomplished on its own, without government interference or "support." Also, we knew, it was unlikely that the government could refrain from regulating an infrastructure that it owned. But if it was in private hands, there was some chance it would be free to govern itself. Of course, at that time, we all perceived the Net as a fine, elite place populated by literate, mature people—a place that needed no regulation. It was, after all, the Electronic Frontier.

The NIIAC

In 1994, Al Gore decided that the government should convene the National Information Infrastructure Advisory Council, composed of private citizens and non–federal government people, to guide the government in its delicate attempts to grow this magical foundation without constructing it itself.

The NIIAC was my introduction to Washington. At the time, I was going to California and to Europe once a month, and to Washington just a couple of times a year. Net or no, my life was actually defined by geography. But I soon got the hang of taking the New York–Washington shuttle.

The NIIAC was a well-meaning attempt to collect a diversity of opinion to make sure the emerging "NII" was useful to all Americans, and it probably did more good than I suspected at the time. (Mitch got pretty frustrated with the ponderousness of its deliberations and stopped going to meetings after the first few months.) The members included the usual suspects: a librarian; a grade-school teacher; a communications workers' union official; the head of BMI, a copyright agency; several telecom executives; several "content" people, including a legal publisher and a music-company executive; an old lawyer friend of the Clintons from Arkansas; a state senator and several other local government officials; my old friend John Sculley, former CEO of Apple (and another friend of the Clintons). The co-chairs were Ed McCracken, CEO of Silicon Graphics, and Del Lewis, CEO of National Public Radio. There was a good representation of women and a sprinkling of African Americans and ethnic Americans—but no kids, who might have had a lot to teach us. It's amazing that we came to agreement on anything, but we did.

Just as Russia taught me about markets as I learned about the country, the NIIAC taught me about politics even as we learned about the

National Information Infrastructure. Ironically, one of the first heated discussions at the Council occurred when Mitch and I and Robert Kahn (one of the Internet's many "founders") suggested that we should all use e-mail to communicate. By the end of the Council's appointed two years of life, most of us were in fact using e-mail, but there were a couple of holdouts.

Our biggest disagreements concerned intellectual property rights. I was in the thick of them as co-chair of the subcommittee on intellectual property, privacy, and security. My co-chair was John Cooke, a senior executive at Disney—someone with fairly strong views about the need for protecting copyright holders' interests! By contrast, I was more concerned with users' needs—and with the notion that intellectual property will lose much of its value anyway as content proliferates on the Net. That wasn't "should," but "will." However, the IP crowd on the Council didn't think I knew the difference ($\Rightarrow$ Chapter 6). There was also an attitude of "let's just leave it alone" when I suggested that we needed to think about the issues that would be raised by pornography on the Net.

Overall, we agreed that privacy is important and that intellectual property should be protected, without going into the pesky details that we couldn't agree on. Our most useful and lasting achievement was project Kickstart, an initiative that eventually morphed into the government's current efforts to get the Net into schools nationwide. Perhaps the most important aspect of Kickstart was that it encouraged local communities to do it for themselves ($\Rightarrow$ Chapter 4).

Back at home . . .

All the while, by the mid-'90s, I was leading a different life in my day job. Daphne Kis, my partner since 1988, was running the business, leaving me free to spend time on other things. We had hired another writer, Jerry Michalski (since replaced by Kevin Werbach), to write the newsletter. I had started investing in information and Net-oriented start-ups, first in Central and Eastern Europe, and then back in the United States.

On the technical side, we now had a direct Internet connection in New York at my company, EDventure, and my e-mail package, Eudora, was easy to use and powerful. I could filter messages automatically and assign them to different categories. I joined a number of mailing lists, and started, just occasionally, surfing the Net. I became one of those people with a secret smile, and I urged my friends to get online so that we could communicate more easily.

There's a funny feeling you get when you see that someone you know is finally on e-mail. They have "come in," as in a spy novel. They're part of the club.

Ironically, as we started using e-mail within the company and with outsiders, it didn't mean I could travel less. In fact, it meant I could travel more and still keep up with daily goings-on at the office. Sometimes when I'm in Russia—where it's still complicated and difficult to phone overseas—I can go all week without talking to the office, but keep in close touch by e-mail. There's nothing that replaces my physical presence, though, either in Poland or in the office in New York. It's just that now they know me well enough in New York that I don't have to be there all the time! (For all the exotic things you can do with e-mail, one of my favorite services is the Daily Soup menu from a little soup shop around the corner from my office in New York. Because it comes every evening by e-mail, I receive it wherever I am. It's a lot of fun to sit in a snowstorm in, say, Gdansk, Poland, and know that back home the specials are Chicken Coconut—Medium $5.95, Large $7.50, X-Large $12.95; Chicken Garlic Bread—Medium $5.95, Large $7.50, X-Large $12.95; Crawfish Étouffée—Medium $7.95, Large $9.50, X-Large $14.95.)

. . . and at the Electronic Frontier Foundation

At the Electronic Frontier Foundation, meanwhile, we had moved to Washington, D.C., from our initial home in Mitch's offices in Cambridge, Massachusetts. We had, almost despite ourselves, became a full-fledged Beltway player, trying to influence government legislation although officially we were "educating," not lobbying. But our hearts weren't in it. Mitch didn't like Washington much and was withdrawing from the organization. Our former executive director, Jerry Berman, left to start his own organization, the Center for Democracy and Technology, which now works together with EFF in Washington on common issues such as privacy. EFF itself picked up and moved to Silicon Valley. I became chairman by default, on the condition that we could find a good executive director to do the real work. We found Lori Fena, a software entrepreneur who had sold her company (to another CEO she met at PC Forum) and was now eager to apply her entrepreneurial talents to something socially beneficial.

(I have since handed the chairmanship on to Lori, and remain as an active board member. In some sense, I have taken the time I used to spend on EFF and devoted it to this book: both publicizing *Release 2.0,* which means giving talks and interviews about the concepts discussed here, and working on *Release 2.1,* as well as keeping track of what's happening, responding to feedback, and so forth. It's much the same sort of work, but to a broader audience. Of course, *Release 2.0* doesn't have a board of independent-minded activists, but I find a lot of those on my travels anyway!)

Whether it was two women running the place or the California influence, EFF has fundamentally changed its focus from keeping the government out of the Net, to trying to figure out how to build appropriate governance from within. We do want rules; we just don't want rules imposed by centralized powers that frequently tend to flout their own rules, often in secret. Instead of just telling the government to keep out, we're fostering initiatives that will let individuals and private organizations perform some of the tasks of Net governance—most notably TRUSTe as a means for people to protect their own privacy (⟹ Chapter 8).

We're leading the fight for freedom of speech on the Net not just by arguing against censorship, but by promoting the notion that people should be able to control the content they (and their children) receive for themselves (⟹ Chapter 7).

Overall, the EFF is a good model of the sort of group you'll find on the Net. It's not a democracy, ruled by votes and opinion polls: It's a self-appointed voice in the discussion, supported by people who choose to join us. We're more interested in gathering adherents by persuasion and illumination than in merely representing existing opinion.

The EFF also reflects some of the weaknesses of fledgling Net communities. At times, it seems to leave the public behind. Both we and the people we disagree with are often too shrill. It's so easy for self-appointed guardians of the digital world to tell their opponents: "We're right and you're immoral!"

We may be right, but we have to persuade people, not overwhelm them. We might even learn something in a rational discussion. My purpose in writing this book is to explain how I came to think the way I do, and to let you judge those conclusions for yourself.

Chapter 2

Communities

By 1997, "community" had become one of the trendiest words around, both on and off the Internet. In the context of this book and of the online world in general, a community is the unit in which people live, work, and play. Most individuals live in several communities online, just as they do in the physical world—family, church or temple, soccer club, professional society, workplace. Some communities are formal, with rules and duties, entrance requirements, and perhaps membership fees; others are less formal groupings with loose boundaries and revolving membership. As the world seems to get more complex and more overwhelming, and public life ever more scary, people look to communities for fellowship and security.

Used right, the Internet can be a powerful enabling technology fostering the development of communities because it supports the very thing that creates a community—human interaction. One benefit of the Internet is that it allows the formation of communities independent of geography. People need only share interests or goals and find one another. Conversely, people are not stuck in the communities they are born in—not entirely, at least. The programmer in India can argue with his peers in Silicon Valley or Budapest about the finer points of the Java programming language. Also, the Internet overcomes some of the barriers of time: both between time zones, and in the sense that it's quicker to send an e-mail than to drive to a community center—let alone cross the world. It's even quicker than finding an envelope and a stamp, and you can do it at your convenience, while the other person does it at *his* convenience.

There will be—there already is—a profusion of online communities. They are easy to find, and relatively easy to form. But what holds them together? Can a single person in fact be a member of twenty different communities, with each getting his attention fifteen minutes a day (for a total of five hours online)? Online communities may engage in conversations and other interaction through the medium of a particular Web site or through mailing lists or newsgroups—people linked together by text messages and increasingly through multimedia virtual places that they enter from time to time. A newsgroup is a virtual bulletin board, which members post to or read on their own schedule. A mailing list (or listserv) is like an active newsgroup; it sends regular messages out to its members, but it also generally maintains archives for people to search.

Online virtual places can be anything from a virtual room where people describe in text what is happening—"Alice looks at her shoes and bites her lip"*—to full-scale multimedia locations where people

---

*This compelling snip of text is courtesy of Amy Bruckman, a grad student at MIT who runs the MediaMOO online community.

Community vs. culture

Communities often have a culture, but there is an important distinction between culture and community. Culture is a set of rules, perceptions, language, history, and the like. It is embodied in books and songs, people's minds, and Web sites. Culture can be learned, even though there are some communities that believe you need to be born into them to be a member (as in Germany and many Asian countries, as well as certain Jewish groups).

In the new sense, a community is a set of relationships. You could (in principle) take a culture and revive it: You could teach people the history, the manners, and the rules, and they could live by them. But you could never revive a particular community, because a community depends on the people in it. Just like education, a community is not a passive thing. Its members need to invest in it for it to exist. An individual can be familiar with any number of cultures simply by studying them. But to be a member of a community he has to be present in it, contribute to it, and be known to other members. Thus, a television channel or an Internet "channel" can create or reflect a culture, but in order for it to become a community its members have to communicate with one another—ideally in the context of some goal. That goal may be only homage to a star, but it could also be political action, a business plan, or a school.

A community is a shared asset, created by the investment of its members. The more you put in, the more you take out.

"The love you take is equal to the love you make."

—The Beatles

COMMUNITY

The Internet will not make a difference at all in the world as we know it. Nothing has changed, nothing will change. Ignorance, racism and supernatural religions based on outdated myths will continue to rule our world because 90 percent of humans do not know how to think logically. The Internet creates communities, yes, but they are the same communities as before. Nothing has changed. Humankind remains essentially stupid, living in fear in a dark cave. We still have a long way to go to realize true community. Maybe another 5,000–10,000 years.

Dan Bloom danbloom@geocities.com

are represented by "avatars"—cartoon figures, images of themselves, or any other symbol they choose. Some of these places support voice or even video. Then there are "buddy lists," which enable you to see which of your friends or colleagues are currently online, and virtually tap them on the shoulder as if to say, "May I talk to you now?" (People can put up "do not disturb" signs, or say something like "Working on Berkman project; don't bother me otherwise.")

Online as offline, what you bring to a community determines what you get out of it. This ranges from a community of two, of which the canonical form is marriage, to a community of two thousand. People's online communities will reflect their daily lives as more and more people go online: their extended families; their colleagues at work, including customers and suppliers and possibly competitors; their school friends; and so on. As people move around physically, from school to camp and college and from job to job, from chance meetings on holidays to various kinds of interest groups, they will join new communities and probably drop out of others.

The great Net hope

For me, the great hope of the Net is that more and more people will be led to get involved with it, and that using it will change their overall

RE: "TRUE" COMMUNITY

Dan, Don't you enjoy participating in—even directing—evolution, at least social evolution? My interest in computer-mediated communication over the past 10 years has grown out of my work as a community development professional and my volunteer work with community based organizations. My initial excitement was in imagining how much more efficient and democratic a community organization could be if its members supplemented face to face and phone communications with online communications. I've put that excitement into practice successfully in a number of organizations. But now I'm beginning to look beyond enhancement of existing organizations to what types of organizations and new communities computer-mediated communication makes possible. Reading parts of Esther's book had further expanded my conceptions of what's possible. At the same time, I've come to appreciate the difficulty involved in building community—perhaps for some of the reasons that you cite. So the question for me is that if the experience and culture of knowing how to build community has been a sign of our "progress" till now (even you look forward to the day when we can surpass current imperfect efforts and form "true community"), then the qualitative increase in community-building success that will be spawned by computer technology will represent a true great leap forward for humankind. Hope you're part of the solution, not part of the problem.

Steve Weinberg nevets2@aol.com

experience of life. Power in one sphere changes one's perception of one's capabilities in general. Right now, politically, the United States is in a sorry state. Only 49 percent of the potential voters bothered to vote in the most recent presidential elections. (Compare that to Russia, where more people voted, but there's even less feeling of involvement.) People are rational, and they know that one person's vote won't change the outcome. Others feel a certain social responsibility, and so they vote anyway. But voting alone does not make a real democracy, any more than taxes are an expression of philanthropy.

From cyberspace to real space

I feel this intensely because it so happens that I have never voted, although I have certainly paid a lot of taxes.* For many years, I just ignored the government and it ignored me. Then I started spending a lot of time in Washington because of the Electronic Frontier Foundation and the National Information Infrastructure Advisory Council, and my attitudes changed. To be sure, even with the advent of the Net not everyone gets invited to Washington, but suddenly everyone is invited to contribute if he or she cares enough to go to any relevant Web site or discussion group. Although I haven't yet voted formally, I feel that I have a meaningful voice and a meaningful stake in what our government does. I'm a far more active citizen than before I raised my voice, and I care about the consequences. This doesn't mean that the folks in Washington are rushing to follow my advice. But if my ideas are valid, other people will amplify them and they will be heard.

The Net will involve a growing portion of the population in this kind of governance, and their feeling of empowerment will spread to other parts of their lives. The secret is that the Internet doesn't actually *do* much; it's a powerful tool for people to use. It's not something worth having, but it's a powerful lever for people to use to accomplish their own goals in collaboration with other people. It's more than a source of information; it's a way for people to organize themselves. It gives them power *for* themselves, rather than *over* others.

Net participation

How many times have you wanted to complain about something, but you gave up because it was just too difficult? I recently flew Delta to Moscow and back from Warsaw, and neither time did they have power

---

*The one time I tried to register to vote I was told I had to go to some office with my birth certificate because I was born in Switzerland, even though I've been a U.S. citizen since childhood. I didn't *have* my birth certificate and it just seemed so complicated that I gave up. I feel a little embarrassed about it; my only lame excuse is that I have other priorities. I now *have* sent in a form to register, but I haven't voted yet.

outlets for my computer, as they had more or less promised in their ads. I complained to the flight attendant. The next morning I went to register my complaint on the Delta Web site. An hour later, I got an automatic notification that my message had been received. And less than three weeks later, I actually got a nice e-mail from one D. E. Coberly that didn't look like a form letter; it specifically talked about the schedule for upgrading the aircraft with power outlets.

Sometimes, I'm in a better mood. I might even like to compliment a company on something in hopes that they'll keep doing it—Marriott's excellent in-room facilities for computers, for example—although in this case I'd rather do it in public so that other hotels will follow suit. (There—consider it done!)

Sometimes I want to write a letter to the editor, but it's just too inconvenient; by the time I get to a computer, type a letter, print it out, and fax it (let alone mail it!), I've lost the urge.

People are not naturally lazy, but they avoid useless effort and are overwhelmed by competing demands. Though we're not quite there yet, in the future the Net *will* make it easier for people to participate in a variety of communities—and do so more effectively. Smart businesses will encourage consumer feedback; smart politicians will solicit and even listen to comments from constituents; smart newspapers will welcome letters by e-mail and foster online discussions.

And individuals will rise to the occasion. The Net will foster activity instead of passivity.

Basic principles

Here are a few basic principles for communities, based on my own experience both on- and offline:

* Each participant should be clear about what he is giving and what he hopes to get. Overall, those desires should mesh, although they may well be different for each individual.
* There should be a way of determining who is in the community and who is outside it. Otherwise the community is meaningless.

* Community members should feel that they have invested in the community, and that therefore it is tough for them to leave. The ultimate punishment in a strong community is banishment, expulsion, excommunication, exile. . . . All those words signify the terror of being cast out of a community.
* The community's rules should be clear, and there should be recourse if they are broken.

Communities fail when these principles are not observed: for example, the marriage in which one person loves a partner who is deceiving him, as opposed to one where one partner provides sex in exchange for a life of ease. Some people might see the latter as a moral failure, but it is a valid community. The dance club where people are screened in or out by a bouncer may or may not be a valid community, depending on how well the bouncer knows the crowd and whether they know one another. On the other hand, a good bartender can create a wonderful community, as illustrated in countless plays and television shows, or by Rick in the movie *Casablanca*.

Vested interest

What kinds of investment can one make in a community? There are two things people can give easily, especially over the Net: time and money. Paying $19.95 a month for America Online doesn't really make you part of the community, nor does it make it hard for you to leave (it may actually encourage you to do so to save money), but it does signify a certain commitment. Time is often more valuable. Emotionally, you will want to justify that spending of time or money because you value what you have paid for.

In the real world, community members often contribute (or own) real estate, which is why in the past voting rights were often restricted to landowners; they were considered the only ones with a true stake in the community (and they paid taxes for that privilege). Now, in many countries, language as well as birth is a gauge of membership. In the Baltics, for example, the old ethnic identities are reasserting themselves

GOOD AND BAD (reaction to a radio talk show)

ED: In another venue I might well agree with you on the "morality" argument, but in talk radio I'm just trying to make clear that "community" itself is not valuable; the substance of the community is. And that morality is a good thing. It's complicated—as you illustrate. Believing that races are different is not immoral; treating individuals unfairly (or trying to exterminate them) because of that is.

I wish you would extend your analysis of morality and the web, and get onto more sophisticated and defensible ground. You said that there were healthy communities on the web that were nevertheless "immoral," such as Nazi hate groups. I would restrict the application of the term moral to acts and interpersonal behaviors, not ideas and words by themselves. If you really believe that races are unequal, I don't think it's immoral for you to say so. If we silenced the ignorant, how could we teach them? How would we know whom to teach, or what most needed to be taught? I'd rather know where the Nazis are and what they're saying than try to suppress them and force them underground where their resentment could build. I also want children to know that grown-ups can be more ignorant than they are and that they have to learn to block out falseness even if people are allowed to speak ugly nonsense.

From: "Dean Hannotte" <dhannotte@classic.msn.com> [software architect / social critic]

through language; Russian residents who went to Soviet/Russian schools and never learned the local language are now being disenfranchised in their local geographic communities. In the United States, use of Spanish is a political issue in border states such as California, Texas, and Florida.

Sharing food is another mark of community, reflected in everything from statements about breaking bread together to customs such as potluck dinners. In many communities, people share their labor, building houses for one family after another. On the Net, they share their time, ideas, and experiences—food for thought or discussion, so to speak.

Community rules

A community sets its rules for itself. Often, they're invisible until they're broken or questioned; then they're discussed and somehow issues get decided. The decision could be made by the community moderator; it could be by vote. As it happens, while I was writing this, the question of use of people's comments outside a community came up. It happened on the Online Europe list, started as an offshoot of the 1996 High-Tech Forum in Europe and run by Steve Carlson, a Net entrepreneur in Hungary. About half its members are people who were with us at the forum in Lisbon; the other half have joined through friends and referrals. One point to note: This community does not run itself; Steve is always haranguing us to contribute, to be interesting. Sometimes he poses questions to get the conversation flowing. Recently, Bill O'Neill inadvertently started a discussion that needed no coaxing. Bill, editor of the (U.K.) *Guardian* newspaper's technology coverage, asked if he could quote us freely . . . But here! Read for yourself:

Date: 09:14 PM 5/26/97 0200
http://pk4.com
To: online-europe@isys.hu
From: bill.oneill@guardian.co.uk (United Kingdom)
Subject: Re: online-e question for posting to list

Comments contributed to online-europe are likely to be of interest (and of relevance) to a wider (and less specialised) audience. How would contributors feel if journalists (like me) published the material elsewhere (in my case, in the paper and on an associated Web site)? I'd always assumed that comments to online-europe were not only non-attributable but also off-the-record; in effect, that they provided informed background material, and that's all. However, I now realize that the material is posted on a Web site, which puts that material in the public domain (so that comments are as attributable and on-the-record as the medium allows). In practical terms, it would be foolhardy of me to promise to let anyone and everyone know if their comments are likely to be published elsewhere. But is there any objection to the idea of comments to online-europe being published in another medium, or in a different section of the same medium?

>===============
> Bill O'Neill
> Editor, Online
> The Guardian

From: edyson@edventure.com (Esther Dyson)
Subject: Re: online-e question for posting to list

Hey Bill!
Why not play a version of Tom Sawyer, and offer to republish our witty, insightful commentary for a small fee?
Just kidding! (Seriously, I had no expectations of privacy, and of course I'd be flattered.)
Esther

After my flip answer, a number of more serious people weighed in . . .

From: Steven Carlson<steve@pk4.com>
>===============
I feel a discussion coming on . . .
Bill O'Neill has asked whether your comments to Online Europe are publicly quotable. As a journalist, he (and perhaps others) might find it useful to gather material here.
Esther has stated she finds this okay. Alex begs to differ. He thinks the journalists should ask for permission before quoting.

This is a question of list policy, and I'd like to hear your opinions. As the list moderator, I will make the final decision (somebody has to, after all) but I want to base that decision on the general consensus of the list. Here are my thoughts . . . Whether you are aware of it, or not, this list is automatically archived at <http://www.isys.hu/online-europe/>. Thus, in a very real way what you say on Online Europe is already on record publicly.

Many of us wouldn't mind a bit of publicity, either. Knowing that you might be published in the Guardian (Bill's paper) might raise the value of participating in the list. At least for some.

And finally, Bill's job will be much easier if he can simply grab a quote and tell you later. Journalists usually work with ridiculously tight deadlines. Having said that, online works a bit differently than print. It's more informal. Many of us dash off a quick opinion, perhaps regretting it later, but figure what the hell, it all disappears into the ether anyway.

The people on the WELL long ago developed a policy Alex refers to, known as "You Own Your Own Words." That means, among other things, that others have to ask permission before quoting you in print. It allows us to express ourselves without worrying that those words might come back to haunt us. My suggestion . . .

Perhaps Bill (and others) could ask the list questions, stating that he intends to use the answers in print. That makes it clear that your opinion will be "on the record." If you wanted to answer informally, you would write "off the record" to let him know.

Finally, as a courtesy, I'd like to see Online Europe mentioned in the quote. After all, this list is a form of publication, and is the source of the quote. And now I'd like to hear your opinions . . .

From here on, it's just excerpts, to save you the e-mail "overhead."

From: "Scott McQuade" <smcquade@hotmail.com>(United States)

>Bill O'Neill has asked whether your comments to Online Europe are >publicly quotable.
Of course they are.
1. They are already 'published', i.e., transmitted between two or more people.
2. They are archived in a public place. Bill can make 'fair use' of any material on the Web or any other forum—listserv, Usenet or whatever. Fair use only requires him to avoid repeating the entire contents and to cite the source, i.e., "Steven Carlson said in the Online Europe forum that . . ."
It's nice of him to warn us that he's likely to quote from postings. He's certainly not obliged. However, the operators of the list might best protect themselves by warning participants (e.g., upon entry) that the list is archived on the Web—it seems at least one of us was unaware.
Bill might also make the courtesy of providing a hyperlink to the original. He's already indicated he would advise the list/ contributor once a quote has been lifted—again, something he is not obliged to do.

From: Dale Amon as Operator<root@starbase1.gpl.net> (Ireland)

If you don't want to be quoted, you don't go out to the local with a journalist. . . . One can make different policies on closed groups like this, but again, if you invite a journalist to your pub, you had better be ready to hear the echo of your words.

From: Boris Basmadjiev<boris@bulnet.bg>(Bulgaria)

You know, I strongly feel that what we say and write here is private—in the sense that many people can have a conversation which is private. Many of our remarks can mean quite a lot of different things to laymen, or if quoted out of place and character, etc. So I would suggest that anybody wanting a quote just ask for one—as some have done—and then quote the list, the person who said so, etc.

I would suggest that since this list is for professionals, it deserves the same attitude as (for instance) the conversation of a couple of doctors behind the closed doors of their office, right? Need I say more—we had a writer asking what INET was, and I wouldn't want to have him quote ANYTHING I ever say without prior permission.

Anybody can quote anybody else—as long as they ask for direct permission, I think.

And it goes on and on; online discussions, like other conversations, can get pretty involved. . . . You can see the whole thing at the URL Steve Carlson mentioned: <http://www.isys.hu/online-europe/>. And finally, one more message, from me:

And of course now I have to send another message to all of you, with the quote above, asking each one individually to give permission.

Because my resolution of the discussion would be the following:

Yes, our comments here are public-domain, in that no one could sue for having them used. But if Bill O'Neill, or I, or anyone, wants to remain a member of the community, he has to show both politeness and discretion, and judgment. That is, he should ask to use our quotes, and he should use them in context. Should he correct the misspellings of his own name? Now there's a question!

Okay guys! May I quote you?

Esther

The role of government vs. self-help

Government can play a divisive role vis-à-vis communities. Often, the more government provides, the less community members themselves contribute.* For example, parents tend to identify less with a government-provided school than with a private school they raise money for and oversee themselves. Yet parents can "invest" in public schools too, by taking an active role in school administration, coaching soccer teams, running school events, and participating in parent-teacher meetings. Often, families join neighborhood communities through their children; single people tend to identify with their jobs or their after-work activities. All these facets of human nature translate easily to the online world. It's harder to build houses, but people can get together to build virtual environments, discussion groups, even markets.

It is often just as deadly for the government to take over communities as for commercial interests to do so. And in cyberspace the results are the same: The members fight and then flee. There's a community spirit that has more to do with influence than with voting, more to do with being heard than with ownership.

Commerce and community

As a concept, community is contrasted mostly with commerce. But one of my favorite communities is Jerry Kaplan's Onsale, an online auction house that specializes in computer equipment but also handles jewelry, cameras, and other high-ticket goods. (Their motto: "Put your money where your mouse is.") The traditional notion of online shopping is sterile and lonely—the user and an array of goods and prices, perhaps with a salesperson on call at the click of a mouse. But think of

*Even in the physical world, the government doesn't entirely control the community. A city may think it "owns" the city streets, but at some point, if the government doesn't do its job, the citizens may take those streets back, with their own neighborhood associations or their own vigilante groups. But that process is much slower and more dangerous than what happens in cyberspace.

where people really like to go shopping: They like Loehmann's where they can get an opinion on an outrageous dress from the lady one mirror over in the communal dressing room; they like Borders or Barnes & Noble, where they can sip cappuccino with a fellow literature lover; or they like auctions, where they can bid against other people, not against a computer.

As you can see from the screen shot on page 59, the people at Onsale have personalities, even though they don't have those cute avatars (cartoon representations) that some online services offer. To the members of the Onsale community, SY of Cambridge, AW of Honolulu, and DT of Lafayette are real people: stingy or spendthrift, wise or foolish, earnest or witty. They look to one another to see what's a good deal and what is best left to a die-hard fan of elephant memorabilia.

Many markets are communities, not just mechanisms for setting prices. On Wall Street, traders like to drink together after work. These people have invested in their community. They know one another and each other's reputations. They have watched each person's behavior, perhaps swallowed a bad deal in hopes of getting a better one later. They share history, dialogue, and perhaps common enemies—the guy who never gave anyone an edge on any deal.

These communities are built on participation; their members act and interact.

For-profit communities

So, communities can be commercial, or they can be not-for-profit. The notion of commercial communities often offends people, although most people spend time in commercial environments every day. There are commercial communities at work; there are athletic clubs and hairdressers, bars and bookstores. Someone has to pay the rent—although the rent is usually a lot lower in cyberspace than in the physical world.

Often it works the other way: The "owner"—a company or an individual leader—thinks it owns the community. But then that owner

Auction Number:	84558
Sales Format:	Yankee Auction(TM)
Starting Bid per unit:	$169.00
Bid Increment:	$5.00
Quantity Available:	6
Current Bid Range	$169.00-$174.00
Auction closes at or after:	Wed Jun 25, 1997 12:02 pm Pacific Time
Last Bid Received At:	Wed Jun 25, 1997 8:40 am Pacific Time

PREVIOUS   NEXT   CATEGORIES   HOME

PLACE BID

Go To: Product Information Shipping and Handling Warranty

Current High Bidders

1. PG of San Jose, CA, Wed Jun 25, 8:40 am ($174.00, 1)
2. TP of Enfield, CT, Tue Jun 24, 3:08 pm ($169.00, 1)
3. GC of Haddonfield, NJ, Tue Jun 24, 5:33 pm ($169.00, 1)
4. SY of Cambridge, MA, Tue Jun 24, 7:10 pm ($169.00, 1) : "YES YES YES! the one I need!"
5. AW of Honolulu, HI, Tue Jun 24, 7:19 pm ($169.00, 1) : "Will be useful when working the farm!"
6. DT of Lafayette, CA, Tue Jun 24, 10:36 pm ($169.00, 1) : "My voice is my passport. Verify me."

Product Information

Panasonic 30 Channel 900MHz Cordless Phone with Digital Answering System & 3 Mailboxes

Model: Panasonic KX-T9550

Product Description

COMMUNITIES

I don't believe that audiovisual interaction will replace text as the primary communication channel for this community any more than videophones have replaced telephones, within my lifetime. Why? Because the task of editing and manipulating an audiovisual record to present the sort of coherent and (if I may be permitted to abuse the term) literate exchange that we have become accustomed to still, despite the advances we have made in "multimedia" technology, remains highly labor-intensive. I can see a sort of "avatar" mechanism being used, but behind the avatar will still be someone with a keyboard and probably a mouse assembling and editing the textual material the avatar will speak. There will no doubt be more social communities where the content of discussion will be more casual and less well thought out . . . but they will be the online equivalents of bars and clubs, a new kind of community, but not a replacement for the ones we have now.

Peter da Silva peter@taronga.com

finds out that even though it may own the facilities, collect the membership fees, and provide the towels, golf clubs, alcohol or online entertainment, hairdressing, or editorial services, the community owns whatever it is that keeps people from leaving. The "owner" may make and enforce the rules, but if he tries to change them without general consent, the community may well take over. Worse, it may just up and leave. Something like that faced San Francisco's WELL, where a tight-knit membership rejected new, financially oriented management.

There's no necessary conflict in an owner's making a profit. Conflict occurs when the members aren't happy. Running online communities will become a big market in the long run. Many will be local, closer to an extension of the local shopper paper than, say, *Time* magazine. Some will be sponsored by advertisers or supported by transaction fees. Others will charge membership fees.*

*What's the difference between a tax and a user/membership fee? Basically, one is required and the other is optional. Is the fee we pay to Microsoft for Windows

Like terrestrial communities, good online communities require care and tending. Members need someone to resolve disputes, set the tone, find the sponsors, or collect the fees. Someone needs to maintain the database or whatever software manages the conversations, deal with the vendors who are supporting the community or communicating with it, and define the rules or modify them in accordance with community interests.

Online communities will vary broadly, and some community operators will do a good job while others won't. The criterion of a "good job" is set by the members—both the critical mass who stay, and those who leave. In the end, if the community does not operate in the interests of its members, whoever they are, it will not survive. But the damage is not as great as in physical communities, where buildings deteriorate, criminals take over, and the most defenseless people have nowhere else to go.

Not-for-profit communities

One real benefit of the digital medium is its low cost, at least by developed-world standards. Just as the Net will foster a profusion of entrepreneurs who can now set up in business for themselves with little capital, so will it encourage philanthropic entrepreneurs. The Net lowers barriers to entry in all kinds of activities. Already there are a number of online museums, many online interest groups, and Web sites and mailing lists supporting interests ranging from Native-American culture to the worldwide fight against child labor. Such groups will proliferate.

It used to take market forces or huge amounts of charity to foster long-distance communications and the communities they support; now it's cheap. One of the organizations I'm involved in, the Eurasia Foundation, makes a tight budget go a long way in helping nonprofit organizations in the former Soviet Union keep their community together.

---

really closer to a tax we pay for the sheer benefit of membership in a Microsoft-dominated world?

They can bolster their resolve in difficult circumstances and band together to lobby for new laws or spread information about existing laws that are being ignored by local authorities. The Net provides a continuing lifeline as graduates of Foundation-sponsored economics courses, journalism training, and other programs apply their new skills at home in local communities that often find their ideas strange and their enthusiasm suspect.

Online support for community

But there's more to the Net than just "virtual" communities. There are lots of "real" communities that also exist online. To listen to many people talk, you'd think we're all going to slip off into cyberspace and leave our daily lives behind. People who read about communities in cyberspace often get online, and then wonder what all the fuss is about. Yes, there are those chat rooms, but many of those are for people who want titillation more than community. You can't necessarily find community on the Net any more reliably than in real life.

NO "PLACE" NO COMMUNITY

It is a long-standing contention of mine that a real on-line community (as opposed to the sort of stuff that is claimed to be "community" but really isn't) (a) always involves a true small group phenomenon at its core and (b) requires an adequate "place" within which people are able to interact with one another reasonably well. The present context (which appears to be very similar to, if not actually based on, the Well Engaged software) is one of many examples of one that does NOT provide an adequate "place". To try to communicate with others in a group here (as most other places on the Web) is like being suddenly afflicted with some sort of severe physical handicap. Compared to the environment in the on-line community in which I spend a great deal of my time (the Canopus Research Forum on CompuServe) most of what is out here on the Web is downright hostile territory to real community formation. All the best,

Will Zachmann wfz@CanopusResearch.com

Usually, you get into a community through an introduction, online or offline. Or you have to take a little time to establish your presence for others. Even online, community still consists of the people behind the computers and the intangible—neither physical nor electronic—ties that bind them.

So it makes sense to think of the Net as community *support,* not a community (or communities) in itself. The Net can support all kinds of communities. As I've shown, my own communities tend to operate through e-mail. We use the Net for our communications, for sending and sharing information, for setting up meetings, for catching up on news. Other communities operate through the Web, with people posting and reacting to one another's comments, or even representing themselves as avatars. People can put up their own home pages describing themselves, but what makes a community is the interaction among people, not their mere presence.

Beyond that, I can imagine a lot of physical communities using the Net in more mundane ways: bulletin boards for teenagers offering babysitting services, listings of school events, sites for restaurants with constantly changing daily specials, news of local sports teams. People in companies can use online support to share information about sales prospects or competitors' activities; they can also organize company outings, complain about the state of the bathrooms, or recommend local coffee shops.

In the future, we'll take online community support for granted. Some communities will be mostly offline, some mostly online, and people's physical locations won't matter as much. But that won't be the key thing about any particular community. In any kind of community, the key thing will be its members. A technical system can support a community, but it needs active members to lead it and to make it worth joining.

Community questions

Many facets of online communities aren't yet clear. What is the right size for a community? The answer certainly will vary according to a number of factors, but over time we should have a better understanding, much as we do of cities and villages today. How do communities split up into smaller communities when they get too large, or when a group simply decides to go off on its own for other reasons? One intriguing point, from anthropologist George Gumerman at the Santa Fe Institute in New Mexico, is that homogeneous communities can be relatively indifferent to size, whereas communities with complex social roles need to have the right number of people to fill those roles: one medicine man, one trainer of youth, one village chief, one spiritual leader, and so forth. If the community grows, too many people may be vying for one role; if it shrinks, certain roles may go unfilled. Such communities tend to have strong rules about family size, and about members joining or leaving the community. It will be interesting to see how that translates into online communities: one social director, one head of member programs, one advertising manager. . . .

What doesn't work

Clearly, some things do *not* foster community. You do not need a real identity, but you need *some* identity ($\Longrightarrow$ Chapter 9). You need to have a voice, a reputation, a presence to be part of a community, because it is (at least) a two-way proposition. Thus, "lurkers," people who only read or listen, are not really part of the community. They may fancy themselves to be, but no one would miss them if they left. They are fans, not friends. Lurkers may latch on to a culture, but they do not contribute to it. (That's why fandom is so eerie: There's usually no real communication between the fans and the stars, just lurkers and fantasies on one side and a PR machine on the other.)

Thus, a particular community may contain pseudonymous members who are valued on the basis of what they contribute to it. If someone's contribution is based on falsehood, then that individual may have a problem. But pseudonymity can also be a mask that allows a person to reveal a true identity rather than to hide one, or to allow a true expression of one facet of that individual's character.

Thus, a self-help group of anonymous people is hard to define as a community unless the members at least have persistent (though pseudonymous) identities. A monologue explaining who you are does not bring you into a community, however good it feels and however cathartic or liberating it may be.

There are good experiences without community . . . and there are bad communities. Imagine, for example, a community built around shared hatred of Jews or Serbians or the U.S. government, working on ways to "cleanse" the neighborhood or destroy supposed enemies. It may be a good example of a community, with shared contributions and common interests—but a horrible example of humanity.

That illustrates the biggest danger in the ease of forming and enclosing communities—their ability to insulate themselves from the rest of society. People in most physical communities encounter reality from time to time, be it on the streets of a neighborhood, a network television broadcast, or the front page of a newspaper. Online communities can exist sealed away from reality. Members can trade lies or illusions among themselves without fear of contradiction. (As I have said, the Net is a great medium for conspiracy, while television is best for propaganda.)

Tricky questions: Freedom of speech

Many social norms differ from community to community. They include censorship/freedom of speech, religion, the inclusion of children, and the like. On many of these issues, communities will simply agree to disagree, and observe and enforce the rules they think appropriate internally.

Freedom of speech is one of those near-absolute freedoms that Americans cherish and many other countries think we honor too much. In other societies, where convention governs more than law anyway, the sorts of things we may legally say in the United States are considered appalling and uncultured, to say nothing of offensive or dangerous. Americans (including me) answer back that this is the price we pay for freedom of speech—and our related freedoms to think for ourselves, to criticize our government, to believe as we want.

Communities will set their own standards for what is appropriate.

People who select or receive content from the Net can use filtering tools to determine what they see as individuals ($\Rightarrow$ Chapter 7), but here I'm talking about content within a community—what people say to one another, what they post in public "online spaces," and so forth. What will your company allow you to say about the chairman on the corporate intranet, or even outside on the Internet at large? How rude can you be when you disagree with someone? How much informality or bad spelling is tolerated at work? What about in a community of poets? How commercial can you be in a sports discussion group? Is Juan allowed to promote his sporting goods store when Alice asks a question about fishing tackle? How loudly can either of them criticize the person who sold her the fishing rod she uses now?

The answers to these questions are norms, not laws. Usually a community can handle them for itself. People chide one another; others complain; leaders calm things down. Over time, people in a group learn how to live together—or they go off in search of more compatible (for them) communities.

Many terrestrial governments that fear freedom of speech will probably try to prohibit their citizens from visiting (let alone speaking in) Net communities outside their own countries. In the long run, that makes no sense. Apart from protecting children, the best response to "offensive" speech, however defined, is not to bury it, but to answer it. (The best response to obscenity is to ignore it. And the best response to child pornography, which involves actual children, is to track down and prosecute the people involved.)

More troubling than "indecency" is what to do with genuinely dangerous information such as bomb-making instructions, maps of sensitive security installations, and the like. There is no perfect answer. The kind of bomb-making information available in chemistry textbooks is best left free precisely so that it doesn't acquire the lure of the forbidden. And I do know that most laws against content can't ultimately be effective; they will simply drive information underground, where only the worst people can get at it. Nonetheless, some stuff shouldn't be published by the people who have it. Such information is often classified and can be kept off the Net by law and secrecy agreements at the source, and by the local decisions of communities that don't want the responsibility on their own heads.* Freedom of speech does not mean "obligation to publish."

Government censorship is unlikely to be effective in the long run, even though governments will keep trying. France outlawed the printing of polling information in the prelude to its recent national elections; those who cared simply got the information from the Net, published by French-language news sources in nearby Switzerland. Germany embroiled CompuServe in a lawsuit over porn and Nazi material, now on appeal.

Nonetheless, we live in a world where governments—even democratic governments—still do things Americans and others find unconscionable. As long as governments control people physically, they can instill fear and keep all but the most determined dissidents under intellectual control, too—not just by cutting wires or employing technical filtering tools and tapping lines (with encryption outlawed), but by getting neighbor to spy on neighbor. They will be able to control the overall level of discourse in their countries if they are willing to lose many of the Net's benefits. But they will fail to keep their most dedicated dissident citizens from connecting with the rest of the world.

Changing culture

Clearly, Net culture is changing. It is no longer dominated by upper-middle-class males who speak (only) English. The commercial community has found the Net, and it is increasingly a business medium. But grandparents and social workers have found it, too. Nonprofit organizations are big users, especially in far-flung locations where other means of communication are prohibitively expensive. In the United States and in wired regions such as Scandinavia, the Net is becoming a consumer medium. In most other countries, it's still

*But in fact, way too much information is classified, most of it probably "dangerous" only to the officials involved.

LET'S GO BEYOND COMMUNITIES

The Net is the first medium to come along in decades to empower the American public to take back the power it ceded to the corporate world. The "public airwaves" have been, since 1934 (in the case of television), controlled for the profit and benefit of those non-humans (a.k.a. corporations) who have the rights but not the responsibilities of citizens who are in no real way accountable to the public. There has never before been a communications medium that put the power of broadcast speech in the hands of most average people. If the population can learn how to organize itself quickly enough, it can establish in this medium a completely grassroots communication network that operates independently of the corporate-owned media (which will never permit the public to understand how the corporate-controlled political and economic systems really work). Ultimately, the Net could enable the public to take back political control. But since the intelligence of a group tends to be inversely proportional to the square of the number of its members, I have some doubt about the public's ability to carry this off. But I hope.

Jeff Fox

too expensive and exotic for all but the most sophisticated home users . . . for now.

Eventually, there will be a global society of the connected, laid over more traditional local communities that are usually less well off—in terms of material things, education, connectivity, and even the sophistication to judge the merits of what's online. This global culture (it would be a stretch to call it a community) will probably offend the sensibilities of many "antiglobal" people, but it will grow as a proportion of the world's population.

Some parts of local culture can easily transfer to the Net; others are fundamentally hostile to it. I'm not comfortable saying that everyone in the world should be on the Net. But in the end, everyone will be, except for a few holdouts. The challenge is to make sure that those holdouts are offline by choice, not for lack of it.

Children allowed?

Some communities will exclude children, for a variety of reasons. Some will be "unsuitable" for children because of sexual content; some will simply be adult by default because most Byzantine-art experts or nuclear physicists are adults. But in many cases children may operate successfully and undetected in adults-only communities, showing more maturity than many adults. (Those Byzantine-art experts can get pretty nasty when they disagree!)

Privacy

Communities will also vary in the level of privacy their members expect. What will people be expected to reveal about themselves or other people? What kinds of "omissions" are permissible? What is okay to say within the group, but should not be revealed to outsiders? Privacy on a commercial basis ideally should be handled through decentralized market mechanisms ($\Longrightarrow$ Chapter 8). But privacy among people within a community will be decided community by community, just as in the Online Europe group. How these decisions are made and what they are is part of the identity of each community. Members will take their own norms into account when they decide what to say. Of course, there will be conflicts and broken trust, just as there are when people break confidences, rat on their former employers, or gossip in real life. (The difference is that the impact can spread farther and faster online.)

Community members will also share opinions about everything from people to commercial products, schools, and of course acceptable content, both in unstructured postings and conversation, and in more formal rating systems and services using technology designed for the task. Indeed, some communities will form around people who electronically express common opinions and interests and are matched through such rating services, whether commercial or not-for-profit ($\Longrightarrow$ Chapter 7).

Trust me!

One basic value of a community is trust among its members. In the end, informal disclosures rather than ones mandated by rules, and shared experiences and discussions, create real communities. People can't live by rules alone, and that's why they will inevitably congregate in the company of other people whose presence they enjoy. Cyberspace is just one more place where they can do that, unfettered by the strictures of time and place. But in the end, many are likely to seek one another out in the physical world as well. You just can't share a sunset, a hot tub, or a hot meal over the Net.

Chapter 3

Work

It's five years from now, and you hate your job. Should you go looking for a new one on the Net? How will your skills be valued in the new online world? Where can you check out the opportunities available? Is it realistic to think you could telecommute to a job in another city, let alone one in another country? You're scared to post too many of these questions, in case your current employer may be out there looking, too.

What kind of job are you looking for? If you're a saleswoman, you may want to stay within your field because you know the territory, or you may want to leave the field because you don't want to compete with your current company. You may be moving to a new town and looking for a similar job (with a raise, of course!) in the new location. Or you may be looking for a new opportunity as a sales manager.

In all of these cases, you can find opportunities on the Net. You can check out the Web sites of companies in your field, or you can explore other industries. You can also read news articles, industry analysts' reports, and other objective third-party appraisals of the companies you're considering. To attract interest from them, you can list yourself with an anonymous résumé service, or you can visit one of many career sites where employers post jobs. Or you can send e-mail to the personnel department or to other executives whose names you can find. You can narrow your search to your own hometown or to your preferred new location.

If you're a writer, on the other hand, you may not be looking for a steady job but rather for interesting assignments. In that case, you may be competing with Steve Fenichell, the writer who helped to edit this book as a freelancer. He has written two books of his own (most recently *Plastic*), and edited or coauthored others. Between books, he writes articles. He gets some assignments through his agent at International Creative Management, who calls him on the phone with proposals, requests, and ideas. He also gets calls from magazine editors, very much at random, who think of him from time to time. Sometimes when he has free time and would like to work, his agent doesn't know of anything appealing. Sometimes he has more offers than he knows what to do with. Sometimes there's work to be had, but he and his agent don't know about it.

How will he be looking for work five years from now? Assuming he learns how to use his browser (just kidding, Steve!), he'll probably be finding a lot of work on the Net. He may scan daily listings of editing jobs available; he may also post his own qualifications in search of work. If he's interested in a particular topic, or he wants to justify a trip to, say, Portugal, he might go outside the writers' communities into, say, a Portuguese site and ask for tips on interesting tourist events that he could write up for a travel magazine. (Would that be spamming? It's up to that Portuguese community to decide.)

To demonstrate his qualifications, he may post some of his past articles on his own Web site, where he'll put links to Amazon.com and Barnesandnoble.com to sell copies of his books. There's a lot of competition out there, and he needs to distinguish himself from all the other candidates. But he's nervous about posting new story ideas for fear of losing them to someone else; leave that for a quiet conversation with a travel-magazine editor he can trust.

What will have happened to his agent? Many of her other clients will also be trolling the Net, along with lots of amateurs. But she'll probably still be working with her clients, because her skills go further than just finding work; she can negotiate contracts, give them advice on which publishers to deal with, and the like. She may well do much of this by e-mail, but every once in a while she and Steve will go out for a drink. She knows a lot of inside gossip that never gets posted anywhere, although some of it gets e-mailed. (The people whose business will really be cut into is the messenger services, who will no longer be carrying heavy documents around town; those will all go by e-mail, and even most contracts will have digital signatures.)

While freelancing in almost every field is becoming increasingly prevalent in 2004, Steve is still not the norm. Despite the technical possibilities, most people still have steady jobs with a regular employer and a predictable salary. There are two reasons for this. One, many people prefer the relative security of a steady job, and the teamwork, community, and affiliations they build at work. Companies, for their part, prefer people who have experience and are integrated into the company, who know how things are done, who have so-called "community memory." There's a lot more to a job than just the formal work.

Second, even those who might freelance often find it too difficult and nerve-wracking to generate a steady stream of work. Even if they know that they could find the work, they don't enjoy looking for it, negotiating, and testing their worth every day. These activities constitute what economists call "transaction costs"—the costs of finding and arranging work. The Net reduces them, but it doesn't eliminate the process or the emotional anxiety that comes with it for at least some people. They'd rather find a comfortable place to work, settle in, and focus on the job.

Looking for work

The Net won't change people's innate preferences for security/familiarity or variety. But it will enable those who prefer variety to achieve it much more easily. Indeed, the Net will support people all along the spectrum, whether they are looking for the job of a lifetime or for a week's work.

The way this works will not be through clumsy search engines, but through online communities and specific-market online employment classifieds. The difference is that such ads will be easier to use for both sides. Employers can post job descriptions and reach potential employees worldwide; employees can search—or post their résumés—and likewise reach a worldwide labor market. (Of course, they'll still have to deal with restrictive labor and immigration laws on occasion.) In a few years, the old notion of using paper classifieds—with no way of searching, no way of telling which are out of date, and limited geographical reach—will seem ludicrously archaic. Books may not be replaced very quickly, but time-sensitive, search-ready information simply works best on the Net.

Already, many résumé-exchange Web sites are popping up, many of them industry-specific. For example, Scala, an accounting software company that I have invested in, sponsors the Scala Job Bank, a free online résumé service targeting users of Scala. Accountants and software experts looking for jobs use it; so do clients, companies who already use Scala and need employees familiar with the software. It works as subtle advertising for Scala, but it also offers real benefits: Customers are more likely to purchase Scala if they know they can find workers trained to use it, and software and accounting experts are eager to learn Scala because they know they will be able to find a job. The fluid marketplace around the software makes the software itself more attractive, and the whole thing feeds on itself, occasionally luring in users of other brands of software. And of course Scala itself occasionally hires people through the Job Bank.

But Scala's site is piddling compared to the "Big Three" of recruiting in the United States: Monster Board, Career Mosaic, and OCC (Online Career Center, owned by the same company that owns Monster Board, TMP Worldwide). Monster Board, started in 1994, now lists 25,000 jobs and offers a database of 275,000 résumés to potential employers. It's free to job-seekers, and costs $175 per job (for 60 days) for companies and recruiters posting jobs. Corporate users include PricewaterhouseCoopers, Microsoft, Blockbuster, Fidelity, Nike, Arthur Andersen, Compaq, and MCI . . . but those are companies a job-seeker would consider anyway. What's more interesting is the availability of jobs with companies you'd probably never find any other way. Career Mosaic offers roughly 70,000 job listings and more than 50,000 résumés. Then there's careerpath.com, a joint venture of leading newspapers including the *Boston Globe, Chicago Tribune, Los Angeles Times, New York Times, San Jose Mercury-News,* and the *Washington Post,* with an additional investment from Cox Interactive Media, the Gannett Company, and the Hearst Corporation. These sites are all aiming for the $10 billion per year spent on recruitment advertising in the United States (according to Morgan Stanley).

Many people, however, are also turning to more community-oriented boards: It depends on whether you've just graduated from college and don't really know what you want to do, or you're an experienced paleontologist looking for a new teaching post. Likewise, is the employer looking for generic marketing expertise, C++ expertise, or "trainability"?

While Monster Board and the others are busily forming alliances with a variety of more targeted partners, including industry groups and sites such as Women's Wire, Net Noir, or Rent.Net, start-up Career Builder has an "e-cruiting" network that focuses on special-interest markets through partnerships with magazines such as *Black Enterprise* and *American Banker,* and Web sites such as C/Net's.

And for those who don't really want a *job,* TMP Worldwide also runs betheboss.com, a site of franchising opportunities. . . .

Join a network

But as any job-seeker knows, traditional channels are not always the most effective. Two others often work better, and fortunately they have online equivalents, too. The first is old-fashioned networking: Join the community in which you wish to work, make friends, get your name known, and then look for a job. There is no better place to do that than in an online community. You can do it in a work-specific community—a food-marketing group, for example—or in the traditional, more social way—a religious group, a charitable group, and so on. The kicker added by the Net is that you have far more choice of which groups to join, raising the chance that you'll find a job that you like and that employers will find a suitable employee.

Of course, employers can and should play this game, too. Are they interested in finding subject experts, or general, well-rounded managers active outside their work community?

Don't find your job; define it!

The second neo-traditional way to find a job is to create it for yourself. Find a company with a problem, and propose a solution that involves you. You can do this to sell your consulting or your company's services, or to find a steady job. Again, the Net makes it easier. You may come across a company that you really like, and see an opportunity for its products in a market it doesn't seem to be exploiting, whether it's your own geographical territory or a market segment.

In the case of Juan, an animal trainer and biologist, he might notice that a certain zoo has just expanded its monkey section—as described in the zoo's Web site, focused more on luring visitors than animal trainers. But that's the point. The Net plus a little imagination. . . .

He sends the zoo's Web site an e-mail asking if someone is needed to mind the new monkeys.

Wait! Not so fast!

Now the other features of the Net come into play. Having found some interesting opportunities, both sides can check out their potential partners. Juan can poke through the zoo's Web site at leisure. More interesting, he can read reviews of it in a variety of city guides. Now the news is not so good. The zoo is known for sloppy upkeep, unhealthy animals, and messy walkways. A few problems might mean an opportunity to help fix the situation, but a lot of problems may mean that it's unfixable and not a place Juan wants to work.

Now he's concerned. He searches the Web for some older information on the zoo, and finds the names of a couple of people who used to work there but no longer do. Politely, he sends them e-mail explaining that he's thinking of working at the zoo, and can they give him some insights?

Over at the zoo, the person who filters the nonroutine messages received at the zoo's Web site has forwarded Juan's e-mail to Alice, head of human resources. She is now conducting an investigation of her own. Has Juan written any scholarly papers based on his work as a biologist? Has he commented in any discussion groups? It's pretty easy to find out, through a search engine called DéjàNews, which indexes not only Web sites but most discussion groups. Aha! Not only is Juan a biologist; he also seems to be active in animal photography circles. Fortunately, Alice likes that; she is an amateur photographer herself. But now she looks at some of his comments; pretty fatuous, she thinks at first. Then she notices the dates of the most awkward comments and sorts them to follow his development over time. From an outspoken, uninformed novice, he seems to have matured into a thoughtful, principled expert, with interesting insights on the interplay between an animal's behavior and its size compared to the rest of its litter. She writes a note inviting him for an interview and hits the send button.

Visible reputations

Whether you're an employee checking out companies, an employer checking out people, or even a potential visitor checking out zoos, the free flow of information engendered by the Net will highlight the distinctions between good and bad. (Alice's zoo is in a pretty good position because there's probably no other zoo nearby, but it will be competing with other ways for people to spend their time—whether online or in the physical world. And local people will be better able to compare it with zoos elsewhere based on information on the Net.)

It's all very well for Alice to check Juan out, but this also means that a lot of people will be able to check *you* out. You may feel different about your privacy after you've been on the Net for a while ($\Longrightarrow$ Chapter 8), but let's consider what it means for your job hunt—and your work life. First of all, anything official will probably be available. Where did you work? What did you say? If you had a notable success or a notable failure, people will be able to find out about it.

There will be so much information out there, both favorable and unfavorable, reliable and unreliable, that no one will pay attention to most of it until someone starts to consider you in particular for some reason such as a job. The sheer volume of information will reduce the sting of sensitive items, but you'll need to recognize that they're there. Employers will become more forgiving of failure once it's clear it's so common; the best thing to do is to disclose everything—and explain what you learned from it. In my case, I presided over a disastrous flop in the mid-'80s, with an ill-fated experiment at producing a daily newspaper for the computer industry. It failed for a variety of reasons, including the absence of the reliable online delivery system we would have had today. I ended up having to fire twenty-seven people. And I could tell a prospective employer that I learned a lot!

Now suppose I—or you—had somehow developed an enemy. People may be reading nasty comments about you from totally unreliable sources. As you go on your job search, you should probably take the time to do what your prospective employers are doing: Find out what other people are saying about you. There may be misinformation you want to correct, from a well-meaning but mistaken person. Tell the person, or if it's a public forum, write a correction that links to the original comment.* There may be nasty comments from people who are just flat-out unreliable or mean; one way or another, it's up to you to prove them wrong. But any sensible employer will measure the proportion of favorable versus unfavorable remarks, and can probably distinguish malice from truth. Finally, there may be embarrassing truths that you're just going to have to deal with. You were younger then, weren't you? But the Net certainly will foster truth-telling, if only because you want people to hear your version of the story first. Personally, I think this is good overall. People may become more realistic in what they expect of others, and of themselves. Feedback isn't always pleasant, but it's healthier than illusion.

Of course, some kinds of information just don't get onto the Net. There are always cases where, for example, no one says anything about an incompetent son-in-law. Some truths are kept within closed circles or sent by e-mail rather than posted publicly. Nonetheless, there's usually an astonishing amount of information available for anyone who takes the trouble to look for it. More is being added every day.

More troublesome yet are questions about health and moral issues. Should you disclose that you have cancer in a chat group, given that the news might get back to an employer and companies are reluctant to hire people with health risks (despite laws against discrimination)? Should you disclose that you have a criminal record? Those are much tougher questions, and in many cases they're handled by law. All I can say is that in the long run more honesty could help erase the stigma of certain diseases and conditions—although not the medical costs. The more people reveal their frailties, the more clear it will become how productive they can be anyway.

---

*One problem with much of the Web is the asymmetry of links. That is, I can write my own rebuttal to a comment and point to the original comment, but I usually cannot annotate the comment itself. People need to take the initiative to hear my side of the story. This ultimately could get a technological fix—although a lot of Web site owners don't really want outsiders commenting all over them.

Companies and products have reputations, too

The information flow that illuminates employees' reputations will also include companies, products, and services. Quality and other features of everything from individuals to movies or even Web sites will become easier to determine and faster to have an impact. Better communications, Net versions of ten-best lists, consumer ratings, and overall visibility will cause investors, managers, employees, and customers to gravitate to good companies; they will flee from bad or ineffective ones. Just as the pace at which you live your individual work life will speed up, so will the pace at which companies are created, grow, and disappear. There will always be market anomalies, but the life span of each individual company is likely to become shorter unless it can maintain quality and transform itself regularly. The giant companies created through mergers over the past few years are likely to keep changing their structure—with further mergers, divestitures, and reorganizations—over the years. They will also be competing with and acquiring an increasing number of start-ups, as the barriers to entry into many markets will be lower for newcomers.

Meanwhile, the barriers to a graceful exit will be higher for existing firms. Companies stuck with the wrong things—people, strategies, culture—will find it harder to change. Companies that lose steam will fall behind more quickly, as competing companies keep speeding ahead. The good news is that this "Darwinism" applies more to companies than to people. Bad companies die or get absorbed, but with luck their employees learn something and move on to better companies.

The shrinking company

All this means a tendency toward smaller company size—even though most of what we hear about is mergers and industry consolidation as the media focus on giants. Little companies will find it easier to reach customers without massive marketing efforts even as they stay small, and they will be able to specialize in just one or two functions instead of facing constant pressure to grow to achieve economies of scale.

Those economies of scale will diminish as even small companies get access to just the resources they need over the Net; the transaction costs of finding and negotiating work(ers) will drop for companies as well as for workers.

Most companies will find it easy to shrink or stay small by outsourcing—hiring outside firms to do tasks that were once done inside. For example, some of Microsoft's consumer technical support is done by outside firms. In my own little company, we don't have a data-entry person on staff; we hire one when we need her. Meanwhile, Scala is doing a booming business running clients' payrolls. It's a dull and boring job, but it's difficult, especially in Central and Eastern Europe where the tax laws keep changing all the time and there are deductions for everything from children to military status, and people may be paid in several currencies. In a regular company, this is an onerous task; for Scala, it's a specialty. In the near future Scala will also be getting companies' time sheets and delivering payment information to their banks over the Net. (In Eastern Europe, most people are moving directly from cash to bank cards and electronic banking, without having to go through the stage of paper checks.)

On the other hand, the division of Scala that translates its software could well become an independent company or perhaps merge with another translation firm, as it already has several outside customers. One of its competitors based in the Czech Republic, Moravia Translations, already does a substantial part of its business over the Net, receiving files from customers, translating them, and sending them back electronically. In this way, this 122-person company operates successfully in several countries, mostly using freelancers with whom it communicates over the Net.

From ignored department to respected partner

The impact of outsourcing is often that a secondary function in a large company becomes the core business in a smaller outsourcing company.

A translator in a translation division doesn't have much hope of career growth or respect from the larger company, but in a company focused on translation that translator could rise to become a manager or at least feel that he's an integral part of the company.

Meanwhile, employees are less likely to stay put when companies try to grow larger. All those start-ups that sell out to larger companies will get integrated into their buyers, yes, but the born entrepreneurs will leave to start new companies. Others will leave to work for them or for themselves in smaller, more comfortable environments.

Many people don't necessarily want to grow companies or make a killing; they simply want to work in a small-company environment. The Net will make it easier for non-entrepreneurs to strike out on their own, avoiding both the perils of company growth and the opposing perils of corporate stagnation. They can run a small business without the imperative of grow or die. Change—yes; but growth is optional when you can stay small and productive. Or you can disband and start over. Why stick around when the magic fades?

Silicon Valley syndrome

Like employees, investors are not likely to be as patient in the future as they have been. Turnover will be faster in companies as well as in people.

Modern firms' primary edge will be creativity and innovation: the ability to come up with new products, new services, new business models, and new strategies. The innovations won't always make sense; existing products may work perfectly well even as they are superseded by newer ones. Silicon Valley abounds with examples of companies built around a single product or idea; many of these companies are acquired, or they just wither away. Examples acquired by Microsoft include Vermeer, with the product FrontPage (a Web site design tool), Coopers & Peters, and DimensionX, all software companies; Hotmail, an e-mail service provider; and WebTV. For its part, Netscape has acquired Collabra (groupware), InSoft, DigitalStyle, and Portola Software. The moment something works, someone else will be out there trying to improve on it. Many of these "improvements" will be cosmetic, but they will cascade through the marketplace.

As information flows faster and as innovations are easier to copy and implement, the ability to keep innovating consistently (or to acquire people who can) and time-to-market will provide primary competitive advantage.*

This won't necessarily be a comfortable world to live in. For better or worse, Silicon Valley is becoming a model emulated worldwide— and is a model for the future for all of us. Many foreign people, and especially foreign governments, visit Silicon Valley in the hope that some of the Valley's economic fecundity will rub off on them. Often, they look at the wrong features, focusing just on high-tech rather than on the culture that makes the companies thrive. Malaysia, Bulgaria, Russia, and Hungary, for example, all want to create their own high-tech zones, and are focusing on high-tech infrastructure, government subsidies, and the like. What they may be missing is the entrepreneurial spirit and the cross-fertilization as companies start, merge, break up, and unleash second- and third-time entrepreneurs into the mix.

The good aspects are an openness to change, excitement, teamwork, a willingness to admit to and learn from mistakes. The bad aspects are troubling: obsession with work and neglect of families and human values, impatience, preoccupation with money and stock prices. Many of these companies' founders are more interested in selling their companies to Netscape or Microsoft than in building robust, healthy organizations. Their stockholding employees are more interested in going public, selling stock, and starting their own start-ups. Companies shouldn't necessarily live forever, but they are not simply vehicles for stockholders' or employees' portfolios.

---

*This may sound glib and unrealistic if you have bought anything lately, especially at the corner coffee shop, which has a captive market because of its location, or at

How to form your very own Silicon Valley start-up

Step 1: Go to Menlo Park. Find a tree.

Step 2: Shake the tree. A venture capitalist will fall out.

Step 3: Before the venture capitalist regains its wits, recite the following incantation:

"Internet! Electronic Commerce!
Distributed Enterprise-Enabled Applications!
Java!"

Step 4: The venture capitalist will give you four million dollars.

Step 5: In 18 months, go public.

Step 6: After you receive your check, go back to Menlo Park. Find a tree.

Courtesy of Laura Lemay, lemay@lne.com. You can see an illustrated version of this story at *http://www.lne.com/lemay/cartoon.jpg.*

Earning that job

So, you're still looking for that job. . . . As employers check you out on the Net, the efficient market for employment will lead to a widening gap between star employees and adequate ones—or worse. But the skills needed are not just creative brilliance or intelligence; they also include attitude. To the extent that workers can find a culture or community that suits them, attitudes may get better. (Or at least all the

---

a tourist trap where the retailer has little hope of repeat business anyway. But, eventually, the Net may tell tourists which spots to patronize and which to avoid.

complainers will deserve each other!) As you develop or market your skills, there are four broad attributes that will be especially valuable.

Creativity and intelligence

The fundamental talent is creativity—whether artistic or intellectual. As the world becomes faster-moving, companies will stay ahead not with proprietary technology, but with a constant flow of new technology and ideas. Employees will be valued for what they can produce, not for what they have produced.

Most successful will be those who can design innovations to help the company get or stay ahead. The major business of business will be design—of new products, new processes, even new business models ($\Rightarrow$ Chapter 6). It will be much harder for any company to gain a persistent competitive advantage other than with a strong company culture/community that both perpetuates and renews itself through new design.

Employees will increasingly need to be good at thinking, rather than blindly following routine. Routines can be automated or at least farmed out to specialist firms; those specialists, meanwhile, need to implement familiar tasks efficiently, but their core value is—you guessed it!— coming up with new ways of doing the old tasks better.

Those who are good at doing what they're told will be able to survive, but they won't excel in the increasingly competitive marketplace. Nonetheless, support people will be valued to the extent that they can adjust to change while maintaining a healthy corporate culture. They will implement the crazy ideas of the dreamers and risk-takers. Even as the market becomes more efficient and the stars can move around more easily, both companies and coworkers will come to value loyalty and comfort as an antidote to this friction-free world.

Real-time performance

The second key attribute is a performance personality, for want of a better phrase. *People who can think quickly will prevail.* Can you respond quickly (rather than think slowly)? In the age of the Net, there will be

SUCCESSFUL NET WORKER ATTRIBUTES

Much of this discussion revolves around the quote from Esther's book which cites "Real-time Performance" as a particularly important attribute of future successful net workers. It is one of four such important attributes called out in the book, the others being "Creativity", "Self Marketing", and "Emotional Intelligence". But several of the messages below seem to agree that this list isn't quite complete. Joachim Klehe, for instance, reminds us that thinking fast is not necessarily thinking deep enough. Also, I think these particular attributes have always been particularly valuable, and maybe the clue to one that is missing from the list can be found in ancient history: Aesop's fable of the tortoise and the hare.

Paul Hunt phunt3@worldnet.att.net

less time to think, more need for quick response—whether a speedy reaction to e-mail, or a real-time interaction in (electronic) print or a video conference. Real-time performance will outrank careful production. Editors and writers will continue to be necessary, but more valuable will be people who can write and think in real time, participating in and moderating real time online forums. Of course, these same capabilities are what "playing" on the Net hones—just as soldiers, toy cars, dolls, and Play-Doh prepared children for the tasks of the previous century. What people do for leisure, they will also do for pay. (Consider tennis pros, for another example.)

As the Internet's "local loops" become broadband, there will be more need for people who can perform the equivalent of online or telephone interaction in video—in short, remote customer service. The people who used to work in stores will now work online, but customers will expect more than a hand wave and a snarled "Over there!" Highly trained people will interpret complex instructions or give advice to customers who prefer to deal with a person. Yes, things should become easier and easier to use, but people will still want customer service from people, not from expert systems. It's a lot more convincing to have a person tell you a particular sweater will go great with the skirt than to hear it from a machine. Who wants baby-care advice from a computer? Persuasion is still a personal art rather than a computer technique.

My favorite example of a real-time employee performance (or was it creativity?) was by a quick-thinking Southwest Airlines stewardess, back in the days before the Net when they were still called stewardesses. The doors of the aircraft had closed, most of us had found our seats, and she took up the microphone: "Hey y'all!" she drawled. "We got a little problem up here. We don't have the peanuts. Now we can set right here for about fifteen minutes, and catering promises we'll have those peanuts right away . . . but I can't guarantee it. Or, folks, we could leave right away without those peanuts. Now I'm just gonna take a little vote . . ." Before she could even finish, she was drowned out with shouts and cries: "Let's just go!" "Fergit the pea-nuts!" "As long as we got beer, who needs peanuts!?" We left on schedule and no one complained about the missing peanuts. We had a choice, and we had chosen.

Self-marketing

Imagine a company as a physical object. The companies of the past were black boxes that produced products and had a small surface area, composed mostly of PR and investor-relations people, and perhaps a couple of outspoken top executives. Consumer companies had ads, but they rarely involved anyone from inside the company—with notable exceptions such as Perdue and his chickens, Lee Iacocca and Chrysler, and Richard Branson with his Virgin product du jour. General exceptions were service companies such as airlines, competing on the friendliness of their stewardesses, and at least some retailers competing on the helpfulness of their personnel. But most employees were focused internally, designing and building products or perhaps writing ads or documentation. The products and the advertising spoke for themselves.

In a service/information/Net world all that changes. Imagine the black box getting thinner and wider, almost all membrane with very little contained inside. (Or to put it another way: There are fewer people exclusively on the inside to talk to, so employees spend more time dealing with the outside.)

The surface that a business exposes needs to be more than just posted information—even specific, customized information such as Federal Express's track-your-own package service ($\Rightarrow$ Chapter 8). Companies will need to have real personality online—which means *persons*.

Accordingly, there will be a premium on *people who can market themselves*. In a world where competitive advantage comes either from new design or from the attention of people, those who succeed will be those who are good at getting their new designs or themselves noticed.

The person is the living face a company presents to the world. For example, take Jennifer Warf, who has run a Barbie Web site for some years. Other Barbie fans came upon the site, and pretty quickly it became an active center for discussions about Barbie, for trading costumes and even dolls. The site eventually attracted attention from Mattel itself, and an enthusiastic Warf hinted that she might like a job with Mattel when she graduated from Indiana University. But instead of hiring her, Mattel's legal department wrote her a letter with warnings about copyright infringement. She has redone the site to remove all Mattel's content; she is using photos of her own dolls instead.

Unaffiliated with Mattel, she is now doing this as a labor of unrequited love. Of course, Mattel's version of the story focuses on its need to protect its image and its intellectual property, but it seems to me it has missed an opportunity. Unless, of course, it is secretly hoping that she'll just continue to promote its products for free.

Emotional intelligence

I once asked an Italian executive who worked for AT&T what he did as a manager, and I have always remembered his answer: "I absorb uncertainty." As routine is sucked out of our daily work lives, people who can create stability from chaos will be key. This man, Vittorio Cassoni, took the uncertainty out of his employees' lives so that they could go ahead and do their best. He did not tell them what to do, so much as he provided balance in a rocking sea.

These kinds of personal qualities—management skill, leadership, judgment, collaborative skills, risk taking, evenness of temperament—are now called *emotional intelligence*. As change becomes constant, leaders must have the flexibility and vision to handle it. It's the skill it takes to run a meeting effectively, whether in a conference room or over a network, internally or with partners and customers—but you have to do it on a global basis and over the long term. You have to fire people up and calm them down, resolve disputes, uncover the key points in a conflict or a strategy, make firm decisions. All these traits and capabilities inspire confidence and lead a company forward. These traits are the least definable—and their impact is the most visible.

THE COMPUTER BUSINESS

Confronting our optimism

High-tech change can't be ALL bad, and objectivity and independence are good qualities to nurture in navigating the times. But optimism about our future digital designs for living tends to present the changes as inevitable. Sarah wonders if the bubble might not break and she points out three possible dangers: corporate control, investor disappointment, and commodity labor. Now that's a lot to talk about. I think I'll stick to my guns from earlier messages in this topic and say that interest in our rapidly expanding digital world has become too complex to compare with the relatively simple bubble of stock market gambling in 1929. It will even survive the puzzling lack of productivity. But even though Sarah's dangers won't stop the momentum, I have no doubt they will change the course of optimism.

Paul Hunt phunt3@worldnet.att.net

What makes companies appealing to employees?

When goods and machines are cheap and mass-produceable, people with the talents described above are valuable. What does it take to attract them? Other people. It's the other people in a company that will be a key factor in keeping employees. Even though employees will achieve greater freedom to move around because of the fluid job market, few people actually want to get up every morning and find out what jobs are available on the Net. They want stability; they want friends; they want familiarity; they want to be part of a community. What keeps employees as well as customers is the emotional intelligence described above—the presence of people they like to work for and with.

All but the most solitary employees prefer to work with people whose company they enjoy and whose contributions they respect. They want to work with people who can add value to their own work, or with skillful managers who can make mostly incompatible people work together happily and effectively. Indeed, a company is a community. A company's best strategy is to attract employees and then to get them to invest in the company's community—not just by paying them but by fostering an environment that lets them flourish. Great value is created by teams who work together effectively, whether as repair people sharing experiences with balky machines or creative types coming up with a new multimedia extravaganza.

That doesn't mean that all companies will become identical happy families. They will have distinct cultures—perhaps more distinct than now because people will be better able to find an environment that suits them, whether it's aggressive and sales-oriented or technical and reserved, formal or informal. But overall, companies with people enthusiastic about their work are likely to be the most successful. Many people join a company because of the money, but most contribute and stay after joining because of the community they find there. Relationships develop and people get comfortable; relationships stagnate or deteriorate and people move on.

Since both companies and employees will have more options, dissatisfied employees and employers are less likely to stick with an unhappy situation—a company community that doesn't really meet their needs. Now, to be productive, it is usually necessary for an individual to affiliate herself with a large organization. In the future, those who want freedom will be able to work on their own terms without sacrificing as much as they must today. People who aren't much fun to work with will be able to become more independent, operating as one-person bands and contracting out for services.

These two forces—independence and the need for affiliation with a community—often conflict. The way they are resolved will vary from person to person and company to company.

The Net on the job

The Net also changes one's experience on the job. First of all, it will change the pace at which everything happens within the company as well as in competing with other firms. It will make it much easier for everyone to keep in touch, and it will probably reduce the need for middle management; employees will be able to communicate among themselves, rather than up and down a chain of command.

For example, suppose you get that new job as a saleswoman that you were looking for. You'll be thrown into a world of new accounts and new products. To find out what's going on, you'll ask other employees, but you'll also start poking around the company intranet. What has the company previously sold to Wanton Widgets, an account you have a strong relationship with? What are the most effective ways of competing against product X? Is there a technical wizard who's especially valuable on sales calls? Your new manager may ask you to post a report on the intranet on the competitive situation as you see it from the vantage of your old job—but no trade secrets, please!

All these trends will place a premium on reporting into the corporate memory, since there may no longer be a sales manager who knows what's going on in all territories. Employees will have to fill out their sales reports in greater, richer detail than ever before. Good companies will build in incentives to encourage their employees to share information, because it takes time to do so. Technology will help you to *find* information on the company intranet, but it can't do much about helping you generate the sales report—other than perhaps providing convenient forms to fill out and voice-recognition technology that will allow you to dictate instead of type.

And once you've made the sale, you'll be using e-mail to coordinate with your company's customer-service group to make sure your customer stays happy. You may refer some ancillary business from the customer's overseas territory to the international sales group.

To find out more about your new industry, you may join a number of industry trade associations. Soon, you find that your outspoken comments in the industry mailing list are generating interest. You get speaking invitations, offers of other jobs . . . your future is assured!

Telecommuting

Now, should you telecommute? I'm not a big fan of the concept—especially for people-oriented work such as sales. What it does mean is that you can travel more easily to see customers *and* stay close to your office. In my own life, I have found that e-mail lets me keep close to the office from the road, but it does not reduce the amount of time I have to spend away getting to know people, having dinner, having arguments, and just doing the kind of high-intensity communication you can't do any way other than face-to-face.

On the other hand, if you're a programmer, a writer, or some other kind of "knowledge worker," you can work from home much more easily. Many people will do so. You can also work from India or Hungary or any other country for employers in the United States—which means a lot more competition for those jobs. But overall, I think the value of telecommuting for most jobs is overrated. People who work from home full-time are more likely to be independent contractors than permanent employees, since telecommuting reduces a major benefit to both sides of permanent employment, which is team membership. The worker misses the companionship, and the employer misses the productivity enhancement of a tight-knit group. The technology will enable people to communicate more effectively over distances, but the best approach will still be to spend enough time together physically to build that community.

The work community and its rules

Remote or local, when you take a job you're making a decision to join a particular community. That means that you have the ability and the responsibility to find out about the working conditions, and that employers have the obligation to disclose them honestly. "Working conditions" includes all the traditional workplace issues, plus a few new Net-oriented areas where employees' rights can conflict with those of employers—most notably, privacy in the use of e-mail and the Web, and freedom of speech.

Many employers now monitor employees' use of the Net, sometimes using software filters to keep employees from playing games, downloading pornography, or sending out secrets. Some of the same filters used to protect children from porn ($\Rightarrow$ Chapter 7) can be used with timers to keep employees from playing games except on lunch hours and after 6 P.M.

However, employers who treat their workers like children are likely to get employees who deserve to be treated like children. Free use of the Net can be a lure in attracting the best employees, even though it also lures the worst abusers. It's up to the employer to detect the difference.

As far as I'm concerned, employers can read employees' e-mail on company servers and control where they go on the Net (during working hours), as long as they disclose these practices. Of course, defining behavior "at work" gets more difficult as employees start to work from home, at odd hours, or from remote locations. Perhaps it means only when using the corporate ID, or on company equipment, or on company time if you have defined working hours. Companies care because they may be held liable for their employees' behavior—ranging from harassing others or creating a "hostile atmosphere" by downloading pornography, to misrepresenting themselves online, defaming competitors' products, or otherwise acting badly. Companies also care for less legitimate reasons, including thin skin.

What happens if an employee gets on the Net on Saturday night and trashes his own company's products—or its competition, provoking a lawsuit? What control does and should a company exercise on its employees' behavior, given that they represent the company in "public" on the Net? "The opinions expressed are purely my own" may no longer be a sufficient disclaimer.

The Net erodes the separation between the work and the person. Employees are no longer judged only on the products they create or what they do inside the company, but also on the way they interact with the world around them on the Net. Their job is to represent the company, so how can they not be judged for how they do so?

In the old days, employers could sack you if they saw you getting drunk and disorderly in the pub on Saturday night, no matter how well you did your job during the week. Nowadays, that's considered undue interference with an employee's personal life. In the old days, an employer might ask you about your family, and give extra money to the employee with a sick wife.

In the United States, we now have increasing legal restrictions on whatever might be considered favoritism, and strict barriers between home and work. That's the now-old world of traditional government and increasing regulation of working conditions. (Unions have helped redress the balance of power in favor of employees, but many of them have spawned their own bureaucracies and power politics.) In other parts of the world, standard working conditions are still generally unfair toward employees.

Power on the job

But the world of the Net is tending the other way: toward freedom of contract.

I don't have an answer to how this will work itself out. But by 2004, you will find that the balance of power between creators and managers, and between employees and business owners, has shifted in favor of individual contributors, even though you and others may personally be playing several roles. That will give capable employees the upper hand in negotiations with employers—although the employers may not realize it yet. Employees who don't like the working conditions can go elsewhere. Now individuals are starting to have power as individuals rather than collectively, at least in the world of the Net and of well-educated employees. Employers control the tangible resources, but employees have more control over their own lives, more options, and more ways to find out those options. Certainly, independence is a matter of attitude as well as opportunity, but now you can almost always find a work community to suit you if you take the trouble to explore.

Chapter 4

Education

It's 2004 and you've just turned thirteen. Of course, you're smarter than average, and you find school a little dull. You spend a lot of time on the Net, both at home and at school, but teachers asking you to pay attention and the schoolwork itself keep interfering with your attempts to educate yourself. You wonder if there isn't a better school around somewhere, especially since you'll be going to high school next year and you'll have a choice among several schools.

Meanwhile, your parents keep talking with your teachers over the Net. They're aware of your homework assignments; they hear about it when you haven't been paying attention in class. And that episode last week, when you tried to get around the school's blocking software to look at the Playboy site: It really wasn't anything your parents needed to know. But now it's all over the parent-teacher network.

You've considered asking your parents if you can resign from school—except for the sports—and just do distance learning. There are several sites on the Net with courses you're interested in: genetic biology, Swiss history, and (of course) Web site design. But you have also been checking out local high schools on the Net and you're quite excited at the possibilities. You'd even be willing to take a bus, or one of those pickup van services that have become popular because of Net-based logistics.

The one subject you're really excited about right now is French. There's this Swiss-French girl, Sandrine; you met her through the Net in one of those cross-cultural programs. You've been sending her e-mail for some time now, and her English is ten times better than your French. Last week she even corrected your English. It was humiliating! Everyone knows that English will be the language of the Net, so why learn French? Sandrine says it makes you more sensitive to other cultures. Americans think they understand the world because everyone speaks English, she says, but they miss the subtleties around them.

Why education is important

Now, since you're thirteen, you may wonder why you need an education at all. But your parents know that education is the fundamental "asset" individuals will need to succeed in the world of the future. More and more physical work will be done by machines. Some will run by themselves; the people who run the others will need education to run them effectively and to make decisions when things don't work as they should. Others will need an education to figure out how to do things better or do better things.

Moreover, you will need education to make decisions about your own *life*—managing your financial assets, educating your own children, choosing and ideally advising your governments, designing your own communities, buying products. In the information world, people need not just information, but the skills to handle and interpret it. The complexity of our society—and the powers of the digital age—impose corresponding demands on individuals. They need to be better educated to survive economically and to thrive socially. They will also need a moral education in order to make the increasingly complex ethical decisions the digital and eventually the genetic ages will present.

Indeed, at the tender age of thirteen, you're facing a far more complex world than the children of a generation earlier. Although your parents try to shield you, you're already communicating with adults in a way that few kids did in the past. In the old days, precocious children read newspapers, but adults still treated them as kids. Now, precocious kids are unnoticed as they participate in discussion groups about everything from architecture to the merits of the Mets.

It's tempting to think that the Net will resolve many of the problems we face in education today. But six years later, it won't have done so. The Net is a powerful tool, but it leaves us with familiar dilemmas: How can we motivate children to learn? How can we give every child a fair deal without interfering with family culture and local control? What's the line between assistance and interference?

How to get an A

One thing you're doing at school is contributing to the school Web site. This has been an enjoyable project, started in the computer lab a couple of years ago, and it keeps expanding. First, every student in the school had to design his or her own home page. That meant learning to use a number of design tools. The eighth-graders helped the first-graders and the seventh-graders helped the second-graders, and the collaboration had an amazingly positive effect. Several seventh-graders decided they want to become teachers—although one decided he didn't like helping people and would prefer just to be a programmer.

Then the fun started. The football team posted a page of its own, trying to raise money for a new locker room. Within weeks all the

Education and equality

In a just society, people have equal rights and are equal under the law. They are born with basic rights that generally allow them to do things that don't harm others and to control their own lives.

But people are not equal in life. They also receive genes and privileges from their parents. Eventually they earn further privileges, encounter good or bad luck, and make their own lives.

In the old days, if you believed in equality of result, or just wanted to make up for those inherited privileges, you could redistribute society's wealth. That involved forcing those with assets to give them up or share them (as opposed to charity, which means the fortunate voluntarily giving things away, or investing, which means paying someone to do a job and create value).

In particular, you could try to even things out by distributing land to the peasants. A few centuries later, you could raise workers' salaries or even give them profit-sharing or an ESOP. (Unfortunately, none of these measures worked particularly well.)

But in the information, as opposed to the agricultural or industrial, economy, such tactics no longer apply. People prosper less according to what they *have* in their hands or bank accounts, and more according to what they can *do* with their minds. That means that the task of fostering equality, even equality of opportunity, is more complex than a simple redistribution of assets.

The only feasible approach is education, which requires not just giving, but helping people to take, and to learn. Education is a process that learners perform, under the guidance of parents, teachers, and other mentors. Teachers can inspire and instruct; they can tell students how to do things. But in the end the learning is up to the students. (Note that "students" may be of any age.) In short, education is just about the most important job a community can do.

activities were online, and kids could sign up for school trips, after-school sports, and clubs over the Net. The school didn't have enough music-minded students for a glee club, but they connected with another school and formed a full chorus. There was some discussion of requiring passwords and keeping parents out, but that caused too much adult flack and was pretty quickly abandoned.

Recently, Juan downloaded a great new tool for voice recording from the Net, and pretty soon everyone's home page had clips of kids saying silly things, like "I scream for ice cream!" or "She sells seashells by the seashore." Several kids included clips from their favorite singers; Alice, the class wonk, had an aria from *Aïda* (for which she paid a few cents in digital cash; the other recordings were free as promotional material). Pretty soon, kids who hadn't taken much interest in school started staying late to work on their pages. They began sending e-mail to relatives. Fred put up some information about his grandfather, who grew up when the town was still farmland, and suddenly there was a town history page. The amazing thing is, you've worked harder in school than you ever did before, and you thought you were just having fun. (Don't tell anyone!)

How can the Net help education?

Rather than deal with the perennial, insoluble problems of education caused by human frailty, let's consider how the Net can help if used right. First of all, it can serve as a *vehicle* for greater attention to education and can make the public think about how to upgrade education, allocate more investment to it, and attract better personnel. And yes, then it can also be a valuable tool for the process of education itself.

Putting computers and Internet access into schools has indeed captured the public imagination in countries from Poland, Russia, and Malaysia to the United States and the United Kingdom. If that brings more resources of all kinds to schools, so much the better. Just a few years ago, fewer than 10,000 of the nation's 140,000-odd K–12 schools had Net access. "Access" varies from a single low-bandwidth connection and a couple of PCs to a modern setup where most kids have their own computers.

STUDENT PRESS ONLINE

This essay was published on the Net as part of the Markle Foundation's E-Mail for All Universal Access Event. Details at the URL.

Author: Laurie Becklund, Los Angeles–based journalist
E-mail: "Laurie Becklund" <becklund@earthlink.net>

REAL STORIES: Associated Student Press

What models for sustained content development and interaction are emerging, you ask?

Let me describe one, but first the reasons for it.

I am concerned that most of us bemoan, but accept as almost inevitable, a digital divide that may last a decade—more if new wedge technologies emerge to extend it.

While we wire, wouldn't it be helpful to define what sort of information that travels over the Net is critical? And to figure out if there are alternative ways to inform those who need it until then?

I am a former Los Angeles Times staff writer and (during OJ) CBS News producer who tends to look at information pragmatically. For years, I've had advocates call me up to "get word out" about, for example, campaigns to help kids, immigrants, human rights victims. I care about those issues and wrote about many of them. But, I turned down others because they weren't newsworthy on a national level. Yet, on the community level at discussion here, they were critical. Moreover, the people who would have benefited most directly from them didn't read The Times or watch Dan Rather. Many didn't even speak English.

After the OJ Trial ended, I took the Nestea Plunge into volunteer work and helped a friend who started the NetDay movement by doing a news site helping volunteers wiring schools. I cared about wiring schools, but I cared more about relieving children's dependence on the motivation level of adults around them.

The challenge as I saw it was this: how could we get customized, needed, news out to local (school) communities on air or on paper. Then it hit me: the largest network of community newspapers in the country is school newspapers. As early adopters even in poor schools (where newspapers still exist), students are in a pivotal position to take information in over the Internet, then turn around and publish it on paper or on air. Moreover, they instinctively know their readers and can tailor information to their needs.

Yet, these kids operate in near isolation, often with advisers whose first love is coaching football. In California, Delaine Eastin, the Supt. of Schools last year MAILED to every principal an application notifying them they could qualify for 50% technology discounts. Yet, the last I checked, fewer than half had returned them. If a kid had done a story about that in a paper, wouldn't SOMEONE have asked about it? In one demonstration project I did, kids were able to interview [then FCC chairman] Reed Hundt at least letting them know schools/districts were going to have to apply in order to get discounts.

Now, nearly a year of organizing, programming, and networking later, we're preparing to start up the Associated Student Press, which will create the first national databank of student journalism, allow kids to read and re-print each other's work, collaborate on national projects, attend "virtual press conferences"—all via simple Internet connections.

Lots of people and institutions are now coming forward, but we still have many needs to finish development over this summer when kids and advisers are out. Once we're up, expect kids to start defining issues and, I suspect, doing something about them. Critical thinking skills, literacy, technological fluency—all these are skills that must be used in this project—not only to inform communities—but to create a diverse 21st century press corps that just might report the OJ Trial a little differently.

For details, check http://www.schoolwire.org/asp.htm.
Would love your responses and participation.

However, the situation is slowly improving. With encouragement but little funding from the federal government, local school districts all over the country have been moving forward on their own. Momentum gathered with NetDay, the local-turned-nationwide volunteer effort to wire schools for the Internet with labor and equipment donated by local individuals and companies. The first NetDay (March 9, 1996), which started out as an attempt to wire 12,000 California schools to the Internet in one day, brought out an estimated 100,000 volunteers, 2,000 organizers, and 1,200 corporate partners, who together contrib-uted an estimated $25 million worth of equipment and labor. By the end of 1996, NetDay had spread to more than forty states and the

District of Columbia, bringing an estimated 250,000 volunteers together to wire 25,000 classrooms nationwide.

In 1977, the national San Francisco–based organization NetDay 2000, founded by John Gage of Sun Microsystems, effectively rallied enthusiasm for the concept of wiring schools. However, the NetDay model lost steam because of its very success: Across the country, regional groups were learning that setting up a month of Saturdays, or even two months, made more practical sense than trying to do it all in one day. From a nationwide movement it turned back into a series of local initiatives responsive to local conditions. More and more school boards and other organizations are acquiring and installing computer equipment without a formal program such as NetDay.

For example, Silicon Valley's approach was led by Smart Valley, Inc., a local nonprofit organization that incubated such projects.* Its approach had been more oriented to what it called "whole-school change," using technology as a driver to reengineer learning in general. While NetDay 2000's concept was to encourage volunteers to buy $500 "wiring kits" suitable for wiring five classrooms and a school library, Smart Valley learned that the schools had to be better prepared to accept the technology in order to implement it effectively—unfortunately at considerably more than $100 per classroom, or up to $30,000 per school. Even in the "Smart" Valley, decentralization has been the rule—different school districts picking and choosing what they want to do and when they want to be wired. Conclusion: What at first sounds like unhealthy rivalry seems to be an example of healthy decentralization.

So far, with the help of NetDay and other less coordinated efforts,

---

*The most notable Smart Valley project so far is Commerce over the Net. CommerceNet is also a cosponsor of TRUSTe: ⟹ page 254, Chapter 8. Smart Valley has a Web site with lots of technical and planning information designed to be useful to regional groups anywhere. Anyone interested in comparing the two models can check out www.NetDay.org. Smart Valley, having accomplished its mission of starting several such independent organizations, closed down in 1998.

about 80 percent of the K–12 public schools in the United States had access to the Net (as of fall 1997). But that access is unevenly distributed: Among disadvantaged schools (where more than 70 percent of children qualify for free lunches), only 63 percent have Net access. Moreover, a school may have access without many children *in* the school having access: Among the schools with access, only 60 percent offered it in more than one classroom, and only 43 percent in five or more classrooms. Things are getting better, but there's still a long way to go.

One of the leaders behind NetDay, Silicon Valley venture capitalist John Doerr, points out that it lured many parents and nonparents into their local schools for the first time ever. They met teachers and school officials and heard one clear message: Teachers want this equipment, but they aren't sure how to use it.

The first item in any discussion about the Net in schools is that teachers should get proper training and support in how to use the technology. But according to Quality Education Data, average per-pupil spending for teacher technology training in the United States amounts to less than $5 per year. Overall, teachers just don't get adequate training to go with the equipment. A study I worked on with McKinsey & Company suggests that for best results with the Internet schools should spend a third of their money on equipment, a third on connections and services, and a third on teacher training. But that last third usually gets forgotten. Moreover, most schools lack in-house "help" lines, let alone MIS (management information systems) departments. But if schools do get the equipment and teachers get the proper training and support, what can the Net then do?

* It can help connect teachers and other school personnel—to one another, to parents, and to students.
* It can connect children to one another, to teachers, to other sources of information—and perhaps even to their parents.
* Net-based rating services of various kinds can provide a force for better schooling from outside.

Connecting teachers

Before we talk about the Net and kids, let's consider the Net and *teachers*. Don't teachers deserve this most important tool to do their own work?

As a thirteen-year-old, you think of your teacher as someone standing in front of the class or cruising the aisles peering over your shoulder as you use your computer to write an essay, surf the Web in search of information, or send an e-mail in impeccable French to Sandrine. But your teachers lead another part of their professional life outside the classroom, where they are trying to work on lesson plans, keep up with developments in their field, and communicate with your parents (well, you know about that!). Yet your teachers, who are the most important single element in your education, used to have only a pitiful set of tools.

At the end of the twentieth century, a typical clerical worker has several times more equipment at her disposal than a typical teacher, starting with a lowly telephone and ending up with a computer, a printer, and Internet access. Office workers get training in how to use all this equipment, and salespeople are constantly trying to sell them (and their bosses) new and better tools. In the business world, employees are encouraged to communicate with the outside world, learn from the competition, and respond to changing customer needs; teachers rarely have that luxury. Teachers work in isolation; most of them don't have telephones in their classrooms. They have little way of reaching parents or other teachers outside their own school.

Another advantage office workers have over teachers is the existence of a lively market devoted to spreading best practices among companies in a way that's lacking among schools. Most software vendors have little interest in the education market because it has relatively limited spending power. By contrast, commercial companies are always getting advice and information about the newest technologies and methodologies from eager vendors. These commercial customers are always striving to stay ahead competitively, and so they send their employees to conferences, they benchmark themselves against other companies, and they hire people from outside to instill best practices. Not all of this is effective, but overall it works.

By contrast, teachers have mostly missed out on the promise (and the reality) of digital media, because the tools are expensive and there's no quantifiable "return on investment" to justify them. But now the U.S. government and many others are saying that there is a return, even if you can't measure it financially. Getting such figures was one valuable outcome of the National Information Infrastructure Advisory Council I sat on from 1995 to 1996 and its Kickstart project: We commissioned McKinsey & Company to do a study of the costs and benefits of "Connecting K–12 Schools to the Information Superhighway." McKinsey studied the literature and concluded in a carefully hedged statement that there are indeed some quantifiable benefits: ". . . in three school years, students benefiting from computer-assisted instruction can learn almost a full year's worth of material more than students who do not have access to the technology."

Although some of the studies are hard to replicate and anecdotal, others are persuasive. Technology alone can't do it, but I have to believe that technology can help. Despite the controversy over the wisdom of spending billions on computer technology when many school districts are strapped for funds, governments worldwide are acting on that same faith and encouraging and funding initiatives to bring technology into schools and to measure its impact.

Meanwhile, even as governments move ahead despite the costs, the Net is making many of the benefits cheaper to achieve than they would have been just a few years ago. The same McKinsey study estimates that connecting all the nation's classrooms individually (not just schools) would take only 4 percent of the annual school budget. That includes not just installation but also annual operating and connection costs of $4 billion to $14 billion a year, depending on the rate of adoption. Some of that will be offset by discounts on Internet service of about $2.25 billion a year from Internet service providers and telephone companies, mandated by the Federal Communications Commission under its Universal Service policy (although that subsidy is now under political attack).

And of course the major benefit—finding other people and information online—is continuing to grow apace. The Net makes it cheaper

From: "Joseph R. Gotchy" <josephgotchy@email.msn.com>

I am a high school social studies teacher in Federal Way, Washington. Over the past two years, I have led a pilot program within our school that trains students to use Win 95, MS Office Professional, and a variety of other productivity tools in an interdisciplinary curriculum. Every student has a laptop 24 hours a day, seven days a week, along with access to the Web.

Our school nickname is the Raiders . . . hence our laptop program is called Raiderlinks . . . technology linking students to the 21st century as citizens, workers, and members of the world community. Next fall will be our third year . . . Release 3.0. In 1996–97 we had 55 sophomores and we added 70 new sophs for the 1997–98 school year . . . and we have almost 80 more sophs signed up for next year. The 1998–99 school year will be our first with students at all three grade levels. We have a vision which sees us developing an increasingly interdisciplinary curriculum that integrates the laptop, business quality software, and the Internet/WWW in every classroom environment (World Language, English, science, social studies, computer apps, math, etc.). We have been more successful in some areas than others, but are making good progress as a program. The real success stories can be seen in the work our students are doing . . .

I have sent a copy of this note to Mr. and Mrs. Baker whose daughter, Jeannette, is a junior in the program this year. The Bakers have been very supportive of the program and Jeannette is one of our stars. I have also sent a copy of this note to Bruce Case, my colleague at Thomas Jefferson HS who teaches computer apps and careers in tech . . . and is the heart and soul of our program. His work with our students gives them the skills to excel throughout our curriculum . . . but we have a lot of good teachers tied to the program . . . and great teaching will always be the heart and soul of any educational system . . . Bruce and I believe, however, that great teachers of this era must incorporate technology into their classrooms.

and easier for teachers to learn from others, to form networks outside their own schools, to trade ideas, and to learn from the best practitioners in their field. Teachers can use it to communicate with other teachers, share best practices, arrange joint field trips, follow up on contacts they made at teachers' conferences—and of course to find all kinds of information and instructional material. They can also reach

From: WJP@hths.mcvsd.k12.nj.us (William Pollock)

I recently finished your book, Release 2.0, over the Christmas vacation from school. I can see a "village" effect taking place in my school. Although I've been online since Genie and 800 baud was high speed, my school has been using the internet (and the early generations of our groupware) as a major tool since 1991 and more recently began with www in 1993. In cyber time: ancient history. We continue to use groupware (FirstClass) to keep our whole community informed. Parents, students and teachers are all connected and interact in meaningful ways to improve the communications and teaching and learning. That's what is important.

If you would ever like to "lurk" and see how our school community interacts we would be honored to give you the needed account. . . . If you are ever in NJ and want to eyeball the place come to the Brookdale Community College Campus and check us out. An open invitation so you don't need to give us any notice this way you will see the real thing without any eyewash. We are proud of everything our kids do.

Respectfully,

Bill Pollock

Monmouth County Vocational School District
High Technology High School
P.O. Box 119
Lincroft, New Jersey 07738
www.hths.mcvsd.k12.nj.us

out to invite experts or business leaders to come in and speak to a class—or at least send information. (Smart companies will be eager to communicate with the customers and potential employees of the future.)

And they can use the Net to communicate with your parents. They can post class information for all to see, and they can send e-mail to the parents of a particular child about a problem, an assignment, or anything else a parent and teacher might want to discuss. Moreover, parents can get in touch with other school personnel—everyone from the administrator who schedules the bus service to the coordinator of after-school activities.

Parents as well as schools need to be online for this to happen—and that is slowly becoming the case. In some instances, parents who don't have Net access at home may be able to log on at work or at a local community center. In addition to wiring schools, businesses should be encouraged to provide Net access (with proper security) to their own employees.

Education only *begins* at school. For example, one of the significant results of the well-known "Union City Online" project in Union City, New Jersey, was an educational reform effort that made the wired schools a center for community development activities as well as for education. The schools and the Net were just part of a citywide revitalization effort, with support from federal, state, and local authorities, Bell Atlantic, and the teachers' union.

Connecting kids . . . to one another

The Net can connect you to other kids—Sandrine and lots of others. The mere ability of kids to communicate with one another will be a driving force for the use of computers in schools, much as it is in the rest of society. You and your friends like to chat, just like adults; you like to organize events, sleepovers, visits, and other social events, just like adults; and you may want to collaborate on homework and other projects. Kids who meet in summer camp want to stay in touch; kids encouraged by a teacher may form long-distance friendships with children from other countries or just other cities and social circumstances. Having a pen pal used to be a big deal; now it's the easiest thing in the world.

But at the same time, you need guidance—education—in using the Net. You need personal contact you can't get over the Net. Your English teacher, Jonathan, does more than force you to read and discuss novels. He encourages you to think; you're eager to win his approval and so you work a little harder, think a little longer. It's corny, but you kind of like him. Jonathan gives you interesting ideas about careers you might consider and he's . . . well, he's a role model.

He encourages you to use the Net to find out things, but he also makes you think about it critically and ethically: to question and understand the motivations of the people and companies who post information and advertising, to observe others' intellectual property and privacy rights, and to safeguard your own. One of the kids in your class downloaded an essay from the Net to hand in as his own, and Jonathan led a class discussion about why that was wrong.

Connecting kids . . . to schools and resources

You've recently come across the notion that the Net will enable parents and children to escape local schools: Just sign up for the Cyberspace Academy of your choice. Through the miracle of modern electronics, a single good teacher can teach thousands. Better yet, children can educate themselves, surfing through pages and pages of information, sharing ideas with other children, talking to experts. Indeed, the Net does allow children to teach themselves, once they are motivated to do so. In the long run, there are likely to be ever more educational resources online, as teachers and others post their work to the Net. It will allow access to some of the best lessons, lectures, and learning materials to anyone, anywhere.

But somehow you know that without Jonathan and your other teachers, you probably wouldn't have the discipline. The lure of online games and online chatting is just too great. You'd learn a lot, sure, but you wouldn't have the kind of coherent vision of the world that your history, science, and social studies teachers are trying to help you develop for yourself.

The Net is only a tool—valuable to those who have the motivation and smarts to make use of it. The very best teaching for grade-school children is two-way—the kind of genuine interaction between teacher and pupil that *encourages* motivation and smarts. The Net in principle allows for mentoring across long distances, but it can't duplicate a teacher's individual presence and attention for more than a limited number of students. First the children need to pick up the love of learning from a nearby adult. (There will always be kids who thrive in any circumstances, but let's not leave kids to the Net when they should be getting personal attention at home or in school.)

From the other side, reality is different, too: The first time I, as an "expert," got an e-mail from a first-grader, I tried to respond helpfully and fully; by the fifth time, I realized I had too much else to do. I am not a teacher, and I can probably contribute more to the world by writing books and articles than by conversing with first-graders. I don't really have any standard way of responding, but I try at least to be polite and suggest a better source. Sometimes, depending on the topic, I can forward the messages to the Electronic Frontier Foundation staff. (Though there's a good chance I might learn something from a first-grader, I have enough of them in my own family to learn from.)

Mind and multimedia

The Internet is not synonymous with multimedia: Much of what it carries is text-based. And a lot of multimedia (graphics, sound, video, mixed together) exists offline. But clearly they are developing together. What impact will they have on how we think?

Optimists are excited about the possibilities of the Web and its multimedia content for education, for information, for building a worldwide infrastructure of understanding. They marvel at how easy it is to find information. They also trust that children can learn by themselves, exploring the geography of Africa one day and the wonders of biochemistry the next. They can watch a video of Charles de Gaulle giving his victory speech and then link to a page of historical context, an English translation, or a map of Europe in 1945.

Jumble of notions

Instead of dry words such as these here, the optimists continue, we will send one another images, videos, references to Web sites, even real-time video of ourselves as we converse. Certainly it's more *fun* to watch a video, especially a well-made commercial one on the history of France, for example. Imagine being led on a multimedia tour: the de Gaulle speech, a timeline of French history with a few dates, a snippet of the speech in English, a map of France. . . . What will you have learned? The French have famous people just as we do. One of them was a great orator.

Do you want an enjoyable experience that flows through your head, or something more interactive in the truest sense of the word—that is, a book or an essay that makes you think? You have to think to absorb words and transform them into ideas and arguments. To learn, you have to change the model with which you view the world, rather than just add some images to a large store of pictures, factoids, emotional resonances, and sound bites that don't support any structure. If all you do is watch, you'll have a hard time formulating what you learned when it's over.

The downside of our obsession with the miracle of multimedia is that we lose the power of mere words, which are relatively cheap to create (requiring only a single author's time) and cheap to distribute. The challenge is that they require more work and attention—from the recipient, and from the creator, too.

It requires work to create a coherent argument (I know; I'm trying to do it right now), and it requires work to follow the argument. However, that work produces something of value that multimedia, for all its cost, often doesn't: knowledge and understanding.

Surf and sand

It may be fun to surf the Net and follow things randomly, but there's value in structure. The Net is a playground of entropy—the structurelessness that occurs when energy dissipates from a system. Yes, the Net also fosters self-organization, when individuals apply their energy, selecting and filtering information for others (aided by search and filtering tools; ⇒ Chapter 7). But there's rarely much internal structure to what's selected; the structures created by links are usually webs of cross-references rather than a clarifying analytical framework. The Net is good at showing that things are related, but not how. Does this item support that one, or refute it? What was de Gaulle's role in history? What mistakes did he make that we can learn from?

There's much more logical power to an argument about abortion, on the one hand, than to a set of pictures of fetuses, or interviews with women whose lives were ruined by unwanted children or with those unhappy children themselves. Yes, the latter can make us feel, but can they make us think rationally? Pictures can give us texture, but they can't expose the logic of the arguments or the trade-offs implied. What is the cost of raising all those unwanted children, in money and in blighted lives? What would have been the alternative? How can you show a hypothesis?

The word "mother," with all its resonance, is far more powerful and meaningful than pictures of a single mother or of several. Moreover, a picture may have unintended side effects, as when the picture looks like a particular person rather than the reader's own mother—which is presumably what the creator intended the viewer to think of. Often, you *want* the universality of a symbol rather than the particulars of an example.

The question

So what are multimedia and its unnatural timescale of jump cuts and flashes doing to us? I don't want to sound like a Luddite, but I think it's bad for our minds. Images may sell, but they don't enlighten. We're in danger of getting a society where people don't bother to think or assess consequences. It is happening not only in consumer society, but in politics: People listen to sound bites instead of assessing a candidate's overall policies. My favorite example of such thinking is the juxtaposition of two questions in a poll (taken some years ago; I may not have the figures quite right but the contradiction was real). Almost 85 percent of a group of consumers surveyed by an insurance company believed that people with good driving records should get a break on their car insurance rates. At the same time, 70 percent of that same group felt that people with poor driving records should be treated the same as anyone else; the accidents may not have been their fault.

In short, it takes work to get through an argument, whether you're making it or wondering whether to believe it.

Connecting kids . . . to their parents

Overall, you're lucky. Your parents have used the Net with you since you were small. They helped you write your first childish e-mails to your aunt and to your cousin Alice. You still remember the excitement when Alice wrote back. Later, you e-mailed General Mills when your cereal was missing the prize, and you booked the family's lodging for a summer vacation in Yellowstone (using your father's credit card). Your mother let you watch how she used the Net to find a new job as a sales manager; your father explored the sports sites with you. They asked you not to go into chat rooms alone at first. They watched over your shoulder as you had your first encounters with a couple of weirdos—until they felt confident you could handle such situations on your own. As in the real world, you learned manners from your parents—not just politeness, but how to put a meaningful subject heading on an e-mail, how to respond to (or ignore) offensive messages, what not to reveal to strangers—and the difference between a true friend and some kinds of people you may meet on the Net. You learned not to give your address out to strangers. (Sandrine, of course, is another matter . . . but good grief! You met her through a school-exchange program.)

Your parents were pleased when you seemed to prefer the Net to television; they were subtly displeased when you spent a lot of time in the chat rooms (and you found out for yourself that they could get pretty boring). You appreciate their trust. You know there are tools that would block certain sites, and your parents have discussed using them. For now, they trust you—and you pretty much deserve it. One of your friends, Juan, got obsessed with pornography, and his parents did install a filtering tool on their PC. You dread the day when Juan asks to come to your house to use your computer, because you know what he has in mind. But fortunately, he's not a very good friend.

Your parents aren't concerned just about "offensive" content. They spend time with you talking about the difference between objective information and information offered in the hope of selling a product or idea. They have also cautioned you about the reliability of what you read online.

So you've already noticed: There are two kinds of education. One is about facts and formal knowledge, and the other is about community (⟹ Chapter 2) and right and wrong. The "factual" side you can get at least partly over the Net, although it helps to have a teacher pushing you along. The moral side, you cannot. It has to happen closer to home. That's where you learn to share things that cannot be duplicated—everything from your mother's attention to the last piece of cake at dinner—and how to do unto others as you would have them do unto you.

That may be an optimistic vision of family life and you're a lucky kid to have such sensible parents, but it's a good model. This kind of education starts early—whether it is done well or not. Children learn selfishness and paranoia, or openness and security, from their parents or whoever is around in their earlier years.

The wrong kind of education

The Net can't solve family problems any more than television can. The only good thing about television is that at least it is relatively harmless and keeps kids off the streets.

By contrast, the Net is both better, because it encourages participation, and worse, because you can get into real trouble on the Net, just as you could wandering outside your home. There still needs to be someone to guide you. And no, you should not necessarily be picking your own friends over the Net. The same freedom that can be liberating—whether it's the sheer ability to wander, or the chance to overcome limitations of looks, disabilities, geography, income, and other constraints—can be dangerous for children (and for adults, but that's another issue).

That's why there's such strong pressure to regulate content on the Internet (⟹ Chapter 7). Cyberspace gives kids as much power as adults, but not as much wisdom. Children can roam from home much more easily and cheaply than they could before. They can get to bad places on the Net much more easily than to most downtowns, nightclubs, red-light districts, foreign countries, or friends' houses. And in cyberspace, no one knows if you're under fifteen—not even other thirteen-year-olds. In our current society, children get exposed all the time to messages meant for adults and not for children (at least according to the cigarette companies). But on the Internet, they have the opportunity to *interact* with other people as adults. Even a socially inept child may be able to convince some adults online that he, too, is a grown-up; adults who are social misfits, of course, may be the least likely to pick up the signals that a person is not an adult—and the most likely to take advantage of that fact if they do.

Your friends who are looking for trouble can certainly find it online. There kids can find one another, and talk about their parents—or drugs or sex—in a medium inaccessible to many parents and teachers. Many parents feel uneasy in an environment that their child may understand better than they do. This particular problem will diminish as you and your generation become the parents and teachers of tomorrow, but the ability of children to operate in an adult world will persist.

The good news is that the Net does allow you to experiment more safely than you could in "real life."

Who's in control?

The Net will highlight the question of who controls your schooling. Whatever kind of education you might seek—social, academic, romantic, or on the fringe—your choices and your time are not determined by you alone.

But the Net is making the education market freer than ever before. You can use the Net to educate yourself. Your parents can use it to bypass the local school system. Local school systems can use it to reach distant resources. And those distant "resources," especially a variety of commercial services or possibly government units, can reach back into local communities and compete with the local education establishment.

In many countries, the Net can be seen as a foreign influence, luring citizens away from the local culture.

This is the promise and the danger of the Net in every aspect of life, but it is particularly contentions in education because education cannot be left entirely to individual choice—either in terms of funding or in terms of content. Society has an interest in seeing that future generations get an education . . . and the right education.

Aside from your particular choice of high school, a looming issue in education overall is at what scale to manage it. If it's managed too locally, there's the danger of fragmentation, of splinter-group teaching, and of lack of a sense of broader community—including national history and ethnic identity. On the other hand, the larger the unit that manages it, the more likely we are to build bureaucracy, an imbalance of administration over teaching, and overall rigidity. This is another issue that won't ever be resolved, Net or no Net.

Education and the market

Now that you're thirteen and heading for high school, you want to explore your options seriously. Unlike six years ago, you have the chance to do so. Primary education, as ever, is primarily funded by the public, not by individuals or their parents. But that doesn't mean there's no room for an education *information* market. In 2004, it's starting to exist.

In your town it began when the local newspaper, *The Valley View,* pressed individual schools to reveal scores on standardized tests (by grade and class, not by individual student). That caused something of an uproar . . . but eventually one renegade school complied, thinking it had the best scores. Then another school countered, with even better scores. Then the parents got into the act and pressed the rest of the schools to publish their information. Of course, it wasn't all smooth. One teacher at one of the schools called the newspaper because her school had eliminated the scores of all the kids who hadn't passed each grade, skewing the results upward. It takes alert people, as well as a system, to make a system work.

The newspaper put all the information onto its Web site, making it available to people moving into the area as well as to real estate agents, vendors of textbooks and educational software, and anyone else. Then, another local Web site, one of a chain sponsored by a large media company, tried a competitive maneuver, and got the schools to reveal how many of their students graduated and whether they subsequently went to college or found jobs. Lively discussions ensued on the schools' Web sites. One Friendship High School board member wanted to sue over a particularly harsh comment, but other members persuaded him that the best response was to ask for parents' help rather than get embroiled in a messy lawsuit. Besides, the criticism was accurate!

In the old days, most of this sort of stuff would have happened behind closed doors. These days, you, as a thirteen-year-old kid, can read as much of it as you can stand. You find a lot of it tedious, but relevant to your future. You're trying to decide between Friendship High, five miles from home, and River Road, in the next township but open to students from your neighborhood under the new school-choice regime. You discover you're learning more from all this than you would ever have gotten in civics class.

You post a question about the schools' French classes, and a French teacher answers. So does a former student of hers, with a decidedly different point of view.

Back to reality

Back in the present, in the United States, there's an appalling lack of information about what our schools are doing in the first place. Kids come home with report cards, but there's no way to compare grades in one school with those in another. Parents can't accurately assess how their kids are doing in comparison to national norms. Likewise, schools suffer from the same lack of information. Delaine Eastin, superintendent of California's school system (with 20 percent of the country's grade school population), has only sketchy information to work with. Based on sampling, she knows how California schools compare with the U.S. average, but she can't discriminate between the schools in Oakland and those in Pasadena, or between one school in Oakland and another. That's how she explained her support for testing standards recently at a press conference promoting national adoption of such standards.

Following up on my stint with the NII Advisory Council, I attended that event, too, along with the president and the vice president. . . . I was a little uneasy about the whole thing. Suppose I don't like the particular set of standards they choose? But the national testing standards pushed by the Clinton administration for "voluntary" adoption by the states are only a start. It helps to have a standard measuring stick as long as it is not the only one. Once you know where schools stand, you need to know why, with more detail. Which teachers' students do better, which worse? Which schools do better in which subjects? And once you find that out, you can't stop there. How do the winners achieve their results? How can you encourage them to share their methods with others? How can you encourage the laggards to learn from the leaders?

An information market for schools

Currently, parents and officials can't compare schools, so there's no market spurring schools and teachers to get better. I'm not necessarily talking about vouchers for school payments (although it's an idea worth considering) or even school choice.

And I certainly don't mean the blunt solution of the government (or whoever) withdrawing resources from troubled schools and giving them to better schools. The concept of parents and children abandoning a school is also troubling: The better students and the children of more concerned parents would move elsewhere, leaving the school even worse off. In the end, schools are not businesses.

But we do need to know which schools need what kind of help, and we need to supply it in all but extreme cases. We need to honor teachers who do a good job and find ways to spread their practices to other teachers. We need to encourage the use of good software and educational resources on the Net and avoid the bad ones.

Markets can work without money when parents and other "customers" have other ways to put pressure on and offer incentives to the people involved, and the knowledge to do so. They can vote officials in or out, but they can also encourage teachers whose classes rate low to get further training. The challenge is to rescue the children and move the good teachers to an environment where they can do their jobs— and to find the worst teachers some other line of work. We can't logically hope for each teacher to be above average, but we can raise the average.

School rankings

The Net has a way of making problems visible, while at the same time making it easier to find potential solutions. One such "solution" is the GreatSchools project, another initiative set up by Smart Valley, Inc. (⟹ pages 122–123). Smart Valley, Inc. reflects this region's foresight both in thinking about education for the digital world and in taking a Net-based approach. GreatSchools will focus on the 500 public schools in Silicon Valley; other regions will no doubt do their own versions, perhaps looking to GreatSchools as a model. Founder Bill Jackson was formerly a local computer-company executive and before that a teacher, of medical students in China and of grade-school kids in Washington, D.C.

To start with, GreatSchools will publish statistics about schools: How many students graduate? At what age? Is the rate going up or down? How many get jobs upon graduation, and what kind? How do the kids do on national tests? At what rate do "limited-English" students rejoin mainstream classes? What foreign languages are offered? How many library books per student? Over time, the best teachers will be described, their methods and approaches publicized. The result will be the survival and dissemination of the best ideas along with the improvement of all the teachers. The service will also include comments from students, parents, teachers themselves, and others. And, notes

From: Bill Jackson <bill@svi.org>

Connecting Politics to Everyday Reality

One of the problems with politics as practiced in America (and probably most places) is that we often spend our time lobbing around big policy ideas at each other without much awareness of (or much interest in) what is actually going on in communities or schools where "the rubber meets the road."

For example, in California now, we have an initiative on the June 3 (1998) ballot that would severely curtail 'bilingual education.' As far as I can tell, most discussion of this ballot goes on without much understanding of what bilingual education *actually means* in California today (i.e., only a third of 'bilingual programs' are actually conducted primarily in a language other than English). [The initiative passed.]

I am excited about the potential of GreatSchools and resources like it (I'd like to create more of them) to help people connect abstract political and policy arguments to the reality of what is really going on around them. So if GreatSchools were up and running today, we would be telling people exactly what kind of bilingual education is going on at each school in the region, including the one near their home or work. The next time that there is a major education-related initiative on the ballot in California, GreatSchools will help people find out what is going on in their school relative to the issue in question.

In this way, I think GreatSchools can be a model for a kind of civic journalism that paints a "big picture" out of hundreds of individual brush strokes and helps people to better connect the concrete-local to the abstract-statewide or national. I think the political process will benefit from this. The more people connect the big picture to the local picture, the more they will understand about what works and what doesn't. The more they know about their own backyard, the more intelligent and careful they are likely to be about the big-picture conversations and decisions.

One of the core tasks of GreatSchools is to provide this perspective with regards to Bay Area schools in an accessible and interesting way. I plan to develop this potential as far and fast as I can with GreatSchools and then to apply it to other kinds of issues . . .

> **[cont'd.]**
>
> **Funding for GreatSchools**
>
> Because school quality is one of the most important criteria considered by families moving into an area, large companies have an interest in providing high-quality information about schools to current and potential employees. We will sell GreatSchools to them as an investment in high-quality information about schools for their employees. This is the Human Resources Angle.
>
> Many companies also believe that better information will lead to better schools. Large companies are investing millions of dollars and thousands of staff hours toward changing traditional ways of thinking and altering long-established power relationships in schools. Many believe that schools won't improve unless citizens—the customers of public education—demand improvement and work with educators to get it. The information in Great-Schools makes for more informed and effective advocates for high-quality schools. An investment in GreatSchools is thus an investment in creating demand for improvement. This is the Community Affairs Angle.

Jackson, he wants to focus not just on absolute rankings, but on how much students improve through the year. Much of a school's overall test ranking depends on the students it gets, he points out, but you can discern its quality in how it helps the students to improve.

In addition to rankings and specific data, the GreatSchools site should "focus attention on the quality of schools across the region, informing and inspiring public debate about policies and practices," says Jackson. "We're trying to help schools overcome their fear of this approach by allowing them to articulate their own goals and the results they're trying to achieve. We don't just put them up against one yard-stick." Moreover, he adds, users of the site can do the same, querying the system to find, say, the schools with the lowest class size within ten miles of a certain address.

As you might expect, GreatSchools has run into a little controversy as it starts up; Jackson spent most of the first year ironing out what information the service should include. The most contentious issue was whether to represent performance data (test scores and the like) by ethnic group. "We couldn't decide whether that would spur people to address problems versus confirm their biases," says Jackson. In the end, the group has decided to publish the rate of eligibility into the California University system by ethnicity and high school; this is a proxy for test scores combined with grades and other measures of performance.

Of course, GreatSchools won't be the only outfit to offer such rankings. Schools may well decide to offer their own. Consumerinfo.com (⟹ page 264, Chapter 8) is considering offering such a service on a paid, for-profit basis. Companies such as CitySearch, Digital City, Sidewalk, and other locally oriented services could provide rankings for the areas they serve. Local newspapers, many of them going online, could add school ratings to their content. People will object that education is official and needs official ratings, but that's exactly the kind of rigid thinking to avoid. The services would be much like the college rankings produced by many independent parties, with some differences. There are many more schools, and a much smaller market for each school. But with the Net, the cost of collecting and publishing such rankings will be far less. What will keep everyone honest? The schools on one side, and the threat of competition on the other.

All this is powerful stuff, as Bill Jackson of GreatSchools found out. Schools and the education establishment will probably resist strenuously, saying nothing is comparable. Airlines and hospitals likewise resist publication of their results on various measures of performance. But this kind of information market is exactly what has made the U.S. economy so successful. It's just what the education system needs.

Chapter 5

Governance

Privatization is sweeping the terrestrial world. Already, many activities that once looked like natural monopolies now look like regular competitive businesses once you divide them up. In the telephone business, long-distance and local service, once combined, are now separate businesses and compete with cable companies as well; electricity, once distributed by monopolies, is increasingly delivered competitively. More and more, former national monopolies are competing not only in their own territories, but extending themselves physically to compete in other territories. What they lose locally they hope to gain nationally and internationally—but they can do so only in competition with others. On the Net, it's the same but more so: No business is limited geographically, but each business must compete globally.

Now, with the advent of the Net, we are privatizing government in a new way—not only in the traditional sense of selling things off to the private sector, but by allowing organizations independent of traditional governments to take on certain "government" regulatory roles. These new international regulatory agencies will perform former government functions in counterpoint to increasingly global large companies and also to individuals and smaller private organizations who can operate globally over the Net.

How the Net should be governed

As the old structures lose sway, how should cyberspace be governed, not only from *within* but *between* Net communities? What sort of regulations and/or governing structure does the Net need internally? How will it be divided up into jurisdictions, since—like the earth—it is clearly not governable as a whole?

Of course, the popular assumption is that the solution to these problems lies in more government: some sort of central world government, which would manage all these issues neatly and fairly, in concert with all the countries of the world and with all the citizens of those countries, who would quickly come to agreement on some basic principles and then get on with the business of government, which is to lay down a bunch of laws and make its citizens obey them.

Well! That didn't happen in the terrestrial world and there's no reason it needs to happen on the Net. An alternative route—let's call it a path of least resistance—would be for everyone on the Net to agree to comply with U.S. laws. After all, the United States still handles more than half the world's Internet traffic, supports more than half its servers, and is the home of more than half its users.

That won't happen either, fortunately! The challenge for the future is to separate the decentralized American *approach* from American *laws* and *culture*. The American approach, as reflected in the Framework for

Global Electronic Commerce proposed by the U.S. White House in 1997—a kind of "Clinton Doctrine" for the Internet—is to avoid letting any one country take charge, even the United States.

That is, instead of a top-down (or follow-America) approach, let's try bottom-up. "World government" should arise as a series of multilateral agreements, among governments and among private parties, rather than as the preserve of a central authority, wherever it could be located.

Power shift

It's common wisdom that the primacy of the central-authority nation-state is on the decline for a variety of reasons apart from the Net—the growth of multinational business, air travel, and telecommunications in general, and the complex interaction of all these factors. This doesn't mean that nation-states will disappear, but that they are losing power to other forces, to multinational businesses and big media, as well as to small businesses that operate worldwide over the Net. Bill Gates is treated like a head of state when he travels, and his products are used by (or should I say rule the screens of) a population equivalent to that of a medium-size country. In general, power is shifting away from nation-states to commercial entities, following a pattern reminiscent of what happened in the Middle Ages, when feudal power gave way to commercial organizations (guilds of craftsmen and merchants and banks) on the one hand, and to nation-states on the other. But this time around, power is not only shifting but also diffusing . . . to small businesses, small media, and to small nongovernment organizations. People who want to change the world will find it easier to choose a small task and take it on, without the overhead associated with the March of Dimes, the Red Cross, or even the NII Advisory Council.

Jurisdiction

Questions of jurisdiction underlie the most vexing issues facing the digital world, in part because the Net has created a new division between "legitimate" terrestrial governments (which own/control physical territory and the people thereon) and "legitimate" Net governments (which control Net territory by consent and indeed request of the governed). In principle, a terrestrial government controls everything in a defined space; a Net government controls a defined sphere of activities of people who may be located anywhere on the globe. A terrestrial government controls its citizens' bodies; a Net government controls only the intermittent presence of people who may enter or leave its jurisdiction at will. You can create a Net service or community for a defined type of activity, and it needs no regulations about other kinds of activities. An online bookselling environment, for example, needs no regulations governing food and drug quality.

Over time, tension will grow, pitting the global world of digital commerce and online society against the more local worlds of traditional governments and of people who aren't part of the "brave new world." Call it the disintermediation of government: Each field of activity attracts its own set of defined-jurisdiction "governments." This is not entirely new: Think of existing organizations, some of them commercial environments, such as trading floors or markets; health-care services with rules for treatment, management of personal data, and the like; or Club Med. Others are not-for-profit, such as Alcoholics Anonymous, the Boy Scouts, or a professional society. As they and similar organizations go online, they will operate in a virtual space of their own that extends worldwide. (Indeed, I believe that nonprofits, especially smaller, noncommercial communities, will take up a greater portion of our lives than their terrestrial equivalents; ⇒ Chapter 2.)

While terrestrial governments are natural monopolies in their own territories, cyberspace governments compete. Terrestrial governments get overthrown when things get too bad; cyberspace governments simply lose citizens, much as a business loses customers. Former members may even go into competition with their old communities. The terrestrial government game is all-or-nothing (despite the possibility of a loyal opposition), whereas Net governments can coexist. "Citizenship" is voluntary.

The layers of jurisdiction

Physical space. Imagine the digital world as a layered system. At the bottom are the physical, terrestrial spaces where people live, each generally governed by a single nation-state. With a few exceptions they don't overlap; everyone belongs in one place or another. Already some people have dual nationality, or live in a place other than their home nation. They may pay taxes in two jurisdictions; under a variety of tax treaties they can usually off-set taxes paid in one place against taxes paid in another. But by and large they must obey the laws of where they are physically located, even when they bring attitudes and behavior with them to new countries in areas ranging from religious observance to child-rearing practices.

The second layer: ISPs. The second layer up is the Internet service providers (ISPs)—the lowest jurisdiction of the Net. An ISP provides us with Net access and e-mail accounts, and may host our Web sites. The ISP is our connection between the physical and the virtual worlds: Through an ISP, our physical selves connect with whatever virtual world or community we enter when we go onto the Net.

In most cases, especially in the United States and in Russia, the ISPs are privately owned, and many compete within a single country. Conversely, some ISPs already operate in several countries, and more are branching out, following the lead of Compu-Serve/America, America Online, UUnet/Worldcom/MCI, and EUnet. Meanwhile, many people and companies use several ISPs—especially companies that operate internationally. Finally, some ISPs also host communities or Web sites, most notably America Online, CompuServe, and Prodigy, as well as offering Internet access. In some other countries, ISPs are state-licensed or even state-owned outfits that pretty much represent the nation-state governments that control them, as in China and many countries with monopoly telephone service.

The third layer: Domains and communities. The third layer up operates across ISPs and across national borders. It's not a neat layer; its different entities overlap and intersect. Here we have both domains (the basic entities of cyberspace, such as edventure.com, fcc.gov, or pol.pl for Poland Online) and various kinds of online communities, operating without respect to international or ISP borders. A domain "name" has only a tenuous connection to physical reality: It can refer to one lonely machine (or even one Web site or mailbox among several on a machine), or it can refer to a company's entire virtual infrastructure with many access points (on many ISPs) all over the globe. (For example, I use the EDventure physical site by logging on to it through different ISPs from all over the world.)

Conversely, a single company or Web presence may own many domain names; Procter & Gamble, for example, has diapers.com and heartburn.com; the CNET online news service has news.com and search.com, among others. To designate a specific machine, you may have to use several subdomains, as in "eng.sun.com," which means the engineering group at Sun Microsystems. Although a community may be based on a single Web site or physical host, the people who participate in it come from all over.

Some online communities have strong borders and may be limited to fee-paying members with passwords and other security devices; others are loose and informal. Some may be real-time, like a chat group or buddy list; others may be intermittent, like newsgroups. Some may have legal standing or be linked to a group with legal standing, such as a company intranet. And some may be restricted by law, in the case of a country that tries to control what passes through and within its physical borders. But most communities have even less relationship to the underlying physical world than domains, which reside on specific machines even though those machines change over time. And a single person may be part of many different communities in a variety of jurisdictions.

The other third layer: Agencies. There's another layer, too, but it's not above the domains and communities in the traditional sense. It's *across* them. It hardly exists yet, but it will. It consists of agencies and other regulatory organizations that don't sit within a jurisdiction, but instead follow the organizations and individuals they regulate wherever those entities may roam in cyberspace. The jurisdiction attaches to the entities it regulates rather than to a physical place or even to a community. It can be represented by a label and some technical authentication, as if to say: This entity is under the protection/jurisdiction of Agency X, or, for a real example, the privacy guarantees of TRUSTe ($\Rightarrow$ Chapter 8). People engaging in transactions with those entities then enter the Agency X jurisdiction themselves, by implied or actual contract.

A Net-based government can operate *only* by consent of the governed. Any Net government must therefore provide its citizens with real benefits if it wants them to stick around. Those benefits may not be just personal goods or services, but rather the broader benefits of a regulatory regime: a clean, transparent marketplace with defined rules and consequences, or a supervised community where children can trust the people they encounter or individuals' privacy is protected.

One down, many more to come

Who then should be the primary enforcers of cyberspace? Instead of theory, let's start with something real but messy that already works pretty well—the community of Internet service providers (ISPs). They are the "property owners" of cyberspace. They manage or rent physical assets, and control physical access to the system. You can find them. And they can (mostly) find their customers.

ISPs connect the physical and the virtual worlds. They know where

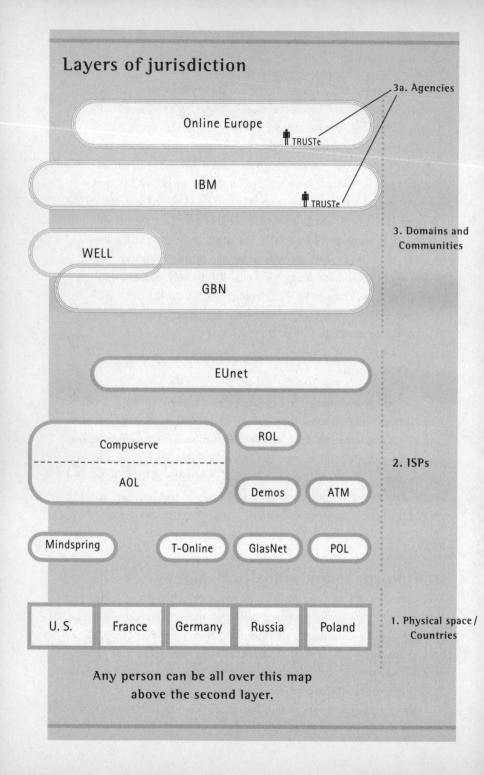

Layers of jurisdiction

3a. Agencies

Online Europe
TRUSTe

IBM
TRUSTe

3. Domains and Communities

WELL

GBN

EUnet

Compuserve
- -
AOL

ROL

Demos

ATM

2. ISPs

Mindspring

T-Online

GlasNet

POL

U. S.

France

Germany

Russia

Poland

1. Physical space / Countries

Any person can be all over this map
above the second layer.

their customers' machines are and they bill them (so they have some interest in being able to find them). They also work with the Net's "authorities" to register domain names for their customers—to give them identity in cyberspace. In turn, governments' main hold on cyberspace will be physical control over the ISPs, who need to be domiciled somewhere, have employees with physical presence (even if they only operate satellites), and so forth.

ISPs have contracts with their users (usually called Terms of Service Agreements or Acceptable Use Policies), and do, on occasion, throw users off the system if they misbehave. They cooperate to varying degrees with the police in physical jurisdictions where they operate, under conditions that they specify to their customers.

ISPs as the first line of governance

Most issues that arise within the Net can easily be handled at the ISP level. The ISPs themselves already decide what is acceptable behavior, driven by a desire to attract and retain customers, although to be honest, ISP customer service is still spotty. To clarify: An ISP is not (generally) a community; it does not tell its members what to do among themselves, but it does de facto govern "external behavior."* Common complaints might concern someone invading a community with junk mail ("spam"), abusive posts disseminated outside a community, or other kinds of harassment; if the misbehaver did not stop his behavior, the ISP could cut off his service. If the ISP did not handle the problem, the invaded community or the aggrieved individual (through his ISP) could petition the community of ISPs to discipline the lax ISP. ISPs that allowed their customers to breach copyright laws, send offensive messages, or otherwise misbehave would eventually find their services blocked out by other ISPs—who would recognize the offensive messages' source—to the annoyance of all its rule-following customers.

The ultimate sanction of cyberspace against a protocol-flouting ISP

---

*ISPs don't read people's incoming or outgoing mail unless someone complains, and then they must follow their own due process as described to their customers.

would be the refusal of other ISPs to communicate with it—the electronic equivalent of shunning. In short, ISPs will police their customers, and ISPs will police one another. All this is already happening; as cyberspace gets more crowded, it is likely to become the norm.

The closest analogy to how ISPs operate on the Net is how banks operate on the terrestrial plane today. In most countries, banks are highly regulated and have a duty to know their customers. Although their primary mission is to serve their customers, to some extent they operate as (sometimes reluctant) arms of government. They are supposed to report not just illegal transactions, but also questionable ones—whenever someone shows up with more than $10,000 in cash, for example. Banks do not particularly like this duty to oversee their customers, but it is a function they fulfill in exchange for their banking license. Now, I would not want to require ISPs to get a license from their local governments, but they do get *equivalent,* decentralized authority from the willingness of other ISPs to exchange traffic with them. In effect, they are guarantors of their customers' behavior. (Likewise, there are rogue banks that law-abiding banks refuse to do business with today.)

In a word, to be part of the worldwide digital society, you have to abide by its rules—but those rules will be derived and enforced in a decentralized, incremental way. How will this work in reality? More important, will it stick? Or will everyone eventually delegate decisions to some convenient agency that will end up becoming a central, encrusted bureaucracy?

How Net government is evolving

Two recent conflicts give a good indication of how self-organizing, bottom-up government is now emerging on the Net. The process isn't perfect, and it involves continued jockeying between various layers of terrestrial and Net authorities. Its very fluidity is its best feature, because it keeps anyone from gaining too much power. The first conflict revolves around the very formal issue of domain names. The second involves "spamming"—how can you keep your space secure from un-wanted mail? (Sometimes these two issues intersect, as in the domain-name spam on page 136.)

Domain names

Domain names are both the real estate and the trademarks of cyber-space; they establish "virtual identity." In real estate, it's location, loca-tion, location. On the Net, it's domain name, domain name, domain name! Battles over property rights are rearing their ugly heads. Re-cently, the most expensive known domain name—business.com—was sold for $150,000 to an undisclosed buyer by London-based banking software producer Business Systems International.

The issue is that in the past trademarks were localized—administered within countries. Large companies have always had to go to the trouble and expense of registering their trademarks all over the world. Now that problem is compounded as companies try to take their trademarks with them into cyberspace; they have to register them in all the virtual domains of cyberspace or risk finding someone else using their name.

So a single name can show up in a number of places with a variety of suffixes: For example, imagine edventure.com (a commercial outfit), edventure.org (a nonprofit), edventure.edu (a school), and then edvent-ure.uk (our new London office), edventure.ru (a Russian affiliate), and so forth. Each of these may or may not have anything to do with what I consider the "real" EDventure. How is anyone to tell? Do I need to register all of them to keep my trademark safe? And what about the educational venture that legitimately wants to use the same domain name?

The suffixes are called Top-Level Domains. The two-letter Top-Level Domains refer to countries, such as .uk for the United Kingdom, both .su and .ru for the former Soviet Union and now for Russia alone, .fr for France, .de for Germany (Deutschland), and so on. These are managed by the countries involved, sometimes through local licenses.

Cyberspace also has so-called generic Top-Level Domain Names or

Announcing . . . domain names for sale

Return-Path: <awall@iagency.com>

X-Sender: awall%iagency.com@smtp.iagency.com
Date: Fri, 30 May 1997 15:42:51 -0700
To: (Recipient list suppressed)
From: Alan Wallace <awall@iagency.com>
Subject: iagency - The Internet Company Sells Prime Domain Names

....

INTERACTIVE AGENCY PRESS RELEASE
       http://www.iagency.com

....

WHAT'S IN A NAME? BROADWAY? PARK PLACE? MAGAZINE.COM!

Real Estate Is A Valuable Commodity—Even On The Internet
Here's your chance to enjoy a penthouse view of cyberspace!

The Internet Company was the first company dedicated to helping business understand the Internet as a commercial resource. As a pioneer and leader in building Web sites and in creating technology for the Internet, the company acquired some of the choicest addresses on the World Wide Web, destinations like Finance.com and Wealth.com, the State Streets, Pennsylvania Avenues and Sunset Boulevards of the Internet.

These are the high-visibility, branded addresses that sales and marketing executives dream about. And now, because The Internet Company has ceased operations, they have fortunately become available.

Whether you are a Fortune 500 company going up against a major competitor, a smaller outfit preparing to take on the big guys, or a start-up hoping to enter the marketplace running, having the right Internet address, such as Market.com or Risks.com, can mean the difference between success and failure. Navigator.com, Messenger.com, and other such names in The Internet Companies catalogue, will be on the business cards of some of the most successful executives and entrepreneurs of the new millennium.

The Internet is as close as it ever will be to a level economic playing field. On the Internet, the best person—or the best product—can win. But competition is fierce: it will be companies that take advantage of every opportunity that will flourish. Addresses like Magazine.com and Sweepstakes.com will give the right companies important boosts, making it easy for established clients to remember their address and for new customers to find the way to their doors.

This opportunity won't last long. Business executives who would like to find out more, should contact The Internet Companies Joyce Dostale at (617)547-3600, x104, or on the Web mail to: jdostale@world.std.com. Don't miss the opportunity of a lifetime.

Here is the complete list of available domain names:

finance.com	navigator.com	alpha-page.com	newsspace.com
magazine.com	gig.com	etech.com	fw.com
market.com	healthcenter.com	caddyshack.com	boomtube.com
risks.com	reason.com	federalsearch.com	hos-usa.com
sweepstakes.com	bixel.com	healthi.com	coin.org
wealth.com	alewife.com	metanews.com	
messenger.com	ear.com	netkeno.com	

— 30 —

InterActive Agency, Inc.
http://www.iagency.com
2701 Ocean Park Boulevard, Suite 201
Santa Monica, CA 90405
(310) 664-6710 (310) 664-6711 Fax

gTLDs for short, which cover the world—suffixes such as .org, .gov, .com, .edu, .mil, and .net ("organization," "government," "commercial," "educational," "military," "network service provider"). Domain names with those suffixes are assigned to users *worldwide* by a private U.S. company (Network Solutions Inc., a subsidiary of military contractor SAIC) under a contract with the U.S. government expiring in the fall of 1998.* Network Solutions parcels the domain names out to name registrars who manage the registration and maintenance of the domain names.

The conflict now is over who has the right to assign the domain names within each generic Top-Level Domain, and how are the conflicting claims of various trademark holders to be resolved? (Note that this problem has not been entirely resolved in the terrestrial world either!) So here you have a mix of country jurisdictions, a for-profit monopoly, and increasing commercial conflicts over increasingly scarce names. But adding more competing gTLDs, one early suggestion, would just make the problem worse.

The domain-name issue has provoked controversy among several different forces of political correctness. Network Solutions wanted things to stay more or less as they were, so it could continue holding a monopoly for gTLDs under contract from the U.S. government. Many foreign authorities understandably don't want the U.S. government involved, and are hoping that an international bureaucracy with broad representation will assume the task of assigning global domain names. Still other parties don't want any bureaucracies involved, and would prefer to see the task handled by small, private companies—but not by a single private company that happens to be owned by a major U.S. military contractor. The traditional Internet community is suspicious of any kind of central authority and also of commercial interests.

In the end, the dispute boils down to inevitable trade-offs: Which is worse—a national bureaucracy, or an international bureaucracy? A commercial bureaucracy, or a not-for-profit bureaucracy? Which is worse—someone profiting off the Net, or government regulation?

---

*.gov and .mil are limited to U.S. organizations in those categories. The suffix .us also exists but is not widely used; most American entities choose from a "gTLD."

Clearly there does need to be some global system of naming, since people can't go around naming their own domains or they will be unreachable by other people. But the actual administration of the names from a common database can be done by a group of competing registrars, thus fostering good service and avoiding a monopoly. That is, no party should have a monopoly on all the names in a specific gTLD, so that you can have the cyberspace equivalent of phone-number portability: You want to be able to keep your domain name even if you go from one competing registrar to another.

By mid-1997, many of the forces of the Net had coalesced under the "International Ad Hoc Committee" coordinated by Donald Heath of the Internet Society. In addition to some old Internet hands with a variety of views, the IAHC comprised some new representatives from large international bureaucracies, including the International Telecommunications Union (which assigns international telephone country codes). Partly because of these "official" ties, and partly because the members conducted some of their deliberations in private, the committee aroused suspicion. Some entrepreneurs who wanted to establish new generic domains felt excluded, and some businesses, worried about their global trademarks, also felt left out. They regarded the international bureaucracies with as much love as they bear toward governments or big business.

Even as many people complained of excessive U.S. influence, the overall lack of consensus persuaded the U.S. government that it should intervene—not with its own solution, but by nudging all the players toward a more open process that *would* lead to consensus, however grudging. The government's first stab, in a much-delayed draft "green paper" in the spring of 1998, suggested some specific new domain names and details on how various interests should be represented. It met widespread derision from all corners: too authoritarian, too commercial, too U.S.–oriented, too accommodating to NSI, too accommodating to NSI's competitors, too bureaucratic. The government threw up its hands and in the summer of 1998 issued a final draft White Paper with fewer specifics, simply recommending the creation of a structure that would be open and "participant-based" and that would generate adequate consensus. At this point, many groups began finally to convene serious—and more open and constructive—discussions about how to structure just the sort of private-sector governance mechanism the government paper calls for. If the board meets the government's criteria, the United States will hand over control. (If not, well, we'll have to try again!) Those criteria are rather vague, and they may put too much faith in the World Intellectual Property Organization to resolve trademark disputes, but they send a clear message that the Net should organize itself.

The original skepticism of almost everyone involved is helping things to work better now, as people realize that no one else is getting a much better deal. The various organizations involved are responding, however reluctantly, to the complaints and criticisms. The U.S. government has fostered a relatively open, fluid process for making decisions and forming a group. Yet the handover of authority to the new governing board will be a formal, discrete event.

Spam in the balance

The second example of emerging bottom-up governance concerns "spam"—a relatively benign form of Net-based misbehavior, but one that grows more troubling as it reaches a grand scale. In principle, spam is harmless: It's electronic junk mail, unsolicited messages sent out to individuals (or posted in newsgroups) designed to accomplish something—usually to make money for the sender. However, political messages, solicitations for charitable donations, religious proselytizing, or even just unwanted information can qualify as spam. Anti-spammers say the direct costs of filtering spam are more than $10 million per year and rising, but that doesn't include any valuation of recipients' lost time, or their frustration.

The e-mail message about domain names (⟹ page 136) could qualify as spam, but since I'm an industry observer it's my job to receive such messages. Besides, this one is unusually polite with a way to "unsubscribe" indicated at the bottom. (But often, if you respond it only encourages the spammer, who now knows there's someone at that

How to interpret an e-mail

Return-Path: <no=+reply@derr98.com>
Received: from ispam.net ([205.199.212.34]) by ingate.edventure.com
(post.office MTA v1.9.3b ID# 0-17671) with ESMTP id AAA197
for <edyson@edventure.com>; Mon, 7 Apr 1997 02:15:16 -0400
Received: from Cyber Promotions' new "Cyber-Bomber"—Details at
http://www.cyberpromo.com
From: no=+reply@derr98.com
X-Shocking-Web-Page: Visit http://www.cyberpromo.com
X-Please-Note: THIS SERVER RELAYS MAIL FROM OTHER SOURCES
ONLY!
X-Important: IF YOU RECEIVE ADULT-ORIENTED MATERIAL THROUGH
THIS SERVER
X-Important2: PLEASE NOTIFY CYBER PROMOTIONS IMMEDIATELY AT
215-628-9780.
Message-Id: <199704070037.UAA06545@ispam.net>
To: hhhkks.com@ispam.net
Date: Sun, 06 Apr 97 22:39:07 EST
Subject: Stealth Emailer
Reply-To: no=+reply@nolre.com

Ironically, this piece of spam from Cyber Promotions is addressed to would-be spammers. . . .

Note that you cannot reply directly by e-mail. All you can do is hold your peace and hope you'll be removed from the list, or call the number to order the product.

This is a ONE-TIME MESSAGE if you do not respond you
will be put on the remove name list.

Yes, you'll be removed from receiving this message again, but you'll keep on receiving others from the same people under different names.

The Sonic Stealth Mailer—$399

"Send your e-mail at up to 250,000 + messages per hour,
even with a 28.8K modem!"

You will be happy to know that regardless of which bulk e-mail software program you
own, you will be able to incorporate this technology with it, as long as you can export
your list of recipients to a text file (1 address per line). The program requires
Windows 95 or NT and will not work with Windows 3.x.

Here's a number to call. The person who answers claims not to know anything about an e-mail list.

....

Better through put than a T1 line, using a 128k ISDN line. Save thousands
per month.
All this, at speeds of up to 250,000 messages / hour with a 28.8k modem.

Call Now!!..212-953-5234

e-mail address.) Most spam comes with fake return addresses, so you can't even complain directly to the sender. In the e-mail on page 140, which I received recently ("How to interpret an e-mail"), there's a phone number listed but the person who answers claims not to know about any e-mail list. However, since spam does not consist of personal messages intended to annoy a single person (harassment) or racist attacks directed at a group (hate crime), in small quantities it should be protected by the First Amendment in the United States and by other countries' guarantees of free speech, where they exist.

That's the problem with spam: It can't really be reliably identified, and in principle and in small amounts most of it is not offensive (unless you consider advertising per se offensive). Some people welcome the spam offers they get or support some of the causes spam celebrates. More often, people despise spam in general, but eventually they respond to a couple of messages, just as they do to the offers that arrive uninvited in a terrestrial mailbox. After all, if it weren't profitable, most spammers wouldn't do it; they'd go out of business. People in the anti-spam community say that the most profitable kind of spam is mail selling mailing lists and anti-anti-spam tools. Spammers have no interest in mailing to people who won't respond, yet because e-mailing is a lot cheaper than sending junk paper mail, they have less incentive to avoid unwilling recipients.

A number of "top-down" solutions have been proposed, including two bills in the U.S. Congress. One, sponsored by U.S. Representative Chris Smith (R–NJ) and based on the U.S. junk-fax law, would make unsolicited e-mail illegal. It would let a company send one unsolicited e-mail and no more to each recipient; senders would have to honor recipient requests to be removed from bulk e-mail lists. Unfortunately, the worst spammers keep switching identities and could simply move their businesses abroad. The other bill, part of the Consumer Antislamming Act sponsored by senators Frank Murkowski (R–AK) and Robert Torricelli (D–NJ), passed unanimously in the Senate and would require any sender to label unsolicited messages with a working return address, full physical address information, and a telephone number, thus outlawing anonymity (⇒Chapter 9). Some groups, including the Center for Democracy and Technology, support the Murkowski-Torricelli bill as a moderate step to handle spam. However, the Coalition Against Unsolicited Commercial Email has attacked the bill for legitimizing spam at all by giving spammers "one free shot" before recipients can get their names removed. States are also getting into the act. In March, Washington state adopted a law that prohibits spammers from misrepresenting the point of origin for their messages. The California state legislature is currently considering two bills similar to the Smith bill that would establish fines or private rights of action to combat spam.

Overall, these laws don't make a lot of sense. For starters, they'll simply encourage spammers to move overseas. Moreover, they're vague, unenforceable, and probably even more futile than the overturned U.S. Communications Decency Act, because the speech they would attempt to control (no doubt in vain) is relatively harmless in the first place.

On the other hand, the U.S. government can and does prosecute fraud, which arguably includes fake e-mail addresses and certainly includes a variety of get-rich-quick schemes that take people's money. The Federal Trade Commission is unlikely to get involved with fake e-mail addresses alone, since the damage is minor, but it has prosecuted a number of pyramid schemes and other frauds committed by e-mail. (The address for complaints is uce@ftc.gov, as in "Unsolicited Commercial E-mail.")

Do-it-yourself spam avoidance

I favor a market approach. Let's start with the concept of clearly labeling e-mail, but without making such labels a legal requirement. Then— and this is primarily a technical issue—simply enable any user to charge the sender before accepting an e-mail. The recipient, not the government, can then decide what kinds of labels to require before accepting an e-mail. And the individual, rather than a mailing house or an advertising medium, would be paid for the use of his address. (This would work unless the sender is a politician, and the money could be considered a bribe.)

Too many mislabeled e-mails would provoke a complaint to the sender's ISP. Several companies are working on the components of such an approach, which depends on payment mechanisms and some kind of authentication and certification of labels. Then it is up to the sender to decide how much it is worth to reach any particular individual, and it is up to each individual to decide how much to charge. (The recipient can also forgive the fee, so that access is not denied to the poor.) Many individuals will simply refuse to read unlabeled, unpaid mail—but that will be an individual decision, not a legal requirement. That's where the authentication comes in: You need to know at least that the sender is good for the money, and most people also won't accept mail without some kind of validated information about the sender—which may simply be a digital certificate from the sender's ISP. Consider it a very smart form of caller-identification service.

How will this work in practice? Suppose it's now 2004, such a system is in place, and you're a busy real estate agent with a lot of clients. It's your job to communicate with these clients, and to look for new ones. On the other hand, you don't want to hear from all the people who want to sell you everything from Caribbean islands to siding for your house (you live in an apartment) or the opportunity to develop a new career in insurance administration.

First of all, you rely on your ISP to handle most of the mechanics: checking incoming messages for the sender's label, managing payments, and sending automated responses according to your instructions. (This kind of extra service will be a standard for ISPs in the future, I believe.) Through your ISP, you charge $1 per message from people not listed in your personal address book or not members of communities or certified by authorities you specify, refundable if you reply. When Alice e-mails you, her software may handle all this automatically, or she may get an automatic e-mail back from your ISP's auto-responder, saying, "You will be charged $1 for delivery of this e-mail by the recipient. The charge will be refunded if the recipient replies. Do you wish to proceed?"

If she selects yes, it will ask her for payment options—either direct billing to her ISP, a credit card, or perhaps e-cash. If you do reply, the charge will be canceled and Alice will move automatically to the list of people from whom you receive e-mail free—unless you specify otherwise. Your ISP manages all the bookkeeping, and, with proper privacy protections, manages your database of addresses. (You could do this yourself if you were very concerned about confidentiality, or perhaps you could find a "data bank" to handle it for you; $\Rightarrow$ Chapter 8.)

It works much the same from your end. When you meet a prospective client at a party or get a referral, you e-mail the person. As you send the e-mail, your software will query you: "How much are you willing to pay to reach Alice Haynes?" You fill in the blank—and as long as she's under your limit, the message goes through without incident, and you pay her fee.

This is just one variant of many ways this could be handled. You could add a filter to select messages with particular words in them, such as the urban locations you specialize in, or a special code number in order to receive messages about the old car you're trying to sell; you posted a message in the online classifieds with that code number.

Each recipient may set his own fees that vary according to the sender, the label, or other parameters (for example: How many other people received this same piece of mail? How long is it?). Rich people or busy people could set high prices; students and others with free time could set low prices—and would probably be perceived as less desirable by the spammers. As a recipient, you could decide to forgive the fee if the stranger turned out to be someone whose attention you welcome. This will be a new social gesture, akin to giving someone your home number. You could also end a relationship that had gone bad by deciding to charge again. That would be tacky, but isn't that the point?

Of course there will be breaches, like the person pretending to respond to your offer of a vintage 1998 Ford Starblazer who is actually trying to sell you an upgrade to your car's global-positioning system. But overall, the system should cut down on rubbish and annoyance.

One way or another, I'm convinced "sender-pays" e-mail will happen. But like other filtering systems ($\Rightarrow$ Chapter 7), it will require a fair amount of work on the recipient's side to figure out what he wants and doesn't want. It will also require the creativity of software vendors to build better tools to enable their customers to set up different categories of e-mail and senders, handle the automated responses and payment details, and work with outside rating services that validate senders' labels.

Let-them-do-it filtering

Indeed, any halfway busy or popular individual will want to delegate the task of defining much of what he wants to receive and what he does not. Many ISPs now act as first-line filters and sell their filtering services as a competitive differentiator. For example, Mindspring, an ISP based in Atlanta, offers a spam-blocking option, but it is all-or-nothing, with no specific control by the user. The ISPs' challenge is to keep out spam while allowing individuals to receive wanted communications from outside their own communities. As an end-user, you can send complaints to any ISP at the Network Abuse Clearing House, at the e-mail address domain@abuse.net, where "domain" is the domain name of the sending ISP. If the problem continues, you can ask your own ISP to help. Given enough complaints—as happened between America Online and the notorious Cyber Promotions spam company—any or all ISPs can ask the provider from whom the messages come to ask its client to desist. Then it's between the ISP and that client. If the ISP can't or won't block the individual spammers, then the other providers will eventually block all traffic from the ISP that sends out offending messages. It's a way of escalating enforcement by making it a group activity rather than the province of a central authority.

And in the meantime, software developers are also coming up with better techniques for identifying and blocking most spam automatically—but of course that does not include messages that are unwelcome just to a specific individual.

How spammers operate

The spammers are developing better tools too, and frequently use fake return addresses and other techniques to hide their tracks. First, a little refresher course on how they work: For years, they have relied on a friendly feature in the most-used "mail transfer agent," or Sendmail, a product available free from Sendmail, Inc., in Emeryville, California. This feature, open relaying, is one of the foundations of the Internet: It makes any host forward mail automatically onward to another host, thus sending mail throughout the Internet. But unfortunately spammers can "relay" their messages through other hosts to disguise where the messages are coming from.

Accordingly, what used to be considered "open" is now called "promiscuous," and that feature is no longer a default in the newest version of Sendmail, out this year (1998). "This should make a huge difference," says Sendmail founder Eric Allman. Of course hosts will continue to relay mail, but pretty much only from other trusted sources.

Sendmail has added other spam-fighting capabilities to its newest version, which is now available in both a free and a better-supported paid version targeted at Internet service providers and corporate mail administrators. It can filter mail based on a variety of patterns in the envelope headers (that is, everything down to but not including the subject line). Such "fingerprints" include invalid message IDs, all-numerical return addresses, and addresses such as "To: friend@public.com." (One I received was from "susiesucker@myownemail.com.") It also detects and rejects large volumes of messages from the same source, other than known mailing lists. It can distinguish between temporary and permanent bounce-backs of returned mail, so that legitimate senders with transient e-mail problems are not blocked for that reason. It can also reject mail from specific addresses or domains, and can automatically use many public-domain lists of known spammers. (All these features are not entirely new, but the new version now makes them more accessible and extensible to someone other than a software wizard. The mail administrator can enable or disable the features and customize many of them.)

Do-it-yourself filtering

Meanwhile, users are getting better at fending for themselves, and vendors are selling them more effective filtering tools and services. End-user e-mail packages that sit on PCs allow users to filter their e-mail on the basis of content as well as headers, a practice most mail services have avoided for privacy reasons. Underlying all this is the conflict between convenience (having a service do your filtering) and privacy (keeping the messages you do want private from such a service). Netcom, the well-known ISP, got into trouble a few years ago over this— trying to filter spam on the basis of the subject lines. Although by and large it was machines, not people, looking at those subject lines, some customers objected, and Netcom stopped the practice. As in other spheres, with a variety of services and disclosed practices, users can pick an approach for themselves. Many individuals also maintain several e-mail accounts for different purposes and know which mailboxes' messages they can safely ignore, forward to a slush pile, or just delete.

Industrial-strength filtering

At the other end of the scale, a variety of companies are jumping into the breach with value-added tools and services for ISPs and mail administrators who can then offer or resell them to their customers. "There are advantages of scale and focus to relying on an outside service. We have a specialized staff devoted to it," says Wayne Correia of

---

SPAM: E-Mail Filters

I use the mail filters included in Netscape Messenger 4.02 and Eudora and have reduced my "junk" e-mail by 90% while allowing my colleagues at my ISP to get them if they choose! Granted, I have to weekly add to my filter list new names, but I never see THAT sender again . . . . they are deposited in the "trash" and deleted from my hard drive at exit.

bobisnow bobisnow@wenet.net

**CHARGING FOR RECEIVED EMAILS AS A WAY
TO CONTROL SPAMMING**

It is the first time I heard about that idea [in Release 2.0] and it seems to be a good one. We will have to wait for a moment before that method of filtering incoming messages becomes a) available b) functional c) accepted. The technical part (a & b) is easier. The only problem is (c)—at first users may react violently: "How dare you charge ME!" But it can work once the concept becomes understood and perceived in a proper context: "OK, the message about the charge for sending my email to you is not a personal message but a general one—a part of a privacy protection system." I'm looking forward to that time because of 3 things: First—there is a clear need for a good compromise between protecting privacy and staying open for new opportunities that may come in a message from a stranger. Opportunities to buy, be informed or experience something that you might miss if you simply cut off all the communication from "unregistered" sources. Second—the protection schemas based on a "register of blocked sender addresses" are easily avoided by clever spammers. Third—because it is a better version of something that already works with phones: "If you call me with a 'Spam' message you pay for it." In the Internet version, the price you pay to get my attention will not be set by the phone company depending on the distance etc., but it will be set by me and based on my choice.

Marek Goschorski mag@msp.waw.pl

Critical Path, the provider of one such service. Altogether, about 5 million mailboxes are already protected by such formal services, in addition to the many informal systems individuals use for themselves. (AOL also filters some spam for its customers; on the other hand, it sends them many marketing messages itself!) Although I still prefer the sender-pays approach I describe above, I think the market will produce a variety of approaches all of which can be successful.

The three companies I describe in the following pages—BSDI, Inc., Critical Path, and Bright Light Technologies—all use the basic techniques outlined above, and all provide periodic updates to their clients,

SPAM AND INTERNET COMMERCE

Every morning I open up my mailbox and delete at least 20 "special offers." I go home and check my personal mail, and delete at least 20 more. I'm afraid to post to Usenet—last time I did, I was inundated with "Adult Site: XXX" emails (and I don't post to that kind of group!!!). It's really driving me up the wall, and diminishing my experience online. It's not like not buying things from spammers is really an effective way to stop them. The incentive structure is all wrong—it's so cheap to send millions of emails that all they need is a couple of suckers to bite and they make money. I've given up on responding to auto-removes. Not only do they never seem to work, but they actually seem to increase the amount of spam I get. Someone recently suggested to me that auto-removes are actually a way that spammers are trying to verify real, live email addresses, and you're better off just deleting. Spammers claim that they're just legitimate business people (not the Make Money Fast people, but the people actually selling things), and that this is just a great new form of direct marketing. The spam I hate most is actually quite similar to the junk mail I hate most: the stuff that masquerades as important, personal mail. Emails titled "Long Time No See!" from addresses I don't recognize . . . Do I open them, and discover that they are trying to sell me a new diet drug, or trash them and miss a chance to get in touch with a friend I haven't seen in years?

Inge

who are usually ISPs or mail administrators for large companies. Their tools treat spam the way the anti-virus tools treat viruses: They get better and better at detecting them, and then block them as the user requests. The problem, of course, is that most users would agree on what a virus is, whereas spam is more a matter of personal taste. So there are a number of delicate issues in filtering spam.

Part of blocking spam is applying rules and recognizing fingerprints like those listed above; another part is simply blocking specific addresses or domains. All these companies are part of informal groups of mail experts and other Net habitués who trade information about the latest developments in spamming techniques and particular cases

GOVERNANCE

I think that it is a flaw in our method of creating laws that anyone is allowed to vote on any issue, which is not always the best idea when not everybody is as deeply involved with, nor as deeply affected by, the outcome of a particular decision as everybody else is. The fact that the voice of the voting majority does rule is great, but criteria ought to be established to where people can vote only on issues that they are actively and directly in participation with.

Jon Lolatte

of spam. The best-known one maintains the Network Abuse Clearinghouse at www.abuse.net. Another group, smaller in size, but large in reach, includes administrators from Netcom, UUNet, AOL, CompuServe, and Whole Earth Networks.

There is also a controversial group, the Mail Abuse Protection System, that runs the so-called Realtime Blackhole List at maps.vix.com/rbl, led by Internet pioneer Paul Vixie. It's controversial because it tends to block people abruptly, asking questions later. (Some consider its approach vigilantism rather than governance.) Companies such as Critical Path and Bright Light, concerned about backlash, are a little more careful before they cut people off. (And BSDI leaves it up to its customers.) Both Critical Path and Bright Light carefully maintain databases detailing what they block and why. That way, they can respond to people who complain about being blocked—and it also helps in recognizing repeat offenders. Again, there are always trade-offs and compromises. What is happening here involves not just laws and services, but people learning how all these things work in practice.

Berkeley Software Design, Inc.

Berkeley Software Design, Inc., the company that distributes the original UNIX OS from the University of California at Berkeley, is one of the many software companies that incorporate Sendmail into their own products. Among other products, it offers an add-in mail-filtering black box plus updating service called MailFilter. MailFilter is easier to use even though it has somewhat more flexible detection technology than Sendmail alone, and it includes automatic updating from BSDI. The box costs $2,300, including the updating for four months; updating costs $2,100 per year thereafter. Administrators can manage the black box to specify kinds of mail or specific addresses that should be rejected outright, tagged, or handled in any other specific way.

Critical Path and Bright Light

Critical Path was founded in 1997 by president David Hayden, former CEO of McKinley Group (creators of the Magellan search engine), and chief technology officer Wayne Correia, a longtime entrepreneur/ engineer in the field (Apple, MCI, and others) who also helped EFF with its Web site. Critical Path indirectly offers the service to several million mailboxes within 65,000 domain names. It actually runs the mail service for its clients.

By contrast, Bright Light Technologies sells software tools that corporate customers and ISPs can install into their own e-mail systems and manage for themselves. Bright Light (in which I have invested personally) started operations in early 1998 and now serves (through ISPs) more than 2 million potential customers. Bright Light was founded by a team of five people, including president Sunil Paul, formerly America Online's first Internet product manager and then the creator of FreeLoader, one of the first "push" services.

Both companies use the kinds of filtering techniques described above, but with more complex recognition rules. They also limit the use of relay services except for mail from known providers. And of course they impose no-spamming policies on their own customers (and their end-user customers) in turn.

In addition, they use one more trick—what CP calls "bait" e-mail addresses and Bright Light calls "spam probes." That is, they set up fake e-mail accounts for fake people and then use software tools to do the usual things that attract spam: register at Web sites, comment on

Web sites or in newsgroups, and the like. Since these are fake people, they have no real friends, and any mail they get must perforce be unsolicited (if only from some really lonely people as opposed to marketers). Neither company will talk about exactly how it does this, in order not to let the spammers figure out how to recognize the probes. Both companies receive the bulk e-mail that those addresses attract and quickly add their senders to the database of known spammers.

Meanwhile, of course, the spammers are busy figuring out how to foil these techniques. "We're going out and buying up all the spammers' tools and figuring out how they work," says Sunil Paul.

(I can imagine a cyber-insult of the future: "He's the kind of guy who tries to start conversations with a spam probe." Or, "He makes a spam probe look intelligent.")

Receiving spam as a service?

One outfit that attempted to deal with spam in a kinder, gentler way was actually a big source of spam—AGIS (Apex Global Information Services of Dearborn, Michigan). Founded in 1994 and one of the original Internet companies, AGIS had a number of spam-generating customers, most notably Cyber Promotions, the celebrated spammer that filed a restraining order when AOL tried to block its messages. The idea was that AGIS would run a sort of monitored spam service, allowing spammers to use its network in exchange for following certain rules of good conduct (and service fees, of course!). Users presumably would get a discount for agreeing to receive the stuff. But CEO Phil Lawler eventually dropped the plan in frustration: "Spammers can't be trusted," he told CNET. Meanwhile, Cyber Promotions' founder, spam king Sanford Wallace, has quit the business to go into legal practice on the anti-spam side. The computer press carried lots of discussions about whether he was sincere. Who knows or cares? From my perspective, the market is making him sincere: He sees more opportunity fighting spam than creating it.

Global agencies

Although the story isn't over yet, all these decentralized, bottom-up efforts are a model for what will happen more broadly on the Net. This kind of informal cooperation requires no laws, and it depends on no particular jurisdiction. It also handles many of the problems raised by anonymity without making it illegal, but by just giving individuals their own defense against unwanted intrusions ($\Rightarrow$ Chapter 9).

Sincere or not, profit-oriented or not, the companies and ISPs whose spam solutions are described above are examples of the kind of global "regulatory" bodies that will increase in influence as the Net expands. The Net will *make* them be effective, or they won't survive. No government commissioned them (although the threat of government action certainly prompted their existence); no one "allowed" them to be created. They will derive their authority from their members' need to be perceived as regulated, and from acceptance by the public. If they have no teeth, more effective companies or agencies will compete with them and win. Agencies and organizations such as these make up for the fact that the Net puts us all in contact with strangers from outside our communities. They create a web of trust with no center; ideally they will weave a strong fabric with few holes.

Such global agencies will operate across communities in a new way: Companies, individuals, e-mail, and other entities will voluntarily submit to regulation and label themselves as "certified by such and such an agency," in effect carrying their jurisdiction with them wherever they go on the Net. Then individuals or local jurisdictions, whether physical or online communities, will interact with outsiders on that basis. Potential partners (or victims!) will be able to query secure, authenticated Web sites to make sure that the certification labels are valid.

From vertical to horizontal

Over time, the current vertical, geographical structure of jurisdiction will give way to something more horizontal, at least over the increasing proportion of human activities that are Net-based. To forestall this inevitable erosion of their power (even to international agencies that they may have sponsored and fostered), many governments will require their citizens to operate only within certain approved Net jurisdictions and under tight government control. Notable examples include China (which has hired Prodigy to manage a countrywide "private" network) and Singapore, which is doing the job for its 3.2 million citizens itself and through strictly regulated licensees. Of course, there are technical ways to cross these barriers and break the law, but the overall effect will be to keep control in state hands.

Meanwhile, the free spirits of the Net will object to any regulation at all as a reimposition of "government control" on the Net. One example is the confusion of voluntary content-filtering with government censorship—but sometimes the impact is the same. Free spirits worry with some reason that semivoluntary regulatory organizations—"you don't have to join, but don't try to post your comments or do business with anyone otherwise"—will resemble their government forerunners and be susceptible to the same ailments—bureaucracy, corruption, and rigidity. They may become captives of the markets they regulate, working in the interests of their members rather than of their members' customers or the market as a whole.

But no regulation at all would mean chaos and a dark, murky Net. The best hope is a profusion of competing organizations and a strong culture of disclosure. Competition and turnover among these agencies are the best forces to make them responsive, flexible, and truly devoted to the public interest. There is no system that will work without unruly citizens and upstart start-ups willing to challenge that system.

Commerce: the first global activity

Governments will try to contain Net jurisdiction to international trade and keep authority over other matters local. That will work for a while, since the first areas to undergo globalization involve commerce, mostly among companies that presumably can protect themselves. But consumers are getting into the global-commerce act and beyond it; more and more of people's lives will eventually be conducted online.

Currently, most countries are bound by a wide variety of multilateral treaties covering commerce, intellectual property, and taxes, while private parties operating within those countries are also bound by contracts, industry-association rules, and other codes of practice.* The concept of conflicting jurisdictions is not new, but they have never mattered quite so much. (We'll make more use of lawyers than of officials!)

The United States is in the forefront of the movement to foster international electronic commerce, as it should be, given the proportion of Net activity that occurs within the country or involves U.S. entities. It is mostly trying to keep government *off* the Net, but proposing joint efforts on developing a common commercial code, guaranteeing reciprocal treatment of commerce, limiting taxation, and defining how the many contradictions between any two countries' laws should be handled. The idea is not so much to have a world court, as to have a reliable way of specifying which court or arbitration process applies in any particular case. Overall, the United States is trying to push as much of world governance as possible into the realm of commerce, since commercial law arouses much less emotion than other kinds. The more you can make things a matter of contracts and market bargaining, the less government—and the less agreement among governments—you need in the first place.

For example—investor protection

In each sphere of activity, we'll need competing agencies to design and enforce rules with specific requirements. This all may sound weird, but

*International bodies and treaties governing commercial transactions include the United Nations Commission on International Trade Law (UNCITRAL), all the organizations that weighed in on the domain-names issue, and the European Union. It's worth noting that the European Union began as a commercial, economic union but is broadening to cover almost every aspect of Europeans' activities. A United States domestic model is the Uniform Commercial Code, which fosters common rules for commerce across state boundaries. The White House's "Framework for Global Electronic Commerce" outlines its policies, goals, and basic principles for worldwide electronic commerce. It urges the United States to

you can see how it is already occurring seminaturally in the world of corporate finance—even before widespread use of the Internet. The U.S.–based Securities and Exchange Commission is gaining worldwide influence even as it competes with other regulatory regimes outside the United States. Even more encouraging, this international competition seems to be fostering more transparent markets overall.

Because companies all over the world increasingly see the United States as a primary source of capital, they are voluntarily subjecting themselves to U.S. standards of financial disclosure to raise money. The Securities and Exchange Commission is de facto becoming financial regulator to the world. Many newer stock exchanges—for example Poland's—are adopting many of its policies. Over time SEC–style rules should prevail simply because in a competitive "market of markets," investor preferences will win over those of the firms who want investors' capital. Not all countries are likely to adopt precisely all the rules of the Securities and Exchange Commission, but anyone who raises money from U.S. investors is subject to them. And in every country it's fair to require that people be truthful in the information that they do disclose (including a statement that "we have included all relevant information required under SEC regulations"). In that case, a company could be sued under whatever jurisdiction was specified for misstatements about conforming to SEC requirements. The penalties might vary (and so might enforcement), but the general level of investor protection would be consistent.

Gullible investors who have lost money in Albania and Russia, among others, would have benefited enormously from such a system. People with little experience in such matters could not see the flaws in what most U.S. investors would immediately have recognized as a scam. You can argue that only sophisticated people get onto the Internet in the first place, but that will not be true over time. Of course,

---

work with UNCITRAL on a new version of its regulations for cyberspace, recognizing the validity of virtual contracts and the need for technical tools such as encryption and authentication. Of course, the framework formally covers only U.S. policy, but it is intended to serve as a model for governments worldwide. Disclosure: I was an informal advisor on the framework project.

con artists would prefer to operate under an Albanian-style system—terrestrial or virtual—but they will eventually find a shortage of victims. (The tragedy in Albania is that many of the crooks were part of the government—which is why a little competition among jurisdictions is not a bad thing!)

The challenge is to get the word out that regulated markets are better than unregulated ones. In other words, people have to know that these agencies are available and that they should demand their oversight. Fostering that awareness is a task for honest governments, for Net communities, and for education.

Consumer protection

That's investor protection. What about consumer protection? Governments rightly or wrongly consider it their duty not just to protect their citizens from outright fraud, but to regulate citizens' behavior and protect their safety in numerous other ways, from regulations on labor practices and privacy to those governing what kinds of goods can be advertised and what kind of speech is permissible. Governments now face the loss of some power to protect their citizens online as individuals themselves choose what kinds of authority—if any—they want to live under.

Most countries have their own version of what constitutes an unfair trade practice. The European Union also has many such laws, gradually superseding those of its member countries. As a customer, I like to know that the vendors I'm dealing with are operating under some such scrutiny. Since the legal jurisdiction of the U.S. Federal Trade Commission doesn't extend outside the United States, I can't expect the FTC to regulate, say, an Australian brewery—but I might want to know that the brewery observes Australia's consumer protection laws, that it is subject to the jurisdiction of the Australian Competition and Consumer Commission, and that the FTC considers the Australian CCC to be a valid overseer. Eventually, the FTC may say the same about a Net-based agency independent of any particular government.

Disclosure: Keeping the keepers honest

In the long run many industries will start their own regulatory agencies. It is in the interest of honest firms for such agencies to exist and for them to operate across national borders worldwide. The challenge is to keep these agencies honest: How can we ensure that they represent the public interest rather than become captives of the industry they ostensibly regulate?

The best answer is not a countervailing bureaucracy but an open system that encourages challenges to any group that oversteps or entrenches its authority.

Above all, such a system requires disclosure. Companies, agencies, governments, communities, and individuals in positions of power . . . all need to tell the world how they operate and what their interests are. Disclosure is the fundamental value that makes everything else work. In addition to being embodied in government rules, it should be embodied in public attitudes.

Disclosure enables people to know what rules apply and whom they are dealing with. It is important that there be worldwide agreement that material misrepresentations on the Net should be punishable, so that no one can emerge from an outlaw jurisdiction and wreak havoc in the law-abiding sections of cyberspace.

Second, governments and communities have to establish and enforce strong antitrust laws—which basically means fighting any group that gets too large and usurps power. Antitrust fosters decentralization of power, whether it's in the hands of government or of business. Right now, antitrust authorities are already cooperating across borders on a number of cases, including some involving worldwide companies such as Microsoft and Boeing. But it's hard for any establishment—including governments—to enforce antitrust with enthusiasm, since antitrust is inherently anti*establishment*. Moreover, large organizations often control considerable resources that they can wield to gain government favor—or favors. In the end, any large organization is a threat; all we can hope for is balance of power and continuing turnover so that no single organization—government, corporation, trade association, or even regulatory agency—gets too entrenched.

Do ask; don't lie

Decentralized government can work effectively only if people can see what is happening around them. Customers and partners will learn to look for signs that any given entity is operating under the rules of the appropriate regulatory agency. No one will be required to register with "an authority," but without such a badge people will have a hard time getting counterparts to trust them. Meanwhile, there should be competition among these "authorities"—and information available about how they protect not only their members but their members' customers, investors, and partners.

The best enforcement vehicle for this free flow of power that keeps anyone from getting too entrenched is informed customers and citizens. That requires a vigorous, free press—and an educated, involved citizenry to pay attention to it. To quote Thomas Jefferson: "The basis of our government being the opinion of the people, the very first object should be to keep that right; and were it left to me to decide whether we should have a government without newspapers, or newspapers without a government, I should not hesitate a moment to prefer the latter. But I should mean that every man should receive those papers, and be capable of reading them."*

*To Edward Carrington, Jan. 16, 1787, *Writings,* VI, 57. From the *Treasury of Presidential Quotations,* ed. Caroline Harnsberger (Chicago: Follett, 1964).

Chapter 6

Intellectual property

Recently, 1 had the opportunity to visit Bill Gates's house in the company of 100 high-level CEOs whom Bill (that is, Microsoft) had invited to a "CEO Summit." A subtle marketing exercise, this event exemplified the value we put on intangibles. It was a way to get attention for Microsoft by offering the attendees the personal attention and physical presence of Bill Gates. At the same time, it also offered them the attention of one another. Would they have come if it had been each of them alone with Bill, or with ninety-nine less "important" people? Would Al Gore have come for Bill alone, or only for the opportunity to get attention from these 100 important men (and three women)? Would Steve Forbes?

There's a second part to this story, too. In the evening we all took a boat over to Bill's house—a lavish mansion well described in the press but not open to the public. The house was magnificent but what really caught the fancy of many of us was Dale Chihuly and his glass-blowing operation.* Chihuly is a celebrity glassblower; I can't think of a better way to describe him. He owns a glassblowing studio in Seattle and is known worldwide for his art, most of which is now produced by a team of apprentices. He gets paid for his glass products, but he also gets paid for creating them in public—giving a performance. In addition, he attracts sponsors for his public works.

Much as parents nowadays frequently hire a clown or a magician to entertain at a children's party, Bill had hired Chihuly to entertain at this event. Chihuly set up shop on one of Bill's balconies. He brought three furnaces, numerous tanks of propane, tubs of cooling water, all kinds of tools, and five or six apprentices.

The whole scene was magnificent to watch—and to feel. The hot glass glowed and you could feel its heat from several feet away. The workers rushed about, twirling gobs of glass, poking them into the furnace, pulling them out again, slowly building a work of art before our eyes. A small crowd gathered, including Bill and Vice President Gore. The magic was how real it was. No electronics. No machines, even. Just people, equipment, glass, the force of gravity, heat, and some shaping tools. The colors mixed; the glass swirled in the air; heated, it stretched and melted and bent—and then it turned into a magnificent curved thing that would cool down into a fantastic bowl. It had to sit overnight, but word was that it would be shipped to the vice president in the morning.

Now what's the point of this story? The point is that in many ways the experience was worth more than the physical objects being created. It certainly added value to them. How many physical goods can you

---

*You can read about him and see photos of his work (no match for seeing them made) in his book, *Chihuly over Venice,* © 1996 from Portland Press.

amass? How many glass bowls do you need to hold all the things you don't use? Even, how many commercials can you watch or how many Web sites can you visit? A better way to measure wealth is by how many unique experiences you have had. What has captured your attention and made an indelible impression?

Intellectual property loses value

It's easy to figure out who owns a glass bowl; it's tangible, physical property. One person can give or sell it to another. If it breaks, you're out of luck. A new one can be made for approximately the same cost as the original.

DEAL WITH IT

First of all, there are no guarantees in life. Secondly, there are no guarantees on the internet. Intellectual property is definitely a theory, in that it will probably never be put to practical use. The wonderful premise of the internet is that it is an abundance of free information (for the most part, that is). I concur with the fellow who said it also tends to be a synergistic grouping of idiotic thought. With this, there is absolutely NO guarantee that anything posted on the internet is factual. To give heed to intellectual property is to also imply absolute accountability on the information provider's head. If you want absolute ownership, there is an absolute price to pay as well. If your information contains slander, you're liable for suit; likewise if it contains known mis-information. Can I sue the person who makes unwitting claims about me if they claim intellectual property? Do I get to hold them responsible? How do I know that what they want to register as intellectual property is actually their own idea and not someone else's? Will it be a mad dash to register like the domain name craze? Can I patent anything that hasn't already been patented? My feeling . . . . if money and a flag to stake is what you're looking for, find a publisher. If you seek idea-swapping and thoughtful (or idiotic) expression, come to the internet.

Leslie

RE: OWNERSHIP ON THE NET

The lure of "ownership on the net" is leading to clutter. Although, like all evolutionary systems, the Net is developing self correcting mechanisms, these mechanisms are leading to a segmented, walled-off Net. In other words, the Net is being parceled into members-only sites catering to the specific interests of their members and depriving them of the anonymity of an open free system.

Karan Singh   ksingh@kileiplaw.com

By contrast, potentially everything on the Net, captured as electronic bits, is intellectual property: e-mail "conversations," banner ads, movies and video clips, legal documents, databases of consumer information, even Internet addresses themselves, to say nothing of traditional packaged content such as videos, images, and news articles. One person can give a copy to another, and retain the original. You can send content across the world in a second to thousands of people. Who owns all these things? Who controls their use? Who has the right to benefit?

These are the questions bewildering everyone from grade-school teachers to Hollywood executives, international trade lawyers, and programmers.

Currently there are laws and treaties worldwide upholding the rights of individuals and copyright holders to control the copying of their works. That is, *only the owner of the copyright—not of the physical object such as a book or an electronic object such as an electronic document—has a right to make copies.* Although enforcement varies, copyright laws generally apply throughout the civilized world—or at least the parts where anyone could hope to make money selling intellectual property.* Of

---

*Copyright laws also control the making of "derivative works"—translations, movie treatments, sequels, even the reuse of a character. Of course, none of this is as simple as the outright duplication of content, but straightforward copying is the major concern of the copyright holders at this point.

course, there are some exceptions. Libraries are allowed to make a limited number of copies for their archives (or to duplicate a rare work in fragile condition). The biggest exception is "fair use"—under which individuals may copy small sections of works with attribution for quotation, parody, commentary, and the like. But just being nonprofit doesn't suffice: A teacher cannot legally copy a chapter from a textbook to distribute to students, however worthy her purpose.

Digital impact

This whole situation is about to undergo a transformation due to the digital age. Computers and the Internet that connects them make it easy and almost cost-free to reproduce content and send or retrieve it anywhere in the world. The Net makes light work of what used to be tedious and slow: for example, tearing out a page from a newspaper, putting it onto the copier, and mailing the copy to a friend.

The problem of large-scale commercial piracy existed long ago, but now, like everything else, the same power to mass-produce is available to individuals. You no longer need to own a printing press or a broadcast station or even a Xerox copier; all you need is a PC with a Net connection.

Correspondingly, in the old days the practice of chasing commercial pirates and suing them or closing them down was easy to justify from a business and moral perspective, as well as a legal one. These targets

---

INTELLECTUAL PROPERTY

Ownership on the net

Does information really want to be free? Yeah, I never want to have to pay to get anything on the net, but I would hate to see a graphic I made copied without any kind of attribution. I've heard that digital watermarking exists, but that it's not terribly effective.

Lisa

RE: OWNERSHIP ON THE NET

Information not only wants to be free, we have an almost impossible time keeping it from freeing itself. Think of any piece of information regarding any topic. Those who know it can't wait to share it with everyone they know with never a request for recompense. The sharing of information feeds on itself, inviting the person shared with to share themselves. The biggest problem with the net is not the sharing of information but the pooling of ignorance. Follow any news group and the "experts" are repeatedly answering the same questions and dispelling the same myths. If what you have to share is of value to you then you have to decide what coin of the realm you are willing to accept for it. If more information is an acceptable payment, then the net is certainly a place to participate. But if you seek hard currency, then only share that which will entice others to seek commerce with you. People will always find ways to justify stealing the intellectual property of others and there is no way you can really stop them if they are determined. So position yourself to deal with as many people who are willing to respect your work as you can and ignore the rest.

BRB Bruce Brandt

ran full-scale factories, producing hundreds of videos, tapes, or disks. Others published thousands of illegitimate books, often in poor foreign translations that not only stole revenue but mangled the originals.

But lest we judge too harshly, note that a similar situation prevailed in the United States until 1891. All of Charles Dickens's works were published by pirates in the United States. The readers who bought the books paid normal prices to the publishers, but Dickens missed out on the royalties he could have received had the United States observed foreign copyrights. He came over here on a lecture tour in 1842 in order to recoup what he could by appearing for hefty fees.

Now the situation is far more complex. The people stealing aren't big-time crooks, but individuals. Some are copying one another's e-mail; some are copying textbooks and reference material and commercial newsletters; others are copying entertainment vehicles such as movies; and still others may be copying Web pages, comic strips, or posters of their favorite stars.

Four questions

The Net changes some of the answers to traditional questions about intellectual property as it makes it easier and cheaper to make and distribute copies. The answers to the first two questions don't change (although laws may need some slight adjustment to reflect certain new technical details and capabilities). But the answers to the last two do.

* What is right (moral)?
* What is legal?
* What is practical?
* What makes commercial sense?

In the long run, the answers to these four questions should add up to consistent solutions, or we'll end up with a mess. Certainly, it's *moral* for people to want to control what they have created. That's a simple principle. If someone has created a vaccine against, say, smallpox or a test for Down's syndrome and refuses to share it, that's immoral. But he certainly has a moral right to ask for some compensation. Likewise, the company that makes the vaccine has the right to charge for it and make a profit to fund future growth. These are not absolutes. Competition usually resolves these conflicts, because someone else comes up with something equivalent at a more reasonable price. (The fact that in some cases there is nothing equivalent—especially in the kinds of things often covered by patents—means that these rights confer a monopoly and leads to the concept of compulsory licensing: You have to let us use this information, and in return you can expect a fair fee—to be determined in court if necessary.)

Meanwhile, individual users will continue to break the law, but owners will mostly focus their enforcement efforts on people who are making money off copying rather than those who are simply sharing a

What you should do about observing copyright

What does this mean in practical terms for you as a Net user? The first rule of behavior is simply not to copy stuff that isn't yours. That way you can never get into trouble.

The fact is, I break this rule all the time, and so do most people. Below I'll list some of the exceptions. But the big rule, the one you should never, ever break, is:

Never collect money—whether directly or indirectly—on the basis of something that isn't legally yours to use. That is, you can't sell copies of something that isn't yours. Nor can you put your name to something that isn't yours even if you distribute it free.

What you can do, for example, is to say: "Buy this software from its vendor and I'll teach you how to use it for a fee."

Or, "You've probably read (and bought) John Hagel's book, *Net Gain.* I'm a consultant and I can help you to apply his ideas to your specific business." But don't hand out unauthorized photocopies of the book—not even of a single chapter.

Look at it from the point of view of the copyright owner—and imagine that you are in that position. Would you as owner mind what you are doing as user? (Be honest.)

How to break the rules—carefully

Here are some examples where the owner should not mind. But if you're in any doubt, ask!

Occasionally, actually quite frequently, I copy e-mail from one person to another. I make sure not to invade either the first person's privacy or his copyright. And I usually send the resulting message both to the original sender and the new recipient. The basic notion is, "Hey, Alice! This is what Juan just told me, and I think the two of you should discuss it!" It could be that Alice is looking for a job (sometimes I'll write Alice back first and ask if I may forward her note to Juan, in case her employer doesn't know she is looking). Or Alice may be a PR person promoting a new e-mail filter and I know that Juan is writing an article about that very topic. Or she could be asking me about one of the companies I'm involved with, and I'm forwarding the question to someone better qualified to answer—or at least less lazy. (Legally, the question of copyright for e-mail is still unresolved as a whole—as it is for private mail. Clearly, some principles apply: If you wrote it as part of a job, it belongs to the employer. If you wrote it for a client, it belongs to the client. But if you wrote it as part of a community discussion—that's where we need community rules, not necessarily a law.)

Sometimes, I forward a single issue of an online newsletter to a friend, being careful to include the subscription information. Some newsletters formalize this process and ask their readers to do so. It's a very effective form of marketing.

Sometimes I copy a small part of an article or a press release to quote it elsewhere, *with* attribution. Legally, that is "fair use"—and it depends on how much of the original I use and how much of my own work it constitutes, as well as other factors such as whether I'm charging for my work. On page 318, Chapter 10 (the lucid essay by George Kennan), you can find an article with permission *and* a fee paid.

Sometimes I forward public information from one mailing list to another. In this case, I have to consider both the interests of the original poster, and whether the new group actually wants to read the contribution. (That is, is it a contribution, or is it unwanted spam? This question also applies to my own messages, of course.)

From the other side

For your part, make the other guy's job easier by specifying any restrictions you want to impose to protect your privacy or your copyright. Assume that anything you write may be copied and redistributed unless you specify that it should not be—and don't expect strangers to be trustworthy. That is, if you don't want people to copy or "reuse" your precious creations, don't post them in a public place.

And if you really want to keep a secret, don't tell anyone.

pleasure with a friend.* This kind of distinction is risky to enshrine into law, because it encourages people to do everything just up to what is forbidden. And "profit-making" is not so clear-cut either. The earnest teenager who decorates his Web page with a picture of Bill Gates is probably okay, but what about the teenager-turned-software-consultant who posts the same picture on a Web page advertising his services?

The legal issues

Of course, the content-publishing community (probably more than the content-creating community) is trying to figure out how to stop copying of copyrighted materials. Overall, I believe that the problem (as the content-owners perceive it) is enforcement rather than law. The overall balance between the rights of users and of creators is reasonable or even favors creators in the laws we have now. But because of the broad reach of the Net, copyright-owners are trying to limit fair-use exemptions even as more and more students, libraries, and just plain folks are copying and distributing content with impunity. They are also trying to apply techniques such as clickwrap contracts ("Click here, and you have hereby agreed to all the terms and conditions on the next ten screens of tiny type"). A new Universal Commercial Code provision would enforce clickwrap contracts that revoke fair-use rights, creating a much bigger problem for the balance of interests involved in copyright than the more visible copyright law now in Congress.

Nonetheless, it's worth noting that the World Intellectual Property Organization has pushed hard to get all countries to sign its treaty on online copyright protection, with strong penalties for infringements.

---

*Efforts have been made to use copyright to maintain confidentiality and privacy, particularly by people and organizations wanting to control information about themselves. But this is tricky because bare facts are not copyrightable. Examples include the Church of Scientology's efforts to keep its high-level writings secret and J. D. Salinger's attempts to maintain his privacy. But no one has yet successfully claimed a copyright in his name or address, although that has been tried. Copyright concerns copying and financial loss, whereas privacy concerns disclosure; ⟹ Chapter 8.

From: Brad Templeton<brad@templetons.com> [EFF director, entrepreneur]

. . . It is the lack of enforcement (or general respect at the low level) that is pushing the industry to go for excessive technological [copyright] protections, and in turn to then ask for laws to protect those technological protections. The law is indeed generally adequate already, but it is largely ignored by the consumer. It's hard to find somebody who doesn't have videotaped copies of movies, a few pieces of pirate software and a lot of never-registered shareware.

The interesting social question is, do you deal with this by strengthening the law? In some cases laws exist to in effect stop the need for complex and costly private forms of protection. For example that's one goal of patent law—let people disclose, and not go through complex trade secret mechanisms. Ditto for copyright—let people publish to the winds, and not have to put the copies under lock and key.

The industry, in seeking crypto-protections, clearly thinks it isn't working, that they'll make more from works that are protected than not. As you know, that debate also went on at the start of the software industry, with most programs on copy protected disks or with dongles [hardware locks], and an eventual move to ordinary disks, except in the games area.

I actually think a good answer for the industry would be a mechanism to make money off the public's desire to copy, rather than to lock it down. Perhaps, when it becomes possible, allowing for example the owner of a CD to easily pay $2 online to make a copy of it for a friend.

The U.S. Senate has passed the Digital Millennium Copyright Act, which would implement the treaty, and the House is considering the bill. It affirms copyright protection, which is fine, but it goes too far, I believe, in criminalizing the use of devices that defeat copyright protection schemes, even for legitimate purposes such as archival copies of material and "fair-use" copying. On the other hand, it absolves ISPs from liability for infringements by users as long as the ISPs take down files once a copyright owner complains—which was a big factor in getting it passed. One beneficial effect is to give the ISPs some immunity so they don't have a duty or an incentive to police their users, invade their privacy, and call all the close ones against fair use. (On the other hand, they don't have much reason to fight *for* their users once someone has complained.) If it passes, the Digital Millennium Copyright Act won't change the fundamentals of copyright law, but it will make the penalties much more severe for those who do get prosecuted.

Practical issues

But does a creator or publisher have a practical expectation of controlling the use of content once it is available on the Net? The answer is not that simple. The rights-holder can choose limited distribution in a controlled environment/community, or broad distribution with limited control.

A third option is to tag the content in some way so that its use can be electronically monitored and billed for. In the long run, producers of content will be able to buy better technology for controlling its dissemination and indicating on what terms they want to license it. Already, there is a "Digital Property Rights Language" developed by a team led by Mark Stefik, a scientist at the Xerox Palo Alto Research Center, that producers can use for this purpose. It defines the possible uses and conditions of content, including time periods, number of uses, and kinds of use—e.g., printing, copying, or editing. Xerox has licensed it to others including IBM, which is using it in its so-called Cryptolopes, or protective digital "envelopes" that use encryption and monitor permitted uses of the content with the rights language. For its part, Playboy has started "watermarking" its images so it can detect them wherever they may be copied on the Net. These are just early examples of many such tools.

The challenge is to make such systems easy to use and robust. Most people won't mind the expense of paying a penny or two for commercial usage of content, although others may well object in principle—especially in countries where a penny is still worth something.

Commercial sense:
The new economics of intellectual property

Copyright-holders may take any of the three approaches above according to their perception of the circumstances: How much is an individual

COMMERCIAL VALUE

I agree that the source of commercial value will be people's attention and not the content that consumes their attention—to a degree. The measurement of the time of the attention and the content that consumed that time will be of significant commercial value to the creator of the content. Right now "hits" are a measurement being used to determine the value of the postings (web sites, banner ads). The person who figures out how to measure the actual impact (the time spent, the resulting actions) will tie the commercial value to the content.

Richard

copy worth? Is it easy to collect from the customers? How large is the potential market?

These are indeed important questions, but they miss the most fundamental development of all—a change in how the value of intellectual property is determined. The plain economic fact is that even if you can charge for them, the price of copies will tend to go down overall:

Increasing supply of copies (which are cheaper to create and
    distribute)
plus
stable demand (measured in people's available time)
equals
dropping prices.

The Net won't increase people's available time—which amounts to their potential demand for content—no matter what all the productivity-tool vendors claim and the content-providers hope. In fact, the time spent by individuals creating content competes for the time they could spend "consuming" it. A better way to state the economics of content is the other way around:

"Intellectual Property" will be remembered as a concept that arose with the invention of the printing press, and died with the invention of the Internet and tele-computing. Given how easy it is to copy digital data, and the speed with which it can be propagated, there will be no point even trying to enforce intellectual property rights. This is entirely consistent with the shift from product to service based industries. It is not sufficient to compete just on the clarity of thought, content or vision, but on ability to execute, time to market, and the quality of service provided.

Peter M. Wilson

Content (and the creation of content) consumes individuals' attention.

That is, individuals' time and attention is in short supply; there's likely to be a surplus of content. Content will still be expensive to create (because it takes people's time) as a business endeavor, but many people will nonetheless spend their own valuable time to create it themselves. This overall shift is the opposite of what happened with, say, clothing, which used to be made at home by women. When factories offered economies of scale for owners and salaries for workers, clothing quickly became a mass-produced commodity.

With content, by contrast, the economies of scale that kept production of intellectual property out of the home are dissipating, so it's moving back into the home (or the very small business). It's often more expensive to create content in a large company than at home. Some individuals are doing it for love, and others for money. Whatever their motivation, they and their efforts are competing with commercial content-providers for people's time—whether it's time spent passively watching a movie, furiously playing an online video game, casually surfing the Web, or earnestly answering someone's e-mail.

All this means an ever-greater proliferation of content trying to attract people's attention. This is already happening, because even mechanical reproduction makes content fairly cheap once the original has been created. The addition of "production" and distribution from home is just another giant stride in the same direction. Imagine how special it was to attend a musical performance in the old days before they could be recorded. People didn't get to hear a particular symphony more than a couple of times—although they could sing songs or play a single instrument for themselves. Now we can all reproduce our own performances.

The result of the new economics is that people are often paid for their attention, implicitly or explicitly. They get to see television free in return for watching commercials. Their magazines and newspapers are subsidized or supplied free by advertisers. Nowadays bus shelters, baseball stadiums, and even those little refresher towelettes on airlines such as Lufthansa are supported by advertisers eager for your attention.

You are also rewarded with content according to the "quality" of attention you can provide. That is, advertisers want to know who you are and how likely you are to buy the products or services that your attention is being drawn to. That's why they ask you to fill in those little forms with everything from household income to ZIP code (which tells a lot more about you than you might suspect). Alternatively, if you can influence other people who might buy, or if you're a visible opinion-maker in politics, you're also a promising target for everything from magazines to free product samples. (If you're a sports-clothes maker, just think of the value of having Bill Clinton appear in your brand of jogging shorts.)

Quality, in this context, has everything to do with income and propensity to spend it. Although this is an "attention" economy, the ultimate interest of commercial organizations is how to turn attention into money.

The source of commercial value will be people's attention, not the content that consumes their attention. There will be too much content, and not enough people with time for all of it. That will change our attitudes to everything; it will bring back new respect for people, for personal attention, for service, and for human interaction.

This all sounds wonderful and humanistic. But it also implies an increasing commercialization of relations between people. So let's get down to business and talk about the most important question: What alternative ways can content be used to generate revenue?

Making money from content

Businesses who make content will have to figure out ways other than selling copies to make money, and they will. (Moreover, all businesses will find that a greater and greater proportion of the value they create is intangible—whether it's product design, electronic gadgetry controlling a car, a representation that the workers sewing a shirt were over fifteen and adequately paid, or assurances that the information concerning a transaction will not be reused.) Most of the models they will use are not new, but they will become more prevalent.

In the old days, a company's purpose was to produce goods and distribute them. Eventually, there were more goods available than people really needed. Now, most people in the developed world have far more things than they "need"—clothes they never wear, exercise gear they never use, spare rooms in their house. (None of this is entirely new; Renaissance princes bought art and wore fancy clothes, too. But these practices have spread to the mainstream of society.) Accordingly, vendors started competing to gain markets and to make enough profits to grow. All these trends jumbled together and eventually fostered the formal discipline of marketing—basically, defining needs and the products to fill them, creating an image for them, and getting attention for them.

As long as this goes on, it's clear we can always increase demand for things. But as the world gets more crowded, more of the things we want will be virtual. Instead of wearing sneakers, kids will post their favorite images or videos on their Web pages, expressing their personalities worldwide instead of just within a single high school. What's the cyberspace equivalent of a Rolex watch? Perhaps membership in an exclusive fee-paid community. Or maybe it's just letting the neighbors know that you buy your groceries from Peapod.

Intellectual property and intellectual process

So how then are companies to make money? And how are individual contributors to get paid?

First, let's consider the two archetypal "content" business models of the future. In one, revenues will be realized for the flow of services based on the content, rather than for static copies of it. Call it intellectual *process,* not intellectual *property.* The services include everything from subscriptions to consulting. The corporate "assets" to generate those services will include employees, who will produce the value that lies fallow in the content and who may have intellectual property—or call it intellectual capital—in their heads, in the form of training, experience, or general smarts ($\Rightarrow$ Chapter 3).

The second model is to use the content to attract attention: In other words, to create intellectual capital in other people's heads, in the form of brand recognition (the most familiar model) or perhaps familiarity with your product (the millions of people who seem to know Microsoft Word with their fingers as well as their heads).

The concept of intellectual capital in other people's heads—whether loyal customers or their own employees—makes traditional business-people nervous.* People feel comfortable with "real assets" that you can own—although anyone who's ever invested in real estate, gold, or a disk-drive plant knows that real assets can depreciate as well as appreciate.

Indeed, it is becoming harder and harder to hold on to intellectual capital. Brands seem to be created and disappear overnight; reputations are gained and lost in a single appearance on the Letterman show; employees no longer have loyalty (since few companies display loyalty to them). The speed of the Net shortens the life of intellectual capital unless it is constantly renewed—by those talented, creative people that are in short supply.

---

*What's the difference between owning the content of a magazine and the magazine's capitalized attention? What you really want, of course, is the ability to garner more attention in the future. That means producing interesting content and having the right people to continue doing so. Although every business nowadays points out that people are its greatest asset, few seem to realize how true this is.

Traditional "content" companies—newspapers, magazines, book publishers—will face an increasing challenge because they will have to compete for users' time with nontraditional content providers—merchants with their own Web sites, kids sending e-mail to one another instead of watching television, amateur bands distributing their music free on the Net in hopes of attracting a following.

Basic business models

Many of the business models for realizing the value in content already exist. In the future, they will simply become more prevalent. Most companies use several in combination; the distinctions are soft. The business challenge of the future will be not only creating value, but also figuring out how best to exploit it. The methods involve a mix of selling content outright, adding value to products, attracting people, selling their attention to one another or to advertisers, and providing special services. The one constant is that the value can't be duplicated easily for another customer at no cost, because the experience, interaction, or content is unique for each customer. The approaches include:

* subscriptions
* performances
* intellectual services
* electronic intellectual services
* memberships
* face-to-face conferences
* product support
* spin-off goods
* advertising
* sponsorships
* fostering transactions
* selling copies

Each of these has its place. Each is most suitable for certain kinds of content. And many actual businesses use combinations of these approaches.

HOME COOKING ON THE NET

From an article by Esther Dyson in the (UK) Guardian

The Internet is going to be the foundation of much commercial activity in the future. Everyone, from manufacturers to intermediaries to content-creators, is going to use it to reach and serve customers.

But now that I've paid the necessary homage to the glorious future of the Net, let me explain why I think Net content businesses will have a much tougher time than the pundits tell you.

Let's compare the Net to the restaurant business. Restaurants are hot. And they're a great way to make value out of very little. You take a little bit of food; then you add content (intellectual property) and labor (intellectual process). In the restaurant business, that's recipes, design (how to make things look good on the plate and the décor of the restaurant), and advertising. The "labor" is in the kitchen (implementing the recipes), and more importantly in the dining room and at the bar, serving the customers, greeting them, making them feel welcome, recognizing them and remembering their preferences (where to sit; the potato-leek soup that's not on the menu but that is available to special customers; let's not mention the price we charge, eh?).

From very little, intellectual property and intellectual process can create a viable business. It's the same on the Net: an editorial person specializing in, say, hockey or divorce law, an advertising salesperson, a with-it graphic artist with lots of time after school . . .

Everyone wants to invest in both restaurants and Net businesses; they're the next big thing. You can invite your friends to visit and have a good time yourself. All over New York chefs and maitre d's and restaurant marketing consultants decide to go into business for themselves. Likewise, all over the world writers and artists and marketers are starting their own Websites. A well-known pastry chef announces plans to open a pastry restaurant, and venture capitalists flock to fund him. A soup chef opens several soup stores. Commercial laundries announce plans to specialize in tablecloths, napkins and waitperson uniforms, and join in the excitement. And on the Net side, journalists start online 'zines, ad salesmen start marketing companies and graphic artists specialize in Website design to serve all these start-ups. Funding is easy to find because it's obvious that restaurants and Websites are the key to success in the next millennium—well, the next decade, anyway.

Of course, a couple of years later it's obvious that no one can eat more than three meals a day, or look at more than a few Websites. And management isn't easy. The pastry chef, brilliant at crusts and filllings, is a failure at books and management. The soup wizard can't manage soup sous-chefs. The journalist can't attract a big enough audience to sell ads. The graphic artist is rude to so many customers that they find another supplier. Moreover, observers and would-be millionaires alike are not noticing all the other people who are trying to get into the same business, and worse, others offering equivalent services for free—or what I call home cooking.

Interestingly, in this regard the Net and the food business are going in opposite directions. Restaurants and mass food-processing have made the process of feeding people into a commercial business. Meanwhile, the Net is turning the business of content creation back into a cottage industry, where many people do it for themselves and their (virtual) neighbors. By contrast, home cooking, such as it still is, mostly serves families and close friends. Yes, I walked into an airport lounge the other day and found a plateful of home-baked biscuits, clearly made by an attendant who was doing it for love rather than compensation. But that's the exception nowadays. On the Net, it is normal. Lately, whenever I give a talk I have asked the audience the following question: "How many of you devote a substantial amount of your resources, whether personal time or money, to creating free content for the Net?" Of course, I depend on the individuals to define for themselves what "substantial" means, but the answer is always interesting. Usually, it is between 20 and 25 percent of the audience. That's an awful lot of home cooking.

It means that all those people and businesses eagerly creating commercial content for the Net are competing not only with those free efforts, but also that many people in their potential audiences are spending their time creating their own content for pleasure rather than—gasp!—consuming the commercial stuff put out by companies and advertisers. Much as in the restaurant business, there will probably be a bifurcated market of giants: chains such as McDonald's or Burger King on the one hand, and the Union Square Café or La Grenouille on the other. They will make money through sheer mass or as destination sites/brand names/whatever.

But there will be very few successful medium-size sites. Instead, there will be a profusion of people hoping to grow their businesses with money from venture capitalists, and others who do it for sheer pleasure. Overall, the business will probably be unprofitable, but people will still keep entering either because they don't care—they enjoy creating and sharing content—or they hope to hit the jackpot.

If you're serious about money, you should probably have something to sell. In the food business, that means attaching yourself to a hotel, a store, a manufacturing plant or perhaps a fee-charging tourist attraction. Likewise, a Website needs to be attached to something offering chargeable value—whether a store with off-price jeans, an editorial service with compelling news (which generally takes more than a single journalist), or an active community with active (and paid) community managers and the like. It's easy to be a one-person band on the Net, but it's not easy to be even a 20-person company—and compete with all those one-person bands.

Subscriptions

Subscriptions are a simple way to generate revenue for copies of content on a continuing basis. Although this is a subtle distinction, customers aren't paying for the content itself so much as they are paying for reliable delivery of it from a trusted source. A subscription, moreover, implies an ongoing contract, however impersonal, between the producer and the recipient. The recipient must undertake to do (or not do) certain things with the content. Meanwhile, the producer (or some intermediary) usually knows who the recipient is. Often, subscriptions offer subsidized content, because the subscribers' attention is sold to advertisers. There are also benefits for the advertiser: First, the subscribers are identified and usually more valuable to advertisers than random customers through a newsstand (or ones who don't pay at all because they get the content from a friend). Second, subscribers are presumed to take a more intense interest in the content (including the ads) than people just passing through. (That's one reason, aside from economies of scale, that subscribers pay less per copy than single-copy purchasers.)

The distinction between whether a "subscription" means delivery by e-mail or simply access to a restricted Web site is vanishing; most online publications offer either, at the user's option. But most are finding it difficult to charge. The *Wall Street Journal* online, with a circulation of several hundred thousand registered users when it was more or less free (or included in other services), now has about 200,000 paying online subscribers, but it is unusual and its content is unique and business-oriented. Time Inc.'s Pathfinder, which once hoped to charge, is still free. And the *New York Times* has an interesting strategy that prices according to value to the customer: Its online version is now free (although you have to register for access). As of mid-1997, the *Times* still charged subscribers outside the United States and had 4,000 overseas at $35 a month (the price of home delivery of the paper edition in the United States). But in 1998, the rate for overseas subscribers was dropped in the interest of competitiveness and long-term international growth potential. Most by-subscription online publications are high-value, industry-specific newsletters or research reports.

Performances/events

A performance is the way in which a single creator—usually someone who has garnered some attention or celebrity through free or subsidized content—can earn money by performing. A notable example is the band The Grateful Dead, which encouraged fans to tape its concerts and distribute the tapes. Instead, it earned money from concert tickets, and from licensed T-shirts, hats, and other paraphernalia. Band members also get royalties from tape sales, because some people will pay for them even though free copies are also available through "informal" distribution channels. Many other bands now make a living by giving semiprivate performances at corporate events.

Other examples include stars who endorse products and make personal appearances (also a form of advertising and sponsorship), and of course paid speakers, lecturers, athletes, trainers, and glassblower Dale Chihuly.

It's a small distinction, but "performances" are mostly entertainment, as opposed to intellectual services such as consulting, teaching, product support, or medicine.

Intellectual services

Intellectual service is the concept of interactive performance enhanced with some content—usually the kind people have in their heads, such as knowledge of a special field, a special skill with people, or sheer intelligence. Usually, a performance is simply an experience, whereas intellectual service involves some kind of tailored solution or result— which is what people pay for (although sometimes they pay for the process without getting the desired result). For example, the point of seeing a doctor isn't to watch her perform (usually) but to have her perform a specific task on you with a tangible result.

Another typical example is the services of consultants. They often write books that they mostly hand out for free or articles in scholarly journals that their firms reprint. That free content enables the consultants to charge higher prices for actually implementing their advice— which involves not just the theory, but understanding the corporate politics of the client, knowing whom to listen to and whom to ignore, understanding how the theory applies to the particular problems of the client and its market. In one egregious case, the authors of *The Discipline of Market Leaders* went further than just free content: Their consulting firm, CSC Index, arranged for its secretaries and consultants to buy masses of the book at bookstores in an attempt to get it on the *New York Times* best-seller list—which actually happened. But the scheme backfired when it was revealed. Just a couple of consultants applying their understanding of attention as a marketing mechanism!

Indeed, the consultants' wisdom is often free, and certainly not protectable. But the ability to put it into practice and actually solve people's problems is a real skill with actual results worth paying for. Everyone knows you should focus, respect your employees, and do all the things consultants always advise. But how many know which employees to respect and which ones to fire, which business lines to focus on, how to implement a network instead of a hierarchical reporting scheme, how to foster a culture of knowledge-sharing in practice? To illustrate, consider the difference between a self-help magazine article and a marriage counselor who knows how to get people to apply the knowledge in the article to themselves.

Electronic intellectual services

Yet another form of intellectual service—one that is replicable and generates economies of scale—is selling the limited-time use of software, rather than a copy of it with a license to keep it and use it at will (though not to duplicate it). Software is already something of a hybrid; software license prices sometimes depend on the number of concurrent users or the size of the machine it's used on. But the services model is where the owner keeps possession of the software and simply provides the service result—processed data, a payroll, or the like—to the customer. Selling the service rather than the license is a good way of generating revenue from software that may be expensive to create, hard to protect, and possibly not frequently used (so that someone would be reluctant to buy it, but might pay a relatively high amount for one-time use).

In this case, the property owner manages a service using the intellectual property. The client pays only for as much use as he needs—whether it's using a high-end, expensive package to create some technical designs, or a lower-end service such as payroll, which may also involve the use of people to answer employee questions and software developers to update the software continually as new laws are passed, new kinds of benefits are added, and so forth. This approach has a number of benefits for the vendor: a continuing revenue stream, good protection for the software (including aspects that aren't really protectable by copyright), and also the ability to sell in bite-size chunks to customers who might not be willing to pay up front, but who may end up paying just as much over time as they discover how useful the software is. (On the other hand, if clients don't like it, they can drop out—which is a good way of forcing vendors to deliver on their promises.)

Memberships

Memberships involve using content to attract members, and then using the members to attract one another. You could call this business model offering a paid subscription to intellectual services, content, and attention from other members. The "intellectual property" members pay for is the design of the concept: What is this organization about? It may also include static but updated content such as monthly reports on city politics, or continuous updates in a particular field such as sports. It can include the services of a moderator who manages the conversation, introduces topics, encourages participation, tones down excesses, and acts as a virtual bartender. (That is a performance of sorts; you could also call it intellectual service, depending on the level of the discussion.) The service may also include the presence of prequalified vendors who offer tailored products or discounts (or who are just easier to find as part of the community), special events, and so forth.

The organizer needs to keep working to bring in a stream of changing content and services—and new members—tailored to the membership. The resulting membership organization could be anything from a book club to a group of midcareer executives looking for new jobs, getting support from one another and professional counseling from the service provider.

One real-live example I'm involved with is the Global Business Network. Its paying members are corporations, some online and some less so, who pay $35,000 a year. In return, they have access to GBN's ongoing online conference with a cast of stellar members, their employees can attend several face-to-face conferences and GBN training sessions a year, and they get a monthly mailing of interesting books (or documents or magazines), selected and interpreted in a newsletter by Stewart Brand (who founded the WELL, page 296, ⟹ Chapter 9). They also have the opportunity to hire GBN for custom consulting. We jokingly call this the world's most exclusive book club, with just about a hundred corporate members, but the real value is the interaction among the members, who mostly manage long-range strategy for their companies, and a group of outside "big thinkers" (including me) who get their membership free in exchange for their intellectual contributions. The membership is not entirely online and not entirely offline, but the electronic network supports the people network. (Typical of the new business models, GBN offers a hybrid of products and services, both tangible and intangible.)

Face-to-face conferences

Conferences are a mix of performance, intellectual service, and membership. The provider gets people to come together—sort of temporary membership—for a short time to experience all varieties of intellectual processes/value, including the presence of their peers. This is a business model I know well, for it has funded most of my activities since 1982. My company runs just two conferences a year, and each is a one-time event. They are profitable, and people continually ask us why we don't simply run a few more each year. The fact is—and it's the reason the ones we do run are so valuable—that these events cannot be easily duplicated. Each requires its own mix of speakers, attendees, new topics, and performance by all of us: my partner Kevin Werbach and I, who pick the speakers and topics, write the conference program, organize the software demos, and moderate the panels (a real-time performance indeed); my other partner Daphne Kis, who knows almost everyone and designs the logistics and manages the whole event; and the rest of our staff, who run after everything, handle everyone's problems, and keep the whole thing going.

Sure, we could sell tapes, but we don't because we strongly believe that watching tapes of the formal sessions is a poor pretense at the value of being there. We do publish transcripts, with photos and our own (funny) captions. But even if we could duplicate all the organizing work, we couldn't get the same mix of people more frequently, and that is a great part of the value. Ironically, we don't own or even control the people (and except for the speakers, *they* pay *us*)—yet bringing them all together is a big part of what we do. For what it's worth, the noncommercial, nonintellectual version of this is called throwing a great party!

We are thinking of extending the conferences into an online conference, or a membership service, but that would require finding an extra person with the right talents to manage it. The value of what we do can't be copied and resold; it's a service that requires a person to produce it in real time.

Product support

Product support deserves its own category because it's going to be such an important part of the revenue stream for most software developers over the long run. It's also important for many "product" companies whose products actually comprise a lot of intellectual content (electronic controls), such as most tools, business equipment, machinery, and electronic appliances.

The need for product support is why software companies have less reason to fear piracy than do producers of entertainment content, which generally doesn't require technical support. (If a game crashes, it's more likely to die in the marketplace than to generate support revenues.) In a sense, software is advertising for the product-support services that follow. Software vendors are increasingly making less and less money on the initial sale of a software package, and more and more on the support that follows it. (Just consider the pricing for BSDI's spamblocker, page 150.) The challenge for the vendor is to make sure it gets those revenues for itself rather than leave them to some independent company. One way to do this is to sell through third parties, license them as dealers, and charge them for training, training materials (more content), and the like.

Moreover, you may even avoid developing the software in the first place. One company I sit on the board of, Cygnus Solutions, does a very good business providing support and consulting for *free* software, which customers can copy and distribute legally over the Internet. IBM recently announced it will distribute and support Apache, public-domain Internet-server software.

Ultimately, the vendor gets paid in proportion to the ongoing work it performs—which I believe is more "fair" than getting paid millions just for having been lucky once with a best-selling product.

Spin-off goods

This is a fairly simple idea—selling licensed content for T-shirts, logo lunch boxes, or stuffed toys, or selling the items themselves. On a grander scale, this is what advertising becomes when the advertising premium matters more than the product. That is, you produce the product to take advantage of the advertising, rather than advertising the product to enhance its appeal (and price). Examples are stuffed toys based on characters in movies, mouse pads, all kinds of licensed products, and so forth. Even as you read this book, you may well be wearing a "content-enhanced" T-shirt. The distinction is subtle, but it means you paid extra for the logo itself rather than for the quality promised by the brand behind the logo.*

Advertising

Advertising right now funds a lot of offline content—magazines, radio, television, and the like. Business interests hope that advertising will also fund a lot of Web content. So it will, but advertising itself will change as it moves to the Net. Yes, advertisers will pay for content that draws attention to their products or that gathers a crowd of potential customers to a Web site where they can interact with them. Several companies offer free e-mail to people in exchange for the opportunity to send them offers or expose them to advertising.

But in the long term, advertisers will recognize that simply posting a banner or broadcasting a commercial can be done more cheaply on a television screen, a billboard, or a bus shelter. The Internet is a fine *physical* medium for television and other broadcast media, but the Internet as a commercial or social concept is a two-way medium for interaction.

---

*Personally, I have what is probably the world's largest collection of advertiser-*subsidized* T-shirts, ranging from vintage Apple and Microsoft to one-of-a-kind collector's items from companies that commissioned T-shirts to honor products that died before they could deliver. These are shirts I did not pay for, because someone was using them to advertise rather than to collect revenues for the embodied content.

TRADING MY ATTENTION

It strikes me that there's nothing new in ED's formulation. I always trade my attention for something. It sometimes is a physical ambience, as in a Barnes & Noble. At this point, the book purchase may be only tangentially related to the content, but the transaction takes place. Ditto a concert? So what's generating the dollars? And does the ambience of the Web necessarily change this?

Owen Quattlebaum
Owen170@aol.com

Simply advertising yourself on a mass basis over the Net is a waste when you could be delivering actual value to the customer, finding out more about him or her, or doing something more useful. Think of a Web site not as glorified television, but as a glorified 800 number. Advertisers need to figure out how to offer real value based on intellectual property and tailored to the individual customer, as in most of the other business models described here. Advertising must either be specifically useful to individuals, or pay attention to them. In other words, just like other content, it is most valuable when it is delivered as a tailored service rather than as just some eye-catching content.

Sponsorships

Sponsorship is when the sponsor/advertiser promotes the content itself rather than a separate product. Right now, many rich people and some organizations fund the creation of content simply because they want it to exist. Many magazines, especially political ones such as *The New Republic* and *Reason* magazine, are sponsored by people who want certain opinions publicized. These magazines also carry some traditional advertising to help defray their costs. (Some "sponsors," particularly of art, are in fact advertising themselves.)

On the Net, there will be a profusion of content entrepreneurs, some for-profit and some not. The low costs on the Net will allow a

From: "David P. Reed"<dpreed@reed.com>[iconoclast computer and communications systems expert, formerly with Lotus and Software Arts]
Subject: striking juxtaposition of an ad and a news story . . .

Thoughtful wordsmith friends:

While I agree with Berst and Markey as quoted below, the quality of Berst's complaint is somewhat tarnished by the ad attached to it! It's a new age in journalism, I guess.

Are we to presume that GTE/BBN actually sponsored the specific story, as a literal reading of the words would imply??? Does anyone care about the appearance here? Should Berst himself care, or is the check in the mail to him already?

How did we get to this point? It might be worth a thoughtful analysis of how the traditional media ever stabilized around creating a level of editorial independence, as it apparently did.

What about those media or their audience is the essential difference from the "ad-sponsored Internet" that is going "downhill" so rapidly? Is this a case where evolutionary processes are making a different choice that will generate a different stable ecology of sponsorship, opinion, and fact? I'd be interested in your thoughts—to me it's a somewhat surprising effect of where the trends in e-commerce are taking non-obvious turns.

And from a practical point of view are writers who don't seek explicit sponsorship missing out on the big bucks? Shouldn't you start selling paragraphs in your columns and books?

David

From today's ZDNET anchordesk email:
_____*Berst Alert*_____
WHY I HATE THE PHONE COMPANIES (AND WHY YOU SHOULD TOO)

http://www.zdnet.com/chkpt/adt0105ba/www.anchordesk.com/story/ story_1613.html

The phone companies are thumbing their noses at the law requiring them to compete fairly. They're wasting millions on lobbyists and lawyers instead of building the high-speed Internet access we all need. Wait until you read about their latest shenanigans. You'll be as mad as I am—and as eager to see Congress keep its promise to put them under scrutiny.

Sponsored in part by GTE Internetworking. In 1969, BBN built the forerunner to the Internet. Now, BBN has joined forces with GTE to create GTE Internetworking. To learn more, visit us at www.bbn.com

lot more people to sponsor content who could never afford to own and run a magazine. Many of them will simply "sponsor" their *own* content: That is, they will publish for free and make money by doing some other day job. This is nothing different in principle from the singer in the church choir who makes money as a secretary, or the political activist who works in a bank, or the poets William Carlos Williams, a doctor, and Wallace Stevens, an insurance executive.

Right now, university professors and most scholars make their living sponsored by academic institutions. Their content is often free; indeed, many scholarly journals charge their authors rather than the other way around. My father spent most of his adult life as a scientist producing content—papers and talks—sponsored by his employer, the Institute for Advanced Study. The Institute itself was sponsored by donors who simply wanted it to exist although it had no visible commercial value. (A committed free-marketeer, I didn't realize that my entire youth was funded by philanthropy. But a free market *includes* philanthropy.)

Fostering transactions

This model is similar to advertising, except that the content and the money-making sales are handled by the same organization. That is, the content advertises the organization's own goods or services. The purpose of the content is to bring people in, and also to add value to the goods themselves. Often, the content is somehow incorporated into the product. In essence, that is the purpose of all the content that Amazon.com provides—book reviews, readers' comments, even links to others' sites. However, building profitable retail locations on the Web is going to be a big challenge, as I describe in the essay on pages 179–181.

Selling copies after all

Many technology companies and inventors are working on various schemes and tools that will allow content creators to control distribution and certain kinds of machine-detectable reuse of their works—i.e., forwarding, copying, printing, and the like. The problem is that the price for most individual items will be so low that the transaction costs will eat up much of the revenue. The inventors counter that they will use e-cash, refillable purses, and other mechanisms to make it practical. I'm sure some of this will happen, but I don't think it will work as well as rights-holders hope. Customers don't want the bother of confirming payment each time, nor do they want to carry an account without knowing how much it's likely to cost them. Moreover, the vendor ends up annoying precisely his most valuable, most frequent customers.

Besides, there's all that competing stuff available for free. I'm sure that some content—especially valuable market-research reports, downloadable movies, and the like—will end up being controlled. (And secret documents will certainly be protected from all but the intended recipients.) But I believe the vast majority of content floating around on the Net (as opposed to corporate intranets or restricted communities) will simply be free.

Paying the creators

The business models described above work mostly for established organizations, not for individual creators. How will the creators themselves get paid? The world will change a lot less for individual creators than for the giant content-providers, who have traditionally controlled the copyrights for individuals' works. They are now having to shift in whole or in part to the models above.

Individuals, by contrast, have almost always done work-for-hire, despite the dream of creating a best-seller—book, music, or software program—and retiring on a continuing stream of royalties and residuals. Often, if they want to make money by creating products (as opposed to continuing services), they will discover that it's easier to get so-called work-for-hire (produce something as a service) than to sell products themselves. Although more of them may now be working for themselves, they will be using the same intellectual-process-as-opposed-to-intellectual-property approach. Content-providers need content tailored to their particular service, so they want creators to produce content to order for use in one of the business models discussed earlier. (There will be a lot more competition for people's time, as I mentioned, from people who create content for free. However, the market for people paid to produce content to order is not likely to suffer as much. All the free or cheap content that is available probably doesn't precisely suit the advertiser's needs; better to hire David "Blue Velvet/Twin Peaks" Lynch to do your commercial than to license something already created.)

Thus, creators will increasingly be paid for working, rather than for their work. As individuals, they often won't have the means or clout to protect their copyrights or to exploit them. Starting out, creators may even want to give their work away in order to earn enough of a reputation to get a job or sell performances or services.

The bad news may be less opportunity to sell the products and get rich. But the good news is that the Internet will offer individual contributors a way to find work on their own terms, rather than become long-term employees ($\Longrightarrow$ Chapter 3).

Is it fair?

All this may seem unfair, since it changes the rules we grew up with. And perhaps the change itself *is* unfair. But the result seems more fair: In the old days, if you produced something that happened to be widely valued, you got compensated out of all proportion to your effort. In the new system, with some exceptions, you tend to earn in proportion to the effort you put in. The rewards will go to the creator who keeps creating, rather than to the person or corporation that might own rights to the product. In other words, if you produce good stuff they have to keep paying you to produce more good stuff. And you, on the other hand . . . you have to keep working!

Community-based control

The business models discussed earlier are all ways of using intellectual property to deliver a service or capture attention: transforming it from intellectual property into unique intellectual processes. To some extent these models are based on "moral rights" as opposed to copyrights—basically, the right to maintain the integrity of your work and to assert that you are the creator. You want to be able to exploit your creation of the work, or to charge others for exploiting it.

However, in the digital world it is not only easy to reproduce content perfectly and claim association with works that you may not own, it is also easy to alter content slightly: incorporate pieces of it into new works, snip out the can of Coke and replace it with a can of Pepsi, remove Madonna's face and insert your own, or put Juan's voice with Alice's video.

That violates not just copyright but also "moral rights." These practices are all illegal when done without permission, but they happen all the time, and they will continue to happen more and more. Musicians call it "sampling"—combining pieces of others' content to create a new work of their own. There's no denying that there's real creativity in some of this activity, and real artistic value in some of the results. But it's illegal.

What do I really think will happen? I think we'll probably handle the problem in typical Net fashion, by creating some communities where it's accepted practice—and taking care to keep copyrighted content from getting in where it can be altered without the owner's permission. In these communities, people will be free to "reuse" others' work—and others will be free to reuse theirs. But they will not be allowed to bring in "protected" content from outside. Many traditional advertisers will probably stay out of such a community, not wanting to open their free but nonetheless protected content to modification. The community managers will enforce the policies in order to keep their communities from being boycotted by the rest of the online world.

Of course there will be some leakage, but probably not much. People who like the fluidity of malleable content will enjoy these places; others, who prefer the "original" products, will stay away. Inside, the communities should be hotbeds of collaboration and creativity, as artists build on one another's work. (For a glimpse at something similar, consider the Oracle, where anonymous authors collaborate on creating and implementing the character of the Oracle; $\Rightarrow$ page 288, Chapter 9.)

And then the market should work. Community members could decide which rules they prefer for their own community, but could not impose them on others (or others' content). Creative people who like to reuse others' works could be as creative as they wanted, but only with the works of people of a similar persuasion. Many advertisers may decide that in the end they'd rather have their icons and images broadly seen and "reused" rather than strictly protected. But it will be their choice.

Community rules for copyright may seem a sloppy, unsatisfactory approach to today's copyright-owners, but it's the most realistic solution I can think of for this kind of creativity.

Caching and mirroring

Another "content-integrity" issue on the Net is caching, or mirroring. Caching is the practice of copying a popular Web site or certain pages, so that it's quicker and easier to download. This is what your own computer often does when you surf the Web, on the assumption that you might want to look at the same page again in the same session. (That's why it's often much quicker to go "back" than to download a page the first time.) Mirroring is basically another term for the same practice, but it has a slightly more formal feel to it. Caching is what you do for your own convenience; mirroring is a formal arrangement where one site maintains a full copy of another. The intellectual property issue, of course, is when does caching become more than fair use and require a formal mirroring arrangement?

For example, services such as America Online cache the most popular pages from Web sites such as Netscape, Pathfinder, ESPNET SportsZone, GeoCities, Excite, and AOL Netfind so that their customers can get to them quicker, avoiding congestion both on the Net and at the particular Web site. It's the usual 80/20 rule; 20 percent of the sites get 80 percent of the activity, so why not make extra copies of them?* Actually, the numbers are probably closer to the top 20 *sites* (a minuscule percentage) getting 80 percent of the activity of AOL customers, but the company doesn't release such information. Companies and services overseas also often cache or mirror remote Web sites. Although the Net in theory is global and distance makes no difference, in practice transatlantic access is often slow because bandwidth is still limited.

This all sounds fine, assuming the sites are free. But free or not, they *are* copyrighted. Who could object to additional distribution of content made freely available worldwide? There are two major problems: First, the time lag. Once someone caches a site for use by others, what obligation does the cacher have to keep the cache up to date? For example, Juan in Silicon Valley may be delighted to have Alice in Australia cache his Web page with all the latest gossip about Netscape and Microsoft and Marimba. But if she doesn't update it more than once a day, he's going to get embarrassed when Netscape's latest acquisition isn't mentioned until the day after it happens. If he's offering stock prices or something that regularly changes minute by minute, forget it! (A medical site would be less likely to have such a problem—until the hour after someone discovers a cure for lung cancer or a gene for common sense, or Dr. Ruth gets the Nobel Prize for medicine.)

Second, if Juan sells advertising for his site, he can't accurately count the visits made to Alice's mirror site and include them in the rate base he promotes to advertisers. Of course, both these problems can easily be solved by contract, as long as you have a basic agreement among ISPs that Alice does indeed need some agreement with Juan to mirror his site. Alice can promise to update the site every hour—or whatever negotiated frequency matches her desire to mirror the site with Juan's sense of urgency. Likewise, Alice could undertake to inform Juan about who visits his site. She might even be able to charge Juan a commission for all the visitors she delivers from Down Under. (Of course, she

---

*AOL has formal marketing agreements with some sites, and no agreements with others. It will stop caching any Web site that objects.

needs to honor those visitors' privacy preferences in whatever information she delivers to Juan.) But should I need any kind of agreement to cache Juan's pages in my own machine for my own personal use? No.

Linking

Linking is a seemingly simpler issue, but it can lead to complications, too. One of the great features of the Net is that it *encourages* linking instead of copying. That is, instead of sending someone something by e-mail or posting it in a discussion group, you can just refer them to the original in its pure form at some Web site. For example, I could have just referred you to David Sewell's article at the *First Monday* site instead of quoting it in this book ($\Longrightarrow$ page 289, Chapter 9). That way, you could be sure it was presented the way *he* prefers and in full. If he happened to change his mind about anything or do further research, you would be able to find the current version. Indeed, the version in *First Monday* is an update of something that appeared previously in *EJournal,* another online publication. A link also helps avoid any possible misunderstandings about copyright, a typo, or a misattribution.

However, imagine some other scenarios. Suppose I wrote a long essay about how ridiculous or dangerous Sewell's ideas are, and then pointed to them as an example of stupidity? Sewell would probably welcome the chance to open a dialogue and would point back to my site with some answers.

But there are already many examples of people and companies who have objected to being linked to. Many corporate sites, for example, are linked to by negative sites established by disgruntled former employees, unhappy customers, and the like. Companies can sue if the content gets too nasty, but they are usually better off responding to legitimate criticism and showing that they have a sense of humor.

There's another interesting example—surely the first of many—in a small battle between Microsoft and Ticketmaster. (The fact that Microsoft cofounder Paul Allen was an investor in and sat on the boards of both companies just adds to the gossip value of this particular little spat.) The situation was this: Microsoft's Sidewalk service, which describes dining, shopping, and entertainment opportunities in a variety of cities, linked to the Ticketmaster ticket-selling site from Sidewalk's descriptions of various events. The problem, from Ticketmaster's perspective, was that Sidewalk linked directly to individual Ticketmaster pages for each event, instead of sending the customers through the "front door" (Ticketmaster's home page), which displays advertising and establishes Ticketmaster's own identity. By the summer of 1997, Ticketmaster had blocked all links from Sidewalk with the message: "This is an unauthorized link and a dead end for Sidewalk."

From Ticketmaster's point of view, Microsoft was stealing its identity and its potential advertising revenues. (Another factor may be that Ticketmaster has an agreement with CitySearch, a Sidewalk competitor, where CitySearch actually pays for the privilege of linking to Ticketmaster. But that may not last.) You could say that Ticketmaster should solve the problem by highlighting its identity on every page, but space is limited. Besides, it generates extra ad revenues by forcing users to come in through its front page and click past banner ads as they hone in on the event and the tickets they're seeking.

The immediate situation has been resolved with an agreement that stops Ticketmaster from linking to Sidewalk, but the lawsuit drags on. Moreover, Paul Allen has since sold his interest in Ticketmaster to Home Shopping Network. But this was a really stupid dispute that should be resolved by a contract, not a lawsuit. You'd think Ticketmaster would appreciate the extra business. There's an analogous situation that works: Amazon.com's relationship with its so-called Associates, who link to the Amazon site. Far from suing the linkers, Amazon actually pays them a commission on the book sales they generate.

Framing

Another controversial practice is framing. Framing is a fine technical innovation: It allows you to put a "frame" around a window on the screen. That is, from within one site, you can link to another site and

SERVING THE USER

Users have told us again and again: they don't care who the information belongs to. They simply want the ability to access the information, compare it, decide whether it has value to them or not and then use it as they see fit. It isn't information that wants to be free; it's users who want to be free. I find it ironic that there has been so much ink spilled about how the Internet will free people who live under the yokes of political tyranny and yet it seems that those who live and die by the concept of free speech (the western media and press) are the first to clamp down on who owns information and how it is used and sold. The management and dissemination of information has long been one of the keys of maintaining power in human societies. The Internet, which fundamentally changes how information is managed and controlled, is certain to become one of the primary arenas of societal evolution.

Roman Godzich rgodzich@totalnews.com

look through the frame into the second site. The problem is with what the frame may conceal—and possibly with what it may add.

Imagine a link to another site where some of the original site stays on the screen, allowing just some of the new content to show through in a frame—with the advertising around it blocked from view. That harms the content-provider trying to sell advertising or simply wanting to maintain its own identity. Second, the frame around the new content may in fact modify it, with everything from criticism to annotations saying "This is not true!" Or it may steal value from the content-provider with its own advertising, in effect using someone else's content to sell its own ads.

That was exactly the case with TotalNews, a site that pointed to other news sites such as MSNBC, CNN, the *Wall Street Journal,* the *Washington Post,* the *Los Angeles Times,* and Time Inc.'s Pathfinder, and sold its own ads around their content. Several of the content-providers sued TotalNews in a U.S. court; the suit was settled in a way carefully constructed not to set a precedent. TotalNews said loudly that it settled only because it lacked the resources to continue the legal battle, and the other side said less. The essence of the agreement was that Total-News agreed to stop framing the sites, although it still links to them. Without quite establishing that there is such a thing as a right to link that they could withhold, the sites have agreed to let TotalNews do so. They can ask it to stop with fifteen days' notice, but in that case they have to go back to court to argue the original question: whether there is a right to link in the first place.

In other words, both sides seem to be saying, "Let's let someone else figure this out." For now, linking is okay, but framing—i.e., using the linked-to content within the framer's context rather than in the linkee's context—may be a breach of the content's integrity and an infringement on the content-owner's rights. That actually seems a pretty fair resolution to me. But it's far from being resolved by the law. That will probably take several lawsuits with more binding resolutions.

The attention age

All along, I've been talking about human attention as a commodity of economic value—whether it's attention from consumers generated by advertisements or the attention given by a consultant who solves your particular problem. Attention also has an intrinsic value to human beings, much like food (and unlike money, which is useful only for trading or spurious self-esteem).

This raises a broader question: What human activities are commercially worthwhile in a world where machines do almost everything? This question brings to mind psychologist Sherry Turkle's insight that long ago children compared themselves with animals—pets or farm animals—and perceived themselves as intelligent and rational. Now they compare themselves with computers and perceive themselves as alive, emotional, and creative, with a will of their own.* After a while, even children perceive that computers can do only what they are told

*Sherry Turkle. *The Second Self: Computers and the Human Spirit.* New York: Simon & Schuster, 1985.

to do. (Yes, that limit is being stretched, but children may be better than adults at perceiving the true nature of these machines.)

Child or adult, we are indeed special compared with machinery. We cannot be duplicated. We can take initiative and make moral judgments. We have goals, and we have a sense of humor. We can perceive patterns and design things—some of us better than others. We can motivate others, and we can reassure or please customers. Our attention is valuable to other people in the way that a machine's "attention" can never be, even if it offers accurate personalized information.

I believe that all the glitz and artificial stimulation offered by the electronic world will ultimately cause people to value human company and attention more. That doesn't mean that we're going to abandon our computers, but that we will value human contact, both face-to-face and through computers, more highly than interaction with the computers themselves.

We need to understand that the Net does not replace human relationships; it is one more way to conduct them, just like the telephone. I use e-mail a lot to keep in touch with friends. Sometimes I e-mail them to call me; sometimes I think of them at odd hours of the day or night and send e-mail for itself. Whatever the words, it says, "I'm thinking of you," and refers to some experience we have shared. Or I may need help: "I was embarrassed to ask anyone else this stupid question, but I knew you'd know the answer: What kind of game do they play in the 3Com Park? Football, baseball, or basketball?"

Sure, I could have looked it up on the Net, but it's nicer to ask a friend.

Chapter 7

Content control

Your thirteen-year-old daughter Alice has been using her computer to go online for several years now, ever since she turned seven in 1998. Like most parents, you bought her a computer with blocking software included, and Alice takes it for granted. She complains that it's clumsy; it keeps blocking her out of perfectly innocent sites, but she has gotten used to it, just as she's used to sharing the bathroom with her messy seven-year-old brother and to not being allowed in the adults' section of the local library. Last week, she was researching a school report on health care, and it blocked her out of a site about AIDS. As usual, she came to you for technical assistance—and you took the opportunity to provide a little moral assistance, too. You had a heart-to-heart talk about AIDS and prejudice. You let her check out the site with your guidance for the medical details you preferred not to describe yourself. Pretty soon, you think, you can trust her to operate without the blocking software. It might be different someday for her brother Juan.

Alice is not likely to go out searching for dirty pictures on the Net. It's more that you don't want her coming upon garbage by mistake. But in your own searching of the Net, you've found it's pretty easy to distinguish "Girls' Toys of the 1880s" on the Family Museum site from "Toygirls and Tooting Tom" on the Naughty Net site. Alice is smart enough to do this for herself, and it's probably time for her to get exposed to the real world, if only so she'll know what to avoid.

Recently, you've been relaxing some of the constraints on the filter; you can adjust it to various age levels in different categories, from violence to sexual content. You can also use ratings from a variety of different services; for convenience, you use the same one as Alice's school but with slightly different settings and with a few handmade changes to the list of blocked sites.

When Alice was smaller, she once started to give her phone number to someone in a chat room, but the filtering tool caught it: You had specified certain outgoing items for it to block as well. Alice innocently came and asked why the software had blocked her, and you explained that you cannot trust everyone—unfortunately. But she's wiser now. You both know that she could probably get around the outgoing filter by expressing her phone number in French or with a variety of other tricks, but she won't.

Of course, you're an ideal parent, and Alice is a wonderful kid. You know of other parents who expect the software to do all the work for them. The neighbors down the street are using the same filtering tool, but they have it hooked up to a different rating service that filters out almost everything except the Family Education Network and a couple of "kid-safe" sites. (Long ago it used to allow Disney, but then Disney lost its "respectability" because of its tolerant policies toward gays and lesbians.) The parents refuse to discuss their choices with their kids, and the kids are rebellious and unruly—unlike Alice, for all the freedom you give her.

How did this come about?

Underlying the filter on Alice's PC is PICS, the Platform for Internet Content Selection, a technology standard launched in 1995. PICS was created by the World Wide Web Consortium, a nonprofit alliance of Internet developers, in reaction to the threat of the U.S. Communications Decency Act, which passed in late 1995 and was overturned (thank goodness) in June of 1997. The CDA would have outlawed the posting of indecent material on the Net, on the theory that it would corrupt and endanger helpless children. It had a lot of problems, which fortunately the Supreme Court recognized. In his decision, Justice John Paul Stevens said the law was too vague and that in seeking to protect children, it trampled on everyone's rights. He referred to "the dramatic expansion of this new marketplace of ideas," and continued, "the growth of the Internet has been and continues to be phenomenal. As a matter of constitutional tradition, in the absence of evidence to the contrary, we presume that government regulation of speech is more likely to interfere with the free exchange of ideas than to encourage it. The interest in encouraging freedom of expression in a democratic society outweighs any theoretical but unproven benefit of censorship." The CDA would have applied not only to porn sites, but to many others concerned with health care, art, medical information, religious discussions, and the like. Moreover, it would have restricted individuals not only in choosing what to see, but in choosing what to say in their own online conversations and postings. Managers of online communities and Web sites would have become afraid to foster lively discussions and would probably have had to pay huge liability insurance premiums or close down.

There are now new "son of CDA" bills proliferating in Congress and state legislatures in the United States, and in other countries. In early 1998 Senator Dan Coats (R-IN), one of the CDA's sponsors, introduced a new, more narrowly written bill, limited to commercial

AN (edited) EXCHANGE ON CHILDREN'S RIGHTS VIS-À-VIS FILTERS

CC: edyson@edventure.com

Dear Ms. Dyson,

Below is one post from a mailing list, fight-censorship, with which you may be familiar. We're having a, um, discussion of your views of content filtering as expressed in Release 2.0.

Specific points have been raised regarding whether you regard minors as having any rights to see content proscribed by their parents, and in fact if use of "filterware" in practice will ever amount to any more than some authority proscribing what can be accessed by someone who has no recourse but to obey.

I wondered if you would care to respond, or join us on fight-censorship@vorlon.mit.edu.

Sincerely,

Jeff Schult

I'm not defending her views. I do wish she was here to do so. Is it possible Esther lurks?;-)

Jeff Schult
[formerly] Marketing Director, JavaNet—www.javanet.com
[now jeff@tftb.com, Tales from the Bitstream]
Internet technology and culture writer, New Haven (CT) Advocate

Thanks. FWIW, the original manuscript (chapter) was *all about* children's rights vs. parents' rights, who should decide who educates children? and free will and so forth, but I realized there wasn't much useful that I could say, so I left it. . . .

Children's rights is a complex issue—off the Net as well as on. Children have *some* rights, but yes, I'd waffle and say it's a question of degree, not of principle. Children are not adults, and who's to say when they grow up. De facto, it's a negotiation between the kids and their parents, and sometimes the resolution is unfair.

Sometimes it's so mixed-up someone should step in. Who's someone? That's why it's complicated. Parents have *some* rights too, vis a vis the government as well as vis a vis other individuals who think they are oppressing their kids. I do indeed believe filterware can be used wisely, just as it can also be used unwisely.

Thanks for inquiring.

Esther Dyson

Web sites, that would prohibit them from allowing children access to material that is "harmful to minors."

Constitutional or not, the Coats bill proposed the same basic approach as the CDA: rendering whole categories of content criminal. In addition, several states have adopted or proposed legislation to restrict online content. New Mexico, for example, recently passed a law that bans the dissemination of material deemed "harmful to minors" on the Internet. The ACLU, joined by the Electronic Frontier Foundation (EFF), filed suit to declare this law unconstitutional and won an injunction against it. As of mid-1998, the ACLU's Cyber-Liberties Web site listed thirteen states that have passed laws to regulate Internet speech, with legislation pending in an additional ten. The argument for the futility of the CDA—that one country could not effectively prohibit speech on an inherently global network—applies with additional force to individual state laws. But as individual bills fail or pass and individual laws now under appeal are overturned (as three have been already, in Georgia, New York, and Virginia), they will no doubt be replaced by new attempts, keeping the ACLU's site full and its lawyers busy.

Meanwhile, Senator John McCain (R-AZ), chairman of the Senate Commerce Committee, has introduced the "Internet School Filtering Act," which would require schools and libraries to install filtering software in order to receive discounted Internet access courtesy of the Federal Universal Service Fund (funded by a tax on telephone charges; $\Rightarrow$ Chapter 4). Vice President Gore has endorsed an alternative to the McCain bill that would require schools and libraries to implement so-called "acceptable use" policies, without necessarily using filters. These arguments will continue as long as some people think governments should be responsible for people's choices of what to see and what to say—that is, forever.

Libraries: More choices requiring more decisions

On the other side, there are lawsuits challenging the mandatory use of filtering tools in public libraries (most notably one entered by the ACLU against the Loudon County Library in Virginia).

Filtering in libraries is particularly controversial because they straddle the divide between government-operated public forums and educational environments for children. The American Library Association has voted—but far from unanimously!—to oppose library filtering. Many individual librarians and city governments, however, do use filtering software, especially on computers in children's sections of libraries.

This is an awkward issue, and perhaps compromise should reign here too: Filtering is okay in the children's section, parents can give permission for their children to use the adults' terminals, and adults should be free to use the Net as they will. In this mode, the library is a point for public access rather than a selector of content. (How the Net changes the role of libraries overall is an interesting question: Their role as financial intermediaries changes from buying books to providing Net access; whereas once they could finesse decisions about controversial books because of tight budgets, now they have to decide explicitly what to do about access to Net-based materials that may offend some in their communities. Meanwhile their role as guides and as community centers is increased, and they must reach out to those who can't afford what better-off people have at home.)

Filtering content

The Communications Decency Act was largely the work of people who consider the Net a borderless cesspool of anarchists, terrorists, dope fiends, and pornographers who can reach out and snatch unwary children. But, in fact, the Net is already full of boundaries—everything from domain names and passwords to language barriers and payment requirements. Even content that is accessible must be sought out and downloaded or visited; except for e-mail, it doesn't come at you unbidden. You have to *join* discussion groups, whether through mailing lists, Web sites, or chats—some restricted, some open to anyone. You must *sign up* for the new proliferating "push" services that send you stuff automatically. You have to *act purposely* to get to all these things; they don't grab you.

Yet there is a problem: Too much of what's out there is not clearly marked. You may follow a link to something unexpected, and offensive. You may get e-mail from someone you don't know . . . and would not care to meet. You may inadvertently leave some data behind that you'd rather not disclose. You may catch a computer virus from a stranger—or a careless friend. How can you tell beforehand?

The answer is to label content and Web sites, and then allow people to make their own choices. Alternatively, governments may mandate the choices, an approach I deplore, but one that is likely to happen in certain countries such as Singapore and China. At least some officials in Bavaria, Germany, which in 1995 sued a CompuServe official for distributing what it considers offensive content, would probably like this approach, too. Ironically, the original prosecutors changed their minds and argued for his acquittal, but the court still convicted the manager, Felix Somm, who had earlier left the company. He was fined 100,000 Deutsche marks, or about $60,000, and sentenced to two years' probation. Of course, the case is being appealed. However, Somm's and the prosecutors' argument was not so much that censorship is wrong, but that it was unreasonable for CompuServe to be expected to block such content with the technology available at the time. That begs the question of how the new filtering technologies might be used, by ISPs or governments. (CompuServe subsequently blocked some of the offending services, began offering filtering tools to its customers, and signed up to support the RSACi filtering initiative; ($\Rightarrow$ page 236.) This case, proceeding differently from the CDA in the United States, continues to foster hot discussion in Germany and all over Europe. In response, Internet service provider PSINet is planning to move some of its Web site hosting servers out of the Bavarian region in Germany. The firm told the *Wall Street Journal* it prefers to operate where "the laws are international, and not Bavarian-like."

In other countries around the world, governments want to limit the proportion of foreign (or foreign-language) material, liquor advertising, or what China memorably calls "harmful material"—as in "harmful to the Chinese government." Government control of content is inherently coercive—and not usually totally effective, fortunately. Yet we in the United States tend to forget that governments can shoot people or lock them up, so that what is technically possible may still be practically perilous. Seeing your neighbor dragged away at midnight has a deterrent effect. Moreover, governments can also find allies for enforcement among local Internet service providers. ISP trade associations have developed joint codes of conduct in several countries, often at government "urging." In these codes, ISPs typically commit to prohibit or remove materials from their sites that violate specified standards of decency or political correctness. In most cases, the rules don't specify exactly what is forbidden, which makes them even worse.

Martin Bangemann, the European Commissioner responsible for telecommunications and information markets, has suggested a "global charter" for the Internet. Bangemann's idea is that the governments of the world would negotiate baseline rules for a variety of Internet policy questions, including content regulation. The EC formally endorsed the idea early in 1998, and the United States expressed qualified support for such an approach. These efforts are hard to distinguish from government-mandated systems; I'd rather see Internet service providers developing their own individual codes and allowing customers to choose from among ISPs themselves—or among different services from a single ISP. (ISPs that allow their customers to behave too badly in what they send to others, as opposed to what they publish for people to see voluntarily, would find themselves blocked; ⟹ Chapter 5 on governance.)

Ideally, a person rather than a government can use content labels to select or filter content. The labeling technology can be inserted into the computer infrastructure so that a user can instruct a browser where to take him or what to avoid automatically. Similar technology can also

Note that this statement does not say censorship is wrong; it simply says ISPs should not be liable.—Esther Dyson

FROM A PRESS RELEASE ABOUT THE COMPUSERVE CASE

eco trade association: Somm verdict a storm signal for foreign investors/eco chairman Michael Schneider: "A German court has seriously damaged the German Internet industry."

Cologne—The conviction of the former Compuserve [Germany] CEO Felix Somm (two years' probation) is a serious blow for Germany as a location in the global Internet market. This was the critical response of eco Electronic Commerce Forum e.V. (Cologne), the German Internet trade association, to Thursday's ruling by the Munich municipal court. eco (whose members handle over 80% of all Internet data flows in Germany through their networks) is concerned that this ruling as the first by a German court that an online provider is jointly liable for a third party's illegal content will send a devastating message to the world.

The statement goes on to express a total lack of understanding for the way that Munich municipal judge Wilhelm Hubbert sentenced Somm despite the united motion for acquittal by the public prosecutor and the defence. eco noted that the example of Compuserve showed clearly that content fed into the Internet outside Germany was virtually immune to control from Germany. ....

Considering further that measures against the misuse of the Internet were still in an early stage of development two years ago, Somm is facing demands which in retrospect are totally out of proportion. "Somm was convicted on the basis of a combination of yesterday's regulations and today's technology," as Schneider notes.

However, today the senior executives of German Internet Service Providers are better protected against conviction for the crimes of others. The measures which eco has taken in cooperation with its members should, according to Schneider, "ensure as far as humanly possible that providers are no longer held liable for the illegal acts of others."

Michael Schneider Chairman, eco—Electronic Commerce Forum e.V.
Director, Regulation and Selfregulation EuroISPA
Chairman, Complaint Commission of the German
c/o Multimedia-Service-Providers Hotline
Michael Schneider & Partners Law Firm, Phone: +49 2242 9270-0
Dickstrasse 35, D-53773 Hennef   Michael.Schneider@Anwalt.DE

filter incoming e-mail for specific words or sources, much as a virus detector scans incoming messages for viruses.

Ideally, all this would work perfectly. Adults could always get what they want and could control what their kids see. The truth is, the filters can sometimes be bypassed by enterprising children, but overall they create a more secure environment and deal with the problems of parental control and offensive content better and in a freer way than any government ever could.

Platform for Internet Content Selection (PICS)

This was the philosophy behind PICS: Give parents or anyone else the tools to filter content for themselves and their children or employees. The goal of the World Wide Web Consortium (W3C) was to define a technology platform (like the Web itself) on top of which people could label their own content. PICS is a set of Web-oriented protocols for how ratings can be expressed, distributed, and parsed, not a rating system in itself. Although the original impetus came from rating content for suitability for children, many of the participants see it as far more extensible than that. And indeed many of the filtering companies are now focusing on the business market. The members of the W3C, which is housed at the European Center for Nuclear Research (CERN) in Switzerland (where the Web originated) and at MIT in Cambridge, Massachusetts, are technical companies interested in standardizing the digital infrastructure so they can compete on innovations around it.

Now, many meetings and much work later, PICS implementations (and non-PICS filters) are showing up all over the place—spurred along by the Supreme Court's decision, which ensures that there will indeed be a profusion of inappropriate material out there that responsible parents will want to filter. The W3C imprimatur, ratified by the Consortium's 160-plus corporate members, gives the standard broad credibility.

PICS is the underlying technology for tools to create and publish labels and for the filters and other tools to recognize them. It allows a Web site owner or a third party to label a site or individual page, and it allows any PICS-enabled browser or other software tool to find and interpret the label or rating. The label can be physically on the site, or ratings can be collected elsewhere by a third-party ratings bureau that users and browsers can refer to automatically over the Net. Anyone can rate and label his own site, and anyone—interest group, commercial service, community manager—can set up a ratings bureau about other sites. And vice versa: A user can specify not just which sites he wants ratings for but which rating service he wants. Just as in other markets, some rating services will be more widely consulted than others, but the PICS standard in principle means an open, decentralized market where content descriptions and people's preferences (for themselves or their children) can be matched.

Service bureaus will maintain electronically readable lists of ratings not posted on the sites themselves. Thus you could go to, say, the Sunny Valley site and find everything about tigers approved by the PTA for kids ages eight to ten. You could also, with slightly more sophisticated software, have your browser consult several services: "I want only sites rated 'A' by the Catholic Church, 'D2' by Healthy Living, and 'suitable for nine and up' by the Sunny Valley PTA."

The system has its imperfections, but it is becoming relatively simple for both self-raters and parents to use as appropriate tools are developed. Parents can set their own desired levels for the various factors, rather than relying on a simple age scale like that of the Motion Picture Association of America. (Your neighbor's fifteen-year-old may be less mature than thirteen-year-old Alice; only you and your neighbor know for sure. And your neighbor may care more about sexual content, while you deplore violence.)

Moreover, there is now a new tool from the W3C called PICSRules, which is a format for creating just such sets of filtering criteria (call them a "user profile") for distribution to others. In principle, PICSRules profiles can be easily modified. In practice, a government could require all its citizens to use the same one unaltered. This has led to predictable concerns by the American Civil Liberties Union (among others) that PICS and especially PICSRules are tools of censorship. Potentially, they are—but they are also tools for individual control.

Over time, this technical approach of labels and selection can do more than just protect children. For example, it could be extended to allow you to select sites according to how the site handles customer data in terms of privacy protection ($\Rightarrow$ Chapter 8). Or more simply, it could allow an adult to find articles rated "insightful" by a favorite critic, all recipes rated spicy by Julia Child, or all sites rated "pure French" by the French government. It could also be part of a requirement by the French government that all browsers operated in France use a special version of PICSRules to measure the user's time spent viewing French and non-French content, sending the user a warning when the proportion of non-French content is too high. Sound ridiculous? Maybe. But like most technology, PICS can support both clever and outrageous applications.

A standard for labels; diversity for ratings

Up to now, most ratings the public is familiar with work something like Annual Percentage Rates for consumer loans or deposits, which specify a set range of information that every financial institution must present. This is the way Hollywood handles movie ratings, and this is the approach the U.S. broadcasting industry is taking for television with the V-chip. The one-rating-system-fits-all method may not technically be government control, but it comes too close to central control to operate much differently in practice.

In fact, there are many different ways to rate, say, sexual material, and many different preferences/aversions among individuals, social groups, companies, and parents. It makes more sense for various groups to have their own standards for content, from age-based ranges to religious issues, violence meters, and the like.

What PICS offers is support for a variety of *rating* systems, through a specific technical standard for *labels*—presenting diverse groups' assessments in a way that lets software as well as people know where to

Filtering out is the wrong idea. You'll never get a significant portion of content providers' cooperation if you tell them that you're trying to make sure that people can't find them. Instead, you filter *in*. Create a XXX-rated search engine. Make it completely free. Give it an obvious name, like search-xxx.com.

Oh, and while you're at it, sell the URLs to the likes of Yahoo, Lycos, Hotbot, Altavista, etc, who could never be in such a business, but would *love* to get your content so *they* could filter out.

-russ<nelson@crynwr.com>http://web.crynwr.com/~nelson
Crynwr supports Open Source(tm) Software|PGPok | Freedom is the
primary
521 Pleasant Valley Rd. |+1 315 268 1925 voice | cause of Peace, Love,
Potsdam, NY 13676-3213 |+1 315 268-9201 FAX | Truth and Justice.

find any label and how to read it. That is, ratings are judgments about a site or anything else; labels are the formal way in which they are expressed. PICS is the equivalent of a packaging standard specifying the location, type size, and structure of a label, without requiring it to be in ounces or grams—or even requiring it to include weight at all. The consumer can decide what he wants to know. PICS also offers a way of specifying the source of the ratings, so that you can search for labels from a rater you trust, and some means of authenticating the rater, the item rated, and the rating. Optionally, of course. Anyone could rate something anonymously, and anyone else could decide whether to pay attention to such unsourced ratings.

How PICS works

I won't go into great technical detail, but it may help to understand how all this works, or at least to know that many smart people and companies have gotten together to figure it out. The system is complex, but it operates relatively smoothly through interaction among users, local networks, Web sites, third-party label bureaus, search engines,

ISPs, and other participants in the decentralized, self-organizing Web environment.

The PICS labels follow a defined syntax. They can be embedded in the content of the site itself, or they can be included in the stream of data (sort of a handshaking communication) between the user and the site. Alternatively, they can be expressed stand-alone and matched to a Web address, or Universal Resource Locator (URL), as happens in the third-party label bureaus. It's equivalent to putting a parenthetical comment in the text, or in a footnote with the text, or in a set of notes at the back of a report that can be published separately, in that order.

A site can create its own PICS label, and it can also incorporate PICS labels generated by others into its site. Independently, third parties can develop and publish their own lists of sites and corresponding ratings. Rating services can include those lists in software updates they distribute to their customers, or they can keep them on their own Web sites, usually with restricted access, for clients to use as they need them. They can also be included on search sites under license. (Typically, when a user uses a separate label bureau, his software automatically checks with the label bureau in the background when he selects a site, just as it does when the "label bureau" is a list of sites resident on his own computer or on a corporate network.) Groups can also create PICSRules profiles, so that users are spared the trouble—or can evade the responsibility—of setting up their own criteria for suitability.

However, buyer beware: The expression "supporting PICS" has many levels. Some tools that can filter PICS labels from some rating services cannot necessarily read all PICS labels from all PICS label bureaus or Web sites. If you plan to use a particular rating service, make sure it works with the particular software you're using. Non-PICS tools usually involve some kind of proprietary update service or label bureau, since they cannot interoperate with PICS label bureaus.

Filtering tools

Where are we now? Although the standard is catching on, it's the usual chicken-and-egg problem. Users won't use the PICS filters until there

MAJOR FILTERING PRODUCTS

COMPANY (product)	NUMBER OF USERS	SITES RATED	SOURCE OF RATINGS	TYPE
Content Advisor	launching 6/98	1,700,000[1]	employees	server
Kansmen (Little Brother)	500,000 desktops	300,000	employees	server
The Learning Company* (Cyber Patrol)	2,000,000+	60,000 NOT 50,000 Yes	teachers/parents employees	server client
N2H2 (Bess)	4,000 schools	400,000	employees	server, 120 ISPs
Net Nanny	1,000,000 copies	100,000[2]	employees	client installed, server
NetPartners (WebSENSE)	2,000,000	200,000	employees	server
Net Shepherd*	NA	500,000+[3]	volunteers	client bureaus, label bureau[4]
PlanetWeb*	NA	50,000+[5]	employees, students	server
RSACi*	NA	90,000+	self-rating	label bureau
SafeSurf*	NA[6]	100,000+	self-rating, volunteers	label bureau
Secure Computing (SmartFilter)	NA	250,000	employees	server

COMPANY (product)	NUMBER OF USERS	SITES RATED	SOURCE OF RATINGS	TYPE
Solid Oak (CYBERsitter)	1,500,000 licensed copies	100,000[7]	employees, self-rating	client, server
SurfWatch*	8,000,000 copies	100,000[8]	employees	client, installed contractors, server, label bureau

Client means a tool on the user's PC; server means a tool controlled by a school, employer, or ISP.
[1]Total database entries; sites can have multiple entries. The number of separate sites is much smaller, but the company will not provide an estimate of it.
[2]Includes sites on words and phrases list; 20,000 sites labeled.
[3]Total of 2 million URLs; over 500,000 represent the main page of a site.
[4]Distributes labels that can be used with other companies' software.
[5]161,400 database records covering 50,000 complete sites.
[6]Previously offered Internet Filtering Solution.
[7]Estimated blocked sites. Works primarily through phrase filtering.
[8]Number of rated sites in database; ratings provided by others.
*Indicates ratings that are PICS-compatible.

are enough PICS-labeled sites, and sites won't bother to rate themselves and label bureaus won't get established until enough users are using PICS filters and search tools. But slowly the momentum is starting to build—pushed along by the overthrow of the CDA and the attendant publicity. (The demise of the CDA has resulted in a lot of stuff out there that deserves filtering.)

In the long run, filtering and labeling will probably turn from a capability used for blocking "unsuitable content" to broader use for *selecting* desirable content, in a world where the whole Web is vast and confusing. The need for additional signposts to help make sense of what is out there is just overwhelming. (Pundits note that one way or another sex helped kick off many new markets, for example, cameras, home video, and VCRs. The Internet is just one more example.) In some sense, labeling is really just one more way to make search engines more effective and relevant. The tools for this to happen are beginning to proliferate.

On the filter side, both Microsoft and Netscape—covering about 95 percent of all users—provide PICS filtering capabilities within their browsers. In the case of Microsoft, it's called the Content Advisor, and can be switched on or off with a variety of filtering options. In the case of Netscape, in line with Netscape's open approach, it's available in two parts: the underlying functionality is in Navigator (below "security" in the help menu). When you click that, you end up on a separate page that can be easily updated for new label bureaus, filtering criteria, or other options without adding new code to the browser. Currently the page describes what NetWatch does, and provides information and access for RSACi and SafeSurf. Users create their own passwords to configure filtering options, which are then in force as they surf away, until (again with a password) they are changed.

Microsoft's Content Advisor defaults to no controls, but if you do want to filter what you or your children or employees receive, the RSACi ratings (⟹ page 236) are the default choice. (But competition from Microsoft and Netscape is not great news for companies trying to sell filtering tools. Most of them will eventually focus more on providing ratings than on trying to sell software, I believe.) Microsoft also has a page on its Web site that lists and links to most of the filtering tools and ratings providers.

CompuServe provides the PICS-oriented Cyber Patrol filtering tool free to its members (including Cyber Patrol's ratings). America Online offers its own parental controls based on Cyber Patrol technology and uses Cyber Patrol as its Web content-control system (as part of its Kids Channel and Teens Channel). It also filters its own proprietary content through a variety of other means including word matches, editors, and real-time human monitoring. (On the other hand, AOL successfully argued in court that it was not responsible for the content produced by "journalist" Matt Drudge, even though he was under contract to AOL.) AOL estimates that about half its member accounts that include children uses these controls.

Overall, a survey by *FamilyPC* magazine early in 1998 found that about a quarter of families who are online use some kind of parental controls, usually something supplied by an ISP or within the browser. Only 4 percent had gone to the trouble of buying and installing a stand-alone product or service. The newest generation of filtering capability vendors—companies such as Content Advisor, N2H2, Kansmen, NetPartners, and Secure Computing—now tend to offer their tools configured for servers that can be managed by an expert, rather than for stand-alone PCs connected directly to the Internet. (That also helps them avoid competing with what the browser vendors offer for free.)

By 2004 filtering technology will be absolutely standard in just about any Internet tool a consumer could buy, and probably on most search engines (or "portals"—entryways to the Net). Net Shepherd ($\Rightarrow$ page 235) offers a filtered version of Compaq/Digital's AltaVista search engine, and N2H2 plans to provide a filtered version of the Inktomi search service. The distinctions will be in how easy a tool or service makes it for the user (or the user's parent or boss or librarian) to select rating services, define criteria for acceptable content, and develop filters for outgoing information such as phone numbers, addresses, and other personal/family information a child might inadvertently release. PICSRules will help a lot in this regard, but it's still a good idea for parents to know what they're selecting or avoiding rather than just to sign up for something blindly.

Almost all the user tools do more than just filter the Internet based on labels. They can filter based on the presence or frequency of specific words in the content itself or in its Web address, such as my company's www.edventure.com or the more-likely-to-be-filtered www.sexygirls.com. Some can also block all graphics files or all downloadable software, which might be games (harmless or otherwise) or could contain viruses.

Filtering what goes out, not just what comes in

As noted, another capability is filtering what a child or employee sends out, such as a revealing home address, a credit card number, or confidential corporate information. "If you can define it, we can block it," says Net Nanny, vendor of one such tool. "I know it when I see it" isn't precise enough for such systems, but character strings such as a credit card number are easily detected and filtered. Says Net Nanny:

"At least they won't be using your credit cards!" However, the technology isn't foolproof, even though Net Nanny uses powerful underlying pattern-recognition tools. It may block innocent but misspelled words, or let out slight variations of sensitive information that may be revealing, offering a false sense of security.

Network-software vendor Novell is promoting similar capabilities in its newest version of NetWare, in an approach called "border services" that supports monitoring of what comes in and what goes out of any corporate intranet. Filtering is now a corporate concern as well as a parental one; it is often available as a package deal with corporate firewalls.

Labels

As of mid-1998, I estimate that about 3 million unique Web locations were rated, one way or another. ($\Longrightarrow$ table, pages 217–218.) That's out of a total of more than 300 million Web documents worldwide. These numbers are even squishier than the numbers cited for Internet users: Some filter vendors refer to pages (of which a single site can have hundreds); others include sites blocked because of the presence of certain words although no person has ever judged the nature or quality of the site. And a single Web site such as GeoCities or AOL can be home to many thousands of individual users' pages. Nonetheless, the numbers indicate that the approach is gaining momentum and covering most of the most-visited sites on the Web.

Nor are all the self-ratings "good" and all the third-party ratings "bad." For example, of the 90,000 sites self-rated through the industry-backed RSACi rating service, about 30 percent rated themselves as having some sex, violence, nudity, or vulgar language. Many adult sites are eager to keep children—and government scrutiny—away. Indeed, says RSACi executive director Stephen Balkam, "The early rush was porn sites." Other rating services provide detailed ratings but also offer their own black-and-white lists of "blocked" or "safe" sites, or what the Cyber Patrol service calls CyberNOT and CyberYES lists. Parents can either limit their kids to "good" sites, if they want full control, or simply block out bad sites, if they have less concern or more trust about what their kids are up to. Other services are listed in the table (⟹ page 217) more are showing up every week. And some now focus on particular concerns: For example, Cyber Patrol and the Anti-Defamation League are working together to create a rating service to identify hate speech.

How ratings work

Rating content is not an easy task. There is one broad distinction: between ratings done by a site/service itself, and those done by third parties.

In principle, self-ratings are likely to be most accurate since Web sites know what they are offering. There are two major problems: The sites may have an incentive to fudge the truth (in order to gain a wider audience, for example). Second, Fred's criteria for rating his site may differ from Kris's criteria for rating hers, even though they use the same terms and the same rating scale. For example, Kris thinks throwing a grapefruit in someone's face is "violent"; Fred thinks it's funny. But Fred grew up in a strict household, and he thinks a passionate kiss is "sex level 3," whereas Kris would rate the same lingering kiss "sex level 2."

There's no real way to overcome this problem; or rather, this problem is the foundation of the whole issue—that people have different preferences and perspectives. RSACi offers "objective criteria"—e.g., "revealing attire"—which are as close as you can get. But in the end, people will just find a rating service that seems to match their perspective (or use one recommended by a friend), just as one might select a magazine or a school for its overall worldview. Each will have relatively consistent humans calibrating themselves against one another. All these problems will get ironed out over time; the most important first step is to identify the clearly offensive and the possibly questionable sites so that parents have some options and the concept of freedom of speech is not besmirched.

DON'T CENSOR ME!!!!

Content Control don't censor me!!!! Don't censor free speech! No one has the right to do that.

Louise

RE: DON'T CENSOR ME!!!!

Dyson is NOT advocating censorship, if in fact your plea ("don't censor free speech!") is in reference to her excerpt on content control. Perhaps "content control" is the wrong phrase to use (as it sounds suspiciously like "mind control"), but look again at what she is saying. In fact, what she suggests can help prevent censorship. Labeling what you write has the same effect as giving a subject heading to your personal emails—it allows the reader to make an informed decision on whether or not to read your message. This way, you may write whatever you want and you don't have to worry about your audience. They will censor [for] themselves. Instead of someone stumbling on your "offensive" website and then calling everyone to arms in an effort to control it, your self-created "label" will act as a warning. This gives both parties more autonomy and protection, for such a label will, as Dyson writes, "allow people to make their own choices." How can you say that is censorship?

Simone

Third parties: Decentralized ratings

Unlike, say, television or the software business, the Internet covers territory much broader than a relatively defined universe of a few thousand movies, shows, or games a year. It includes not just software and packaged content, but also mailing lists, chat rooms, discussion sites, newsgroups, and, of course, constantly changing streams of content at news and other timely sites.

So the ratings can't be static either. By a "ratings database" (or a label bureau), I actually mean a constantly changing flow of updated

RE: DON'T CENSOR ME!!!!

The premise behind having a subject field to promote self censoring is a great idea . . . . but how to enforce it is a whole other ball game. One of the main aspects of the net that sets it apart from any other medium is its cultural diversity. What I think is a good idea, is probably not shared by even 30% of the world's population. Many people on the net LOVE the aspect of shock value. They like to post a site with a certain heading, that has a holistically different content. My site could have "Christmas Ornaments" as the subject line and "XXX Material" as the content. In order to get me to "comply" with the subject field guidelines, a certain element of censorship would have to be adopted. Where do we draw the lines for how we want to structure web content? I'm all for the subject line idea. Every day when I search the net I get so tired of looking through pages that have NOTHING to do with what I'm looking for. It's not the browser's fault; it's the editors fault. But then who will write the standards for how to categorize the material so the subject lines are easily referenced, therefore easy to self-censor? I certainly hope it's not the same people who organize the yellow pages or I may abandon the web for good!

Leslie

RE: DON'T CENSOR ME!!!!

This suggestion of content labeling is elaborated quite a bit more in the book. In particular the promotion of labeling standards, such as PICS (www.w3.org/pub/pics) [that] allow different net "communities" to design their own labeling criteria. Users can then select content filters to suit themselves, or their intent of the moment. Of course this doesn't prevent access to material that is not labeled if a user wants that access. The theme of this approach is informed choice where the technology allows content to be organized in ways that are much more advanced and extensible than the Yellow Pages.

Paul Hunt phunt3@worldnet.att.net

information. It has to cover new sites and changes in old sites due to management changes, membership changes, or just continually updated content. The services are an example of the constantly changing intellectual property sold as a service that I see as an important business model for the future (⟹ Chapter 6).

This is ideal ground for a proliferation of third-party raters. One can imagine rating systems for almost any characteristic that is easily specifiable, or for any group's or individual's judgment. They can rate locations or places or communities—online stores, chat rooms, discussion groups, and news services—as well as static content. It's easy to imagine a lively marketplace of competing rating services, just as in the real world there are restaurant ratings, seals of approval, best picks in magazines, reading lists from high schools, rankings of legislators by political groups, top-ten lists, special college issues, and the like.

In the online world, where communities are more far-flung, such systems are even more useful. They help to make sense of what would otherwise be confusing, unmapped territory. Want to know what people think of the hotel you're considering for your trip to Bloomington, the hairdressers in your new neighborhood, or the acupuncturist you met online? When you visit their Web sites, you may find that they're rated by third parties for the comfort, style, or value of the outfits they represent as well as for sexual content and violence. But for now, the focus will be on filtering and selection for suitability for children.

Some rating systems simply look at the discrete words or images, but the more sophisticated ones will make qualitative or editorial judgments: "This site is filled with mature people with an interest in social action; that one is best-suited for teenage girls who want to talk about boys, models, and makeup; that one is for teenage girls interested in discussions about female pilots, doctors, diplomats, and leaders, such as Margaret Thatcher, Kay Graham, Madeleine Albright, and Carol Bartz, CEO of Autodesk."

Most of them use both automated text analysis and human inspection to develop or validate their ratings. In fact, classifying all this content is a perfect job for the new knowledge workers everyone is talking about. It's just that these workers shouldn't be employed by a government imposing its standards on everyone. They should be working in a marketplace of diverse firms and organizations competing to classify subsets of what's out there to meet the needs and interests of specific groups—parents concerned about their kids' exposure to violence, libraries' children's sections following community standards, employers concerned about online game-playing on company time, individuals searching for sites that match their religious or political convictions, and so forth. Imagine a classified ad (online, of course):

> *Forget the entry-level job at McDonald's! Join the knowledge economy by starting as a Web site rater. No experience required! All the Internet access you can stand, at 1MB and above!!*

A profusion of services

As more users take advantage of PICS capabilities with their browsers and other tools, and as rating services become easier for providers to set up and for customers to find, many entrepreneurs and investors will see markets for a variety of rating-related businesses. These business ideas will range from better automated-filtering techniques to a diversity of label bureaus, and their models will range from stand-alone services or software sales to alliances with communities, search sites, and other content-oriented businesses. And of course there will be rating services to rate the other rating services. Customers will be able to choose from a variety of rating styles and business models.

Search sites, "channels," and ISPs

Just as you can now select your search service from the Netscape or Microsoft home page, so will you be able to refine your search query with a rating criterion. In other cases, ISPs might offer either selection services or even content-blocking, which parents could order when they sign up for Internet access (perhaps with different passwords for Juan and Alice). For example, my friend Ron complains that he gets too many sex sites even for the most innocent queries. (That doesn't happen to me, but maybe he's mostly looking at cars and other "boy" things.) He would pay a small amount extra to avoid those on a regular basis, but he would not want an ISP that totally restricted his access. "I might have to do some research or something," he claims with a straight face.

To meet Ron's and others' needs, many ratings databases will end up being bundled in with the various search services, supported indirectly by advertisers rather than directly by customers. (The search services will license the use of the ratings databases to make their search systems more attractive to consumers and thus make their audiences more attractive to advertisers, but the advertisers needn't be directly involved.) The ISPs will include the cost in the fees they charge their customers.

The Magellan search service of Excite, for example, already has its own proprietary list of "green" sites, rated appropriate for children by its own team of reviewers. There's no reason it couldn't offer the SurfWatch, RSACi, or Net Shepherd (and affiliates) ratings as well. The AltaVista search service will be using Net Shepherd's huge 1.7-million-item database.

RSACi has a deal with PointCast, one of the largest content distribution channels on the Net, whose PointCast Connections product aimed at corporate intranets incorporates RSACi, enabling corporate managers to control the content broadcast internally.

As with all such deals, the rating providers, search companies, and ISPs will have to negotiate delicate trade-offs between exclusivity and market share. I hope we can retain the diversity of tastes that a range of rating services will foster, even from the mass-market ISPs and search engines.

Bundled into a community

Many of the most "diverse"—or niche—rating services will be voluntary and membership organizations: schools, teachers' associations, religious groups, and interest groups of various kinds such as the visually impaired who might rate sites for accessibility, or political/moral/

social-action groups such as Girls Inc., People for the Ethical Treatment of Animals, and Mothers Against Drunk Driving. They may
charge their users membership fees, or they may function as a public
service (paid for by donations and sponsors). One of the companies
profiled below (page 235), Net Shepherd, has set itself up to be the
supporting structure for a variety of label bureaus with orientations
ranging from strongly Catholic to agnostic.

Then there will be self-regulatory organizations such as RSACi, a
trade organization based in the United States and operating worldwide,
and the InternetWatch Foundation in the United Kingdom. The European Commission is suggesting that the Internet service providers in
each country form such groups—or it will do so for them!

Many rating services are likely to generate revenues by licensing
their ratings as members-only services offered by commercial communities. The ratings content won't be charged for directly, but will be
included as part of the membership fees for a broader offering.

Collaborative filtering

Some services currently offer "collaborative filtering," where ratings by
people with tastes similar to yours carry the most weight. Collaborative
filtering is a finely tuned technical way of achieving the same clustering
of opinions from a broad database that you could get by selecting a
rating service that matched your opinions overall. It requires additional
technology heavy with statistical algorithms and a lot of information
about everyone's preferences, but it will lead to much better "tuning"
of ratings to match individuals' preferences.

Although these services aren't using PICS yet, pretty soon users
(just like label bureaus) should be able to use PICS tools to express
their opinions as well as to select or filter. In return for using other
individuals' aggregated ratings, you would simply have to post your
own. However, you would have to consider the privacy issues; you
might not want to expose your interests to everyone—just to people
who share them ($\Rightarrow$ Chapter 8).

The value of such collaborative filtering systems is that they celebrate diversity rather than obliterate it. Like-minded people and content can find one another and cluster together, instead of losing out
to majority preferences. Distinctions don't get averaged away but are
reinforced: People who really object to, say, mistreatment of animals
but don't care much about sex or violence in general could get ratings
matching those preferences, assuming the original database was large
enough to include enough similar opinions.

Diversity in content; diversity in companies

Finally, there are the rating bureaus themselves. Describing these companies is a challenge, since they are mostly typical Net companies:
They're in a new market. They change form and business models with
no notice. But that very diversity shows the potential success of PICS:
It is fostering precisely the kind of decentralized, pluralistic profusion
of products, services, and business models that its creators hope to see,
especially since the CDA was overturned. However, they are not typical
Silicon Valley companies; there is not a single dollar from brand-name
venture capitalist Kleiner Perkins among them. Two (Net Nanny and
Net Shepherd) have funding from those oil-oriented investment pools
that populate the Canadian stock exchanges; one (PlanetWeb) is partly
a Silicon Valley restart. Solid Oak and SafeSurf are very private, and
RSACi and the U.K.'s InternetWatch Foundation are nonprofit industry coalitions. Only SurfWatch took the traditional Silicon Valley start-
up route and then was acquired; Cyber Patrol's original parent, Microsystems, is a standard-issue private company based on Route 128 in
Massachusetts. Content Advisor is the first second-generation filter
company; it started out working with RSACi and then got into the
business for itself.

Politically, they range from dedicated everyone-to-his-own values
(Net Shepherd) to targeted-at-conservative-families-and-proud-of-it
(Solid Oak, maker of CYBERsitter). Cyber Patrol is now part of the
Learning Company, which is a traditional consumer-software company,
while SafeSurf is a volunteer effort turned for-profit in order to sustain

its existence. Net Nanny has a strong technical background in telecom and computer security. SurfWatch was a typical Silicon Valley start-up focused on the single problem of parental control; it is now part of Spyglass, increasingly focused on the brand-oriented corporate market and the Internet device (WebTV) market. Industry supplier PlanetWeb sells filter-enhanced browsers to other vendors for game machines and Internet appliances. SurfWatch is generally considered liberal, CYBERsitter conservative—just the diversity you'd want to find in rating services that seek like-minded customers. Others, such as nonprofit RSACi, focus on providing "objective" information and have less visible biases.

Content control at work

Many of the vendors are quickly coming out with corporate versions, designed for employers rather than parents; they can block employee access not just to smut and violence but also to productivity-destroying games, potentially virus-ridden downloaded software, and time-wasting chat rooms. They include audit trails, scheduling tools that distinguish between work time and leisure time such as lunch hours with the rules relaxed to allow game-playing, and user profiles to assign workers to categories with different levels of restrictions. This trend delights "real engineers" at the supplier companies who have been trying to make simple tools for consumers; they can now build elaborate tools for the corporate market, which is willing to accept a higher level of complexity in exchange for granular control and configurability.

CYBERsitter (Solid Oak)

At the vigilantly antiporn, pro-family end of the spectrum of rating services sits Solid Oak. Solid Oak is a venerable Santa Barbara–based development company founded in 1986 that long produced software for other companies; it started selling under its own name a couple of years ago. Its CYBERsitter Internet filter, first released in mid-1995, originally worked only with its own VCR (Voluntary Content Rating) ratings, which were designed to be much simpler to generate than PICS labels—the cyberspace equivalent of Jack Valenti's television ratings, except that they're not imposed on an entire industry. "Those other rating services are free now, but sooner or later they'll start charging," says founder Brian Milburn darkly.

Nonetheless, in response to demand, CYBERsitter can parse PICS ratings. It now blocks about 100,000 sites selected by a review committee at Solid Oak, reported by users, or found by search tools tuned for offensive words and phrases. It also has a considerable backlog of adult sites that want to be rated to avoid trouble.

Milburn sees CYBERsitter as the voice of the people—people too poor or simple to go to a complicated service but eager to rate themselves. "There are about nine companies that do 50 percent of all the really smutty content on the Net, and they are glad to keep children out," he says. "One of them rated twenty different domains that it operates." This company and its competitors have all rated themselves with VCR (now called the CYBERsitter Ratings System), and by now probably with PICS as well. "We target the conservative family; our customers are happy with the sites that we block. That's who we're trying to please—our customers," says Marc Kanter, director of marketing.

The company has gotten into tangles with free-speech advocates who sometimes forget that freedom of speech includes the right to be selective and overtly political about content—as long as that choice is not imposed on others. One organization called Peacefire raised objections not only to the selection of sites CYBERsitter has seen fit to block, but to CYBERsitter's insistence on keeping its list of blocked sites encrypted so that users (or critics such as Peacefire organizer Bennett Haselton) can't easily find out what's blocked—including Peacefire's own site.

While there is bad will on both sides and strong differences of opinion and values, this controversy does raise a legitimate issue: If you believe in openness, shouldn't you believe that the filtering services should disclose the sites they block? That's a tough one, because access to a list of blocked sites or ratings is precisely what a rating service sells. Probably the best resolution is that rating services should answer when queried about any particular site, but reserve the right not to answer more than a reasonable number of such queries from any particular person.* Meanwhile, they should be clear and open about their criteria. Then, the market should work: Who would buy filtering from someone with undisclosed criteria?

Bess

N2H2, Inc., is a private Seattle-based Internet filtering and caching company founded in 1995 by the husband-and-wife team of Peter Nickerson and Holly Hill. The couple named their filtering service Bess after their pet dog, a retriever, and the friendly pooch is depicted prominently on the Bess home page. Nickerson is a former economics professor who wanted to keep his kids away from adult sites on the Internet. He found that children could easily evade client-based filtering products (with the filter on the user's PC), so he began the company to develop a server-based filtering service, where the filtering happens at the ISP or a school's central Net access point.

Bess uses a proxy server to block sites based on a database of hundreds of thousands of URLs. N2H2's employees review every site considered for blocking; less than half of the sites they examine wind up being blocked. In addition to filtering, Bess provides a colorful Web site with links to several dozen kid-friendly sites and Web-based e-mail.

The company initially focused on the consumer market, but today the bulk of N2H2's business is turnkey filtering services for over 4,000 schools. N2H2 installs a proxy server in the school network and then sends updates to the database of blocked sites into each proxy server on a daily basis. N2H2 also provides technical support for the equipment. Pricing varies based on the size of the customer, from $60 per month for a small school to several thousand dollars a month for larger institutions. A similar service is available to businesses and libraries.

---

*This is similar to the approach Four11 takes to the similarly touchy issue of reverse look-up: finding people's names from a phone number or e-mail address; ⟹ Chapter 8.

N2H2 also sells to approximately 120 ISPs, allowing them to offer filtered access to their customers for an additional monthly fee. The ISP partnership program includes the proxy server as well as sales and marketing materials; once Bess is installed at the ISP, the ISP acts as a reseller and can provide the service to individual customers for an additional fee. Finally, users in western Washington state can get filtered dial-up Internet access directly from N2H2 for $24.95 per month. (N2H2 also operates an unfiltered ISP, Rainier.net.)

N2H2 also offers an advertising-supported filtered search service built on the Inktomi search engine.

Cyber Patrol (The Learning Company)—"To Surf and Protect"

At the other end of the spectrum is the Cyber Patrol unit of the Learning Company in Cambridge, Massachusetts. Cyber Patrol also offers a family of products for people with low-vision and motion disabilities, so it's no stranger to social issues. And its parent company has a large presence in the consumer and education markets.

A key player in the PICS consortium (abetted by geographical proximity to Cambridge), Cyber Patrol is committed to the PICS movement. "We were the first Internet access management utility to include built-in support for PICS," says director of corporate communications Susan Getgood. As part of its commitment to PICS, Cyber Patrol has also endorsed RSACi. In 1996, Cyber Patrol delivered the first PICS server, at the same time that RSACi was released. Parents using the Cyber Patrol filter can now read RSACi labels with no adjustments by the user.

The company has carefully addressed many of the issues involved in content control. Its "CyberYES" list includes about 50,000 sites rated as good for children, with no links to any "bad" sites. It also offers the "CyberNOT" listing of over 60,000 sites updated weekly and judged "questionable" by a team of professionals, currently about ten parents and teachers, paid by Cyber Patrol. The company eschews volunteers because they don't provide consistent ratings, says Getgood.

Criteria for the "CyberNOT" list include "partial nudity, nudity, sexual acts/text, gross depictions, intolerance, satanic or cult, drugs and drug culture, militant/extremist, violence/profanity, questionable/illegal and gambling, sex education, and alcohol and tobacco."

Cyber Patrol posts the CyberYES list as a Web site called Route 6-16 with links to the sites on the list, but it keeps the CyberNOT list confidential, it says, partly because publishing it might encourage kids to go hunting down the list. Any Webmaster can find out the rating of his own site and ask how it got that rating. The company also periodically convenes an oversight council of representatives from organizations such as the National Organization for Women, the Gay and Lesbian Alliance Against Defamation, church groups, and other interested parties. Getgood notes that Cyber Patrol permits parents and other "authorities"—teachers, librarians, and corporate managers—fine granularity in adjusting users' access to specific Internet sites. "Parents and teachers may select all or any of the categories to be blocked by general content, time of day, or specific Internet site." A parent who wants a child to have access to "sex education" but not "alcohol and tobacco" may set the system up accordingly. Authorities can also deny access to additional sites not included on the CyberNOT list.

The Cyber Patrol team has partnerships with both CompuServe/AOL and AT&T, who supply it (or a version of it) to their customers free as the default Internet filtering system. The software sits on the user's PC (or the school's or library's server) and can be configured by a parent or other password-holder.

The Learning Company also offers a corporate version of Cyber Patrol, which permits filtering on a proxy server, suitable for controlling Internet content on corporate networks. A prototype of the latest "home" version also allows parents and teachers to set privacy preferences and contains a time-control feature limiting Web usage.

Net Shepherd

Positioning itself not in the middle but across the whole spectrum, Net Shepherd is a Calgary, Alberta–based company traded on the Alberta Stock Exchange through a merger with a capital-pool company called Enerstar. The company was founded in 1995 by Ron Warris, a corporate information systems manager, who was helping a friend to connect a home PC to the Net. The friend imagined aloud how great such a system would be for his kid, but. . . . Warris saw a need and an opportunity.

The company claims to have assembled "the largest ratings and reviews database of English-language Internet sites in the world," and says that as of mid-1998, it had rated 500,000 sites (but of course those numbers are a little squishy). Net Shepherd has formed an alliance with AltaVista designed to integrate its filtering system with AltaVista's search engine. Scheduled to open in the fall of 1998, the service will initially simply offer filtered-search; that is, the sites found will be limited to those that pass muster as "family-safe" according to Net Shepherd's cadre of about 1,500 active content-raters. AltaVista hopes to find a sponsor for the service, ideally "a family-oriented service that wants a 'family-safe' search on their site," says Don Sandford, Net Shepherd CEO.

Net Shepherd encourages multiple site ratings, where individuals and groups can simply add their ratings to the tally for each site. This fosters quality control all by itself, but it results in average ratings rather than the clustering of opinions of "collaborative filtering." Overall, the company says it has collected about 3.3 million ballots for 1.7 million unique URLs, which condenses down to half a million sites when you account for duplicate votes that get averaged and multiple, often different-flavored locations within sites.

The company also has an agreement with Dun & Bradstreet to put its community of raters to work on the D&B Web site database, both ensuring that D&B rates only quality sites, and that the D&B information matches what companies put on their sites. In essence, Net Shepherd has built a community. Now it is helping them find interesting work to do beyond the ratings they provide almost for free (about 2 to

5 cents per page, or enough to pay for their Internet access, notes Warris) out of belief in the Net Shepherd "mission."

Indeed, Net Shepherd is encouraging interest groups or any other kind of community to form their own label bureaus using like-minded raters and criteria, paying a license fee to Net Shepherd for the technology and technical support. Net Shepherd hopes to find sponsors for some of these services as well.

RSACi

In early 1996, the Recreational Software Advisory Council (RSAC), an independent nonprofit creation of the Software Publishers Association that rates computer games (and keeps government heat off that industry), formed a new unit, RSACi (for Internet). It describes it as "an objective, PICS-compatible, content-labeling advisory system that . . . utilizes the nonprofit organization's experience in developing a content-rating system for the computer games industry." It has generated PICS labels covering about 90,000 Web sites. However, the labels are posted directly on each Web site; RSACi does not maintain a label bureau available to the public, although it licenses it with updates to third parties such as Landmark Community Interests for GuardiaNet, a service targeted at schools.

RSACi is a self-rating service: Sites can rate themselves by answering questions over the Internet and RSACi generates PICS labels for them automatically. RSAC charges for its game ratings, but RSACi offers this Web service free—both to encourage use and because it's complicated to pay over the Net anyway, says executive director Stephen Balkam. To fund the project, Balkam successfully approached a number of corporations and industry organizations to become sponsors. He eventually got $100,000 each from Microsoft, IBM, and the Software Publishers Association, $50,000 from CompuServe and PointCast, $10,000 from Disney Online, all the hardware he needed from Dell, and implementation assistance from Web site development firm USWeb—along with a commitment to encourage all USWeb clients and franchisees to rate their sites with RSACi.

To self-rate, a Webmaster goes to the RSACi site and answers a set of branching questions with a yes or no ("Does it have blood and gore?"), and the tool calculates a set of ratings from 0 to 4 in four categories: sex, nudity, language, and violence. RSACi e-mails him the code for the label to place on his Web site, along with a symbol for visual display. Although the service is free, the Webmaster does have to fill out a contract before he goes through the rating process, certifying that he will not willfully misrepresent anything. That gives RSACi enforcement rights if there are any problems later. RSACi has provisions for spot checks—matching self-ratings against those derived by a panel of experts—and responses to complaints from users who disagree with a rating. RSACi also has a Webcrawler (an automated searching tool) to search for inaccurate RSACi labels. As of mid-1998, the number of sites mislabelled by the content provider's Webmaster remained remarkably low, says Balkam. A growing problem, however, was the number of individuals attempting to rate sites that they didn't control. According to Balkam, some of these were malicious, but most were well-meaning attempts by Web users to label their favorite sites. RSACi has revamped its Web site to cut down on the 100 or so such mis-ratings out of 5,000 new ones per month. The goal is to focus on sites that are aimed at children, to make sure they're okay, or to highlight ones that are explicitly aimed away from children, to make sure they're tagged. RSACi no longer has dreams of rating the entire net.

Among notable users of RSACi for self-rating is CompuServe, which has rated all its Web sites (still a tiny part of its overall content, since most of CompuServe is proprietary). Microsoft's Content Advisor defaults to the RSACi labels and Netscape's NetWatch offers them as one of two options, when they are activated.

Content Advisor

The two-person team that helped RSACi implement the PICS-compatible ratings system for use in Microsoft's Internet Explorer has now gone into the filtering business itself. The company, based in Somerville, Massachusetts, and formerly called Coffeehaus Networks, is now called Content Advisor. Based on his RSACi experience, founder Steve Shannon concluded that the RSACi system relied too much on arbitrary decisions about the level of sex or violence on a site, and too much on site creators to self-label. Moreover, as he worked on the problem, he kept coming across sites that were no longer in existence, "adult" sites with multiple names, some rated and some not, and communities with a wide variety of different kinds of personal home pages all linked from a single site. He decided to build an industrial-strength, third-party rating database as an alternative.

Shannon sees technology as Content Advisor's secret weapon. Content Advisor uses a patent-pending distributed Web spider technology to scour the Web for new content (even on old sites) and to help in categorizing it. Instead of examining each page one by one or each site as a whole, it lists all the URLs on a site together so that it's easier and faster for the labelers to do their work, sometimes rating in a batch when, say, forty pages of a camping gear catalogue show up in sequence. Through spot checks and training, Shannon has reached a level of reliability that matches that of anyone in the market, he says. The company's database currently holds about 7 million items, of which 1.7 million have been labeled so far (June 1998), using the company's own staff for consistency and completeness. Content Advisor's staff of six editors is able to classify 250,000 to 350,000 URLs per month into twenty-nine different subject categories, while it finds about 5 million new URLs a month. But with a staff of 100 it could catch up!

Content Advisor has nonexclusive partnerships with several security-oriented and firewall companies such as Check Point to incorporate filtering as an extra feature. The company is focused entirely on the corporate market; administrators can block any subject area defined by Content Advisor that they consider unnecessary or inappropriate for normal business uses. Later on, it may offer Internet service providers a service they can resell to consumers. However, Shannon asserts, he will never sell to a government or to any service that disguises what it is doing.

The company also plans to go beyond filtering to selecting, with subject-specific search engines based on its massive database and classification expertise. For example, someone looking for sports-related information would be able to search a database limited to sites classified in that category.

Beyond filters

In principle, PICS labels could be used by any application, for better or worse. Imagine a tool that automatically selected names from any site labeled above a certain rating for violence and sent out solicitations for guns or dangerous work of dubious character. Or a résumé-filtering tool could check out the URLs of prospective employees' employers to screen (in or out) for various kinds of affiliations. (Or you could do research before the screening, to find out what sort of background correlates best with successful employees.)

Like any standard, PICS will gain value and usefulness the more broadly it is used. Right now, it is starting to show up in various guises: in labeling tools and services, in the proliferation of ratings both from sites themselves and from third-party sources, and in filtering tools and browsers to use them. But in the long run, PICS and its successor standards may support a lot of our Net activity—helping us to find or filter everything from content to people we might like to meet, merchants with privacy practices we prefer, and political discussions with goals we support. Labels in cyberspace, like the signs and shapes and other signals of the physical world, make it easier to understand our virtual surroundings and help us decide where we want to go. In many cases, though, we won't even see them; we'll just see their effect in the sites we are steered to or away from. That's okay as long as we're aware it's happening.

Ownership and control of ratings

In principle, a service that develops ratings—whether they are developed internally or gathered from users and Web site managers themselves—owns those ratings. It may offer the use of them as a service to the world at large (as most churches might do) or to members only (especially fee-paying members), or it may sell the (use of the) data and updates to users or third parties. But it needs to negotiate carefully the shoals between obsessive control and losing a proprietary edge.

Meanwhile, if the service owns the ratings, what rights do the subjects of the ratings have? Who rates the raters? Do the subjects of ratings get to argue back? To erase them? Dispute them? Even see them? Can they see the data on which the ratings are based? What about a rating service that is sloppy, or one that is corrupt and takes bribes? Suppose Juan has a really bad experience at Alice's Restaurant and badmouths it to rating services that base their ratings on customer feedback? ($\Longrightarrow$ Chapters 8 and 9.)

In the short run, that can be a problem, but in the long run—fairly quickly, the way the Net operates—the market should work. The unreliable rating services will lose customers, and Juan will be exposed as a petulant, obnoxious jerk. His restaurant ratings will almost all be negative, and people won't trust his ratings anymore: He'll be rated out of the rating-service feedback loop. (Or people who share his particular demands will flock to his rating service.) Most rating services will use a large number of raters and calibrate them against one another. Some reviewers will get reputations for unreliability, and their views will be disregarded. Some sites will use anonymous reviewers, and their judgments will reflect that. People who find a rating service biased can go elsewhere—and those who share its biases will use it happily.

Of course, for all this to work we need a market that fosters good practices and disclosure—which is what the World Wide Web Consortium is trying to achieve with PICS. The basic assumption is that people can dispute the ratings, and various services may set themselves up as dispute-adjudication boards. Rating services with unreliable ratings will lose market share. In extreme cases, people who feel they've been unfairly rated may sue under terrestrial laws, but that will be expensive and complicated—as it is now. Better to fight back by rating the raters!

Losing control: A new attitude

In the end, people and companies will have to start feeling comfortable with the proliferation of ratings that they don't control and trust the market to sort things out. The fact is, right now people all around your social and business circle are saying things about you that you might not like. But you don't post representatives at cocktail parties to protect your good name. Nor, personally, do you probably know everything that is being said about you on the Net even now.

The difficulty, of course, is that cocktail party conversations usually vanish, or at least are treated with appropriate skepticism. Stuff on the Net lives on. On the other hand, it is easier to find and correct, and comments can be posted to explain other comments. In short, there will be a decentralized, Web-like system, rather than a hierarchy of control, to keep things in check.

Will all this work perfectly? Of course not. But whom would you like to put in charge? And what proportion of the rest of the world would agree with you?

Chapter 8

Privacy

Once again, it's 2004, and you want to buy a turtle tie. You go to the Web and type in "[turtle tie] and not pet or zoo." You're indifferent to the brand name; you just want to see what's on offer—and you certainly don't want to buy a real turtle or visit a zoo. Aside from one jokey story about people "tying one on" at the Purple Turtle nightclub, you get a selection of several stores offering turtle ties. One is a well-known British retailer, another is a mail-order house in Thailand (real silk!), and a third is what looks like a novelty shop. And of course there are Hermès, Nicole Miller, and the like. You decide to check out the Thai shop and your screen flashes a warning: "This site has no privacy rating! Do you want to proceed?" Since it's only a tie you're buying, you don't really care. You check out the site; it looks a little threadbare, and you move on.

The well-known retailer passes your browser's inspection. As you look at the home page, you see a little logo, a "trustmark," which indicates a privacy policy and invites you to find out more. Aha! You click on the logo, and you get a description of what the store will do with your data: It will use it for in-house marketing and follow-up, but it won't sell it to anyone else. But the ties aren't great. Now you try one of the brand-name vendors. Again, your screen flashes a warning: "This site sells data. Do you want to negotiate?" You click on yes, and proceed to the site.

This site displays another trustmark, with the legend "Third-party exchange." Here the details are more complex. The Web site explains that it may sell your name and transaction information to third parties. If you click on "Allow third-party sale," you will get a 2 percent discount on your order (before taxes and shipping charges). Otherwise, you can pay the full price and the site will keep your name to itself.

You could have set your browser to negotiate this automatically according to your instructions, but you prefer to make these decisions each time for yourself. So you consider the one-dollar/2-percent inducement: It isn't much in itself, but you like the feeling that you're in charge and that you are getting paid for your information.

When you order drugs for your asthma and other ailments, you really appreciate the control you have. You have set your browser's "Open Profiling/Privacy Preferences" feature to default to "no data" on any pharmaceutical purchases. Even though the discounts there are higher (because the information is more valuable), you don't want information about your medications getting back to your employer, your insurance company, or anyone else.

Now, how can you trust that the pharmaceutical company will indeed follow your instructions? Is there a law? Let's consider how all this could have come about. It started back in 1997 . . .

Privacy on the Net

By 1997, consumer privacy had become a big issue in the United States. A number of trends had combined. More data was being collected, online and off. Direct marketers, telemarketers, and assorted shady people were invading people's privacy, and press coverage highlighted the issue. The Federal Trade Commission held hearings on consumer privacy, saying in effect: "Tell us the problems and propose some solutions, or we'll have to regulate." In the summer of 1998, not entirely satisfied, the FTC was about to unveil some proposals for regulation.

Meanwhile, the White House had unveiled its Framework for Global Electronic Commerce in July of 1997. Government's first rule for the Internet, said Vice President Gore, should be "do no harm." There were mutterings about privacy, spamming, and the like, but the government, with strong guidance from White House Internet advisor Ira Magaziner, decided to let the industry see what it could come up with.

A year later, not much had happened on the privacy front. Various bills were pending in Congress through 1997/98, changing form over time: the Consumer Internet Privacy Protection Act (Rep. Bruce Vento, D-MN), requiring that ISPs obtain customer permission before releasing personal data to third parties; the Social Security Information Safeguards Act (Rep. Barbara Kennelly, D-CT), to prohibit disclosure of Social Security numbers on the Internet; the Children's Privacy Protection and Parental Empowerment Act (Rep. Bob Franks, R-NJ); the Personal Information Privacy Act (Sen. Dianne Feinstein, D-CA, Sen. Charles Grassley, R-IA, and Rep. Gerald Kleczka, D-WI), to more broadly restrict selling of private data without permission; the Data Privacy Act (Rep. Bill Tauzin, R-LA), which would require an industry working group to draft voluntary guidelines for collection of personal data; and the Communications Privacy and Consumer Empowerment Act (Rep. Ed Markey, D-MA), to require the FTC and FCC to examine online privacy practices and propose regulations if they were inadequate (which the FTC did anyway).

Other privacy bills had been introduced on issues ranging from medical records to identity theft. But as of mid-1998, none of these proposals had made it through congressional committees. In July of 1998, I was asked to testify on this issue before the House Commerce committee. Much of what I said is in this chapter. Meanwhile, in Europe, the European Commission had taken concrete action, and as of October 1998 European citizens were covered by the European Union Data Protection Directive, which among other things forbids the export of personal data to any territory without adequate data protection measures (as certified by the EU). The European deadline was putting further pressure on U.S. entities, whether government or private, to come up with robust privacy-protection measures. These initiatives reflect both legitimate fears and simple fear of the unknown, and they are continuing.

Many people, both potential users and potential government regulators, perceive the Net as a scary, unregulated place. The Net makes it even easier for lots of people, not just well-capitalized mass marketers or obsessive creeps, to get at information and use it for undesirable and even dangerous ends.

Beyond Web sites, beyond labels

These issues of privacy didn't begin with the Internet, and they can't be resolved by controlling what happens on some, or even all, individual Web sites. The problem arises when information travels among Web sites—or away from them to places where people and companies assemble databases of information gleaned from many Web sites and from non-Web mailing lists, directories, news reports, listings . . . and other databases. A lot of this information has traditionally been available to people willing to go to a lot of trouble, visiting county document vaults, calling companies posing as a prospective employer or old boyfriend, or spending several hundred dollars to get an investigator's license. It has also been available on a random basis to criminals in jail doing data-entry work, bored clerks at the IRS, and various other untrustworthy people in trusted positions.

Many companies manage huge amounts of such data and trade it among themselves; they include Experian, Equifax, Trans Union, and several credit card providers and service companies. (Experian is a new company created from the credit-checking operations of TRW combined with a similar company owned by Great Universal Stores of the United Kingdom. Early in 1998, Experian/GUS acquired yet another related firm, data- and list-processor Metromail, from R. R. Donnelley.) Yes, it makes the economy more efficient and keeps revenues up and costs down. But not all of the companies who manage this information are especially honorable—nor are all their employees.

The growing presence of the Web increases the ease both of collecting such data and of assembling it. The interconnectedness of the Net makes safeguarding privacy an increasing challenge: People are rightly concerned about the combination of data from different sources— Web behavior, buying habits, travel history, income data. Often, facts are innocuous until they're combined with other facts.

The user wants a seamless experience as he explores the Web, but he wants to appear as a discrete entity to each place he visits, with a legitimate identity revealed as appropriate—a credit rating, an employment record, a bank account, or a medical history. Indeed, a person's identity gets splashed all over the Net in little fragments—no problem. But then someone in particular—anyone from a benign marketer only after the customer's business, to an employer, a stalker, or a blackmailer—can start collecting those fragments. One version of the problem is when the data are incorrect (and the user is the last to know); another version is when they are true.

In response, markets and governments are setting up systems to foster privacy. As a society, we can't totally guarantee everyone's privacy. But we can create a situation where people can choose the level of privacy they want according to trade-offs they determine for themselves, and provide them with a means of recourse when promises are breached. When that happens, I believe, people will feel more comfortable on the Net overall and no longer fear the visibility it fosters.

Two kinds of information

There are two broad classes of information about yourself that you create on the Net: one kind that you generate when you engage in a one-to-one transaction at a Web site, and another kind that you generate when you do something in "public"—post an opinion, send out a message to several people, or supply information on your own Web site. (You may also appear in someone else's comments; we'll deal with that kind of situation later.)

The "one-to-one" data is created by a variety of individual exchanges and transactions—anything from visiting a Web site to buying a racy book, revealing personal data in order to win a prize, or stating your income on Barron's site for investors. In principle such information is private—but not in practice. Here's one tale of woe from Russell Smith, a privacy activist who testified at the Federal Trade Commission hearings in 1997:

> . . . my every move on the Internet could potentially be tracked. For instance, I recently did a search of newsgroups via the DéjàNews service http://www.dejanews.com. In my search I was searching on my user name "russ-smith." The search turned up an entry in some type of an adult newsgroup. When I clicked on the message it turns out it had nothing to do with me. However, the banner ad I received was for an adult site from a widely used banner network called The Link Exchange. Does my profile now include this information? Is my search criterion ("russ-smith") also associated with this information? Do they have my name and address, since I have purchased products (and entered personal information) at other sites with these banner ads? Is it being sold? How can I find out? Can I expunge it?

Cookies

Aside from data supplied knowingly by users, there are other means of collecting information—most notably "cookies." This is the innocent name for data about a user's visit to a Web site that is, ironically, placed on the *user's* computer remotely by a Web site computer. That explains a couple of things you might wonder about: First, when you visit a

Web site, your hard drive may keep gurgling long after you've down-loaded the page you're looking at. That's your computer and the Web site talking in the background.

Second, if you return to that Web site, it may seem to know more than you might expect. For example, specific pages that you've already looked at are marked in some way (the type is in green instead of gray, for example), or the site refers to something you did last time. (For example, my favorite cities—San Jose, Moscow, Warsaw—are already marked whenever I visit the *USA Today* weather pages.)

The frustrating thing about cookies is that even though they reside on your PC, they are unintelligible to any normal person. (Clever, "bad" crackers understand them all too well and can create fictitious cookies to log on and impersonate another user.) The data that lets a site read your cookies can also be passed from site to site, so that one site, for example, can see where you came from and what you were doing there. Recently, some "good" hackers have developed tools that allow users to erase cookies or to send back a "wafer"—a sort of anti-cookie with a user's complaint on it. Both Netscape and Microsoft now offer users an option to turn cookies off in the latest versions of their browsers—but the default is to keep them.

Cookies, in some cases, *can* be useful—in saving your password or security information, say, as long as it is not passed on elsewhere. A cookie can also contain the information needed to offer you custo-mized news items or your favorite weather report. The issue is simply that this kind of information should be under *your* control. Even if you're willing to give that Thai tie company your information, do you want them selling it to the Bangkok Bamboo Shack?

What do "they" know?

Merchants' growing excitement about the Net stems mainly from the fact that it's so much easier to track a Web user's activities than to correlate, say, what a television viewer watches with his subsequent purchases. Web sites can keep track of what a person looks at, how long he stays, which ads provide the best response, whom he communicates with, what he says (in public discussion groups), how his behavior changes over the course of a day. Do drinkers buy more stuff in the evening, when they've had a few? Are customers of Web catalogs more price-sensitive than customers of paper catalogs? Are people who book airline seats through the Web more likely to be no-shows? Are customers getting so sophisticated that middle seats will have to be priced lower to sell? Alternatively, would you be willing to pay extra for an aisle seat? The possibilities for one-to-one everything are endless.

In principle, a merchant could compare a person's musical tastes to her reading preferences, or the political Web sites she visits to the magazines she reads. The merchant could scour the newsgroups and send e-mail to all people whose comments appeared on a particular site or matched a particular profile (as measured by statistical sampling of words). With birthday and ZIP code, you can usually find someone's name. Using the new directory services, a merchant can match up e-mail, name, and address . . . and all the other data linked to any of these. Try it on yourself. Thought your comments on libertarianism went only to people on that newsgroup? Think again! How did they get your name for that spam about a Caribbean island with a friendly government?

Some of this information is just statistical, but marketers also want it in order to track you individually. Merchants would like to know how ads affect your subsequent behavior: Do you see something online and then go buy it in a store with a credit card? Of course, the marketers don't really care who you are; they just care what you (can be induced to) buy. They want to be able to predict behavior. The problem is that the information they gather has a way of spreading further. . . .

Much of this information is in fact unnecessary, because much of what defines a person is reflected in the communities he is part of. Advertisers should be happy (or at least reconciled) to support those communities without knowing the "true" identities of each of their members. A company can place its advertising where the right customers show up; it's why you have bottled water ads in health clubs and resort ads on airport television. Likewise, community members want to know one another because of shared interests, not because of personal information.

Nonetheless, we have a friction-free market where consumer data is freely traded by giant corporations careless of people's identities—or worse, by small sleazy organizations with no reputations to protect. The companies out there collecting data on you may be small or large; these front-line data collectors get information from forms people fill out, from transaction records, and from various kinds of filings—many of them from government organizations. But the major companies buying, aggregating, and reselling data—Equifax, Trans Union, Experian, and the like—are large and powerful, and are well represented by the Direct Marketing Association. An increasing number of critics, including Russ Smith of Consumer.net, fault the DMA and its members for flouting their own guidelines as well as various consumer-protection laws. Indeed, as companies increasingly form marketing partnerships, purchases from one vendor—an ISP or a magazine or credit card company, for example—may subject you to a barrage of "customer communications" from "related marketing partners," related to the original vendor only by a marketing agreement. The intent of the law is that a vendor may have a legitimate need to communicate with its own customers—about billing or follow-on services, for example—but marketers are stretching this exemption to ridiculous lengths.

Marketers glibly say that the consumer is king, but in practice he's not. In the real world, experienced marketing and consumer-affairs hands will tell you, consumers aren't very good at protecting their own interests. They're too busy consuming, or working, or just living regular lives. The groups that claim to protect their interests often end up with their own agendas, which may have more to do with Washington power battles and fundraising than with genuine consumer interests.

A customer can't easily express her privacy preferences: She may have one preference for a site dealing with computer-industry issues, and another for her neighborhood after-school chat. We present different faces at work, at school, at church or temple, at the doctor's office. The difficulty is that personal information changes character as it travels, in a way that packaged "content" does not. Besides, your concerns for security may depend on the kind of interaction you are having: Are you simply giving your name, or are you transferring cash or revealing deep dark secrets? Of course, you can refuse to supply any data, but greater granularity would be beneficial to both customers and marketers.

Flawed solutions

The solutions most often presented in response to this situation generally miss the point. We don't need new government regulation that stops the free flow of information voluntarily given, outlaws cookies, and makes customization difficult (except perhaps where children and coercion are concerned). Nor do we need a Direct Market*ed* Association—a force equal in power to the Direct Marketing Association but aligned with someone's vision of consumers' interests. After all, consumers don't all have the same interests; what they really need is choice. Among many initiatives in response to these challenges are four notable, complementary efforts:

* *TRUSTe* is a disclosure and validation system enabling a user to reliably control information even after she has given it to a second party.
* *The Platform for Privacy Preferences* allows a user to define, see, and control the information about himself, and to determine which information to reveal to any particular Web site. It also includes a standard vocabulary by which users and Web sites may express and negotiate privacy preferences.
* *VeriSign* is a for-profit, public company that creates digital certificates, technology that allows Web sites or people to prove who they are.
* *Consumerinfo.com* offers a Web-based service that lets consumers check their own credit reports.

They offer a way for all sides to express themselves, and some way to ensure that they are telling the truth. In practice, this means self-rating and honest disclosure, along with third-party verification to ensure honesty on one side and trust on the other. Such verification has an additional benefit: the spread of best practices via firms that specialize in privacy and security methodologies.

Personally, I like all these initiatives because they are not moralistic, evangelistic, or dependent on government—other than for enforcement on the basis of fraud. They are examples of the kind of grassroots efforts at decentralized regulation and customer control that I hope to see proliferate on the Net. The first two are not-for-profit but independent of government; the other two are for-profit start-ups that see an opportunity rather than a duty in helping individuals to control their own information and identities.

Tools for customer empowerment

Much as I hate the term, what I'm talking about here is customer "empowerment," not "self-regulation"—*transforming passive consumers into active customers who can (through third parties) monitor vendor practices for themselves.* That implies some kind of broad movement to give customers the tools to do so, but the actual enforcement and use of the tools should be decentralized into users' hands.

The reason to avoid government regulation is not that government oversight is always bad; courts and other enforcement mechanisms are a necessary backup to systems such as TRUSTe. It's simply that frontline customer enforcement is likely to be more flexible and more responsive to actual conditions and consumer preferences than government regulation. A decentralized system scales up nicely and crosses borders with ease. Customer enforcement will give users greater choice, while at the same time giving them confidence that they can trust the medium. People can pick data-control practices that suit them, rather than be forced to operate in a one-rule-fits-all environment. The overriding rule is that providers must disclose—label—themselves clearly and honestly. And then they must do what they promise.

The goal is not to regulate cyberspace, nor to solve all problems concerning privacy (or content) online, but rather to carve out enough clean, well-lighted territory so that the dark parts of the Net lose their power to scare people away. In the end, most people will prefer to live in safe neighborhoods, while potential predators in dark places will find few victims other than their own kind.

TRUSTe

"Trust, but verify."—Ronald Reagan

TRUSTe is a labeling and certification organization created by the Electronic Frontier Foundation and by CommerceNet of California, another nonprofit created by Smart Valley, Inc.($\Rightarrow$ Chapter 4) in 1996. TRUSTe also has a host of sponsors and partners that should help it gain credibility, including Netscape and IBM. Two well-known accounting firms—PricewaterhouseCoopers and KPMG—helped to design the program and validate Web sites' privacy claims; they see a big business opportunity in conducting online "privacy audits."

The most visible part of TRUSTe is its trustmarks, which highlight and point to a Web site's privacy practices, allowing a customer to choose for himself whether to deal with a particular site.

Site oversight

Of course, the devil is in the details. What exactly will the site owner do with the data, and to whom will it be provided? Are those third parties bound by TRUSTe, too? How does TRUSTe validate the licensees who post its logos on their Web sites? First of all, it talks to them directly, requiring them to fill out a questionnaire and to sign a legally binding contract. It encourages them to have their data-processing systems audited by an accounting firm. It does random spot audits itself. And it has borrowed an old trick from the direct-mail industry: It "seeds" a site with fake data, just as a mailing-list broker seeds a list with his mother-in-law's name so he can find out if a one-time-use list is being used twice or more. Only in this case, TRUSTe applies the technique on behalf of the consumers whose data is being (mis) used.

What happens when someone fails in compliance? That's part of what TRUSTe hopes to determine over the next few years—ideally without too many instances of noncompliance, but enough to show that the program has teeth.* When there's a problem, it can surface through TRUSTe's seeding and spot checks by auditors, through tips from whistle-blowing employees, or through complaints from consumers whose data has been misused.

First, TRUSTe sends off a formal notice and gives the target an opportunity to respond. If the response is inadequate, TRUSTe can pursue it according to contract—revoking the license to use the mark, auditing the miscreant, and publicizing the results on a bad-actors list. The wrongdoer has to pay the costs of determining its noncompliance, and ultimately could be sued for fraud. If the breach appears willful and fraudulent, TRUSTe can call in the local jurisdiction under which the license was signed (usually a U.S. court) and sue. TRUSTe can also call in the FTC or other government agencies in serious cases.

TRUSTe's recourse mechanisms sound reasonable, but they haven't really been tested yet. Notes TRUSTe chairman Lori Fena, "Naturally enough, the first few hundred companies to sign up will tend to be the most sincere. We have contacted people [licensees] about what looked like problems. When you point something out, it's an oversight and they want to clear it up."

Spurred by the baleful gaze of the FTC, more than 150 sites have signed up as licensees, including ten of the top fifteen Web sites. They include America Online, Excite, nine CNET sites, several Buena Vista Internet Group sites (including Disney.com, ABCNEWS.com, ESPN-SportsZone, and ABC.com), GeoCities, IBM, Infoseek, Intuit, Lycos, Microsoft, Netcom, the *New York Times,* Organic Online, PlanetAll, Studio Archetype, Tandem, WebCrawler, four Wired Digital sites including Hotbot and Hotwired, Yahoo! and Yahooligans!, Z Auction, ZDNet—and, of course, my own company, EDventure Holdings. TRUSTe has also

---

*There will also need to be contracts specifying the sanctity of the data as companies form, merge, and break up. Currently, such contracts may be broken in the case of bankruptcy—which is one place where U.S. law needs to be changed.

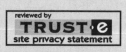

The Trustmark—A Symbol of Trust

The TRUSTe trustmark signifies to users that a Web site is a TRUSTe licensee. As a licensee displaying the trustmark, you are sending a clear signal to users that you've agreed to disclose your information gathering and dissemination practices, and that disclosure is backed by third-party assurance. Each trustmark is linked to a licensee's unique privacy statement, which users can bring up by clicking on the mark.

Privacy Statements

As a TRUSTe licensee, you will display a trustmark on your home page that represents an overall privacy statement; i.e., the privacy practices that pertain to your entire site. Licensees also have the option of displaying a trustmark on other pages where personal information is collected. TRUSTe recommends this practice, as it allows licensees to reflect accurately the disclosure practices throughout their site (besides, users often enter a site at locations other than the home page). A trustmark not on the home page signifies a tailored privacy statement that pertains only to the privacy practices of the specific page or location where the trustmark is displayed.

Whether overall or tailored, each privacy statement discloses, at a minimum:

- What type of information the Web site gathers
- How the site uses the information
- Who the site shares information with
- Whether users can correct and update their personally identifiable information

- Whether users will be deleted or deactivated from the site's database upon request
- Whether users may opt out of giving specific information to third parties

garnered an endorsement from the Internet Content Coalition (representing most major Web publishers listed above and also Pathfinder, MSNBC, CBS Online, Playboy Enterprises, Sony Online, Time Inc., and various Warner properties). That's small compared to the total number of sites, but it's a visible beginning, and it means almost every Internet user has at least seen, if not noticed, the TRUSTe logo.

The Platform for Privacy Preferences (P3P)

The Platform for Privacy Preferences (P3P) is the consolidation of two separate standards efforts: the Open Profiling Standard (OPS) and the World Wide Web Consortium's original Platform for Privacy Preferences. In mid-1997, OPS's creators submitted it to the W3C as a proposed standard that would be complementary to P3P. There was some slight overlap, but by and large the hand-waving parts of each proposal matched the more solid parts of the other one, and it was clear to everyone that it should be absorbed to P3P.

The Open Profiling Standard was originally an independent, complementary response to many of the same pressures that fostered TRUSTe. But while TRUSTe was a creation of nonprofit groups, OPS was a technology developed for commercial use by a company called Firefly Network,* which decided the benefits of seeing it widely adopted outweighed any proprietary advantage it could hope to gain. At the time of the FTC hearings in mid-1997, Firefly and two partners had just announced OPS as an open standard and submitted it to W3C.

*I was a small investor in this for-profit company.

In 1998, Firefly was acquired by Microsoft, which has committed to carry on the mission.

Firefly Network is intimately concerned with privacy issues because its primary business was "collaborative filtering"—collecting information from consumers so that they can match their preferences with other people's. That is, if I like Bonnie Raitt, I'd like to know what other artists Bonnie Raitt fans like. On the other hand, I might not want my preferences too widely disclosed, especially to a whole lot of music clubs.

Firefly's partners in the OPS project were VeriSign, mentioned above, and Netscape. OPS (now P3P) also uses the "vCARD" standard for business cards, with specified formats for basic information such as name, address, phone number, and e-mail address. Like TRUSTe, it had garnered an impressive line-up of support, including Microsoft, J. Walter Thompson, American Express, and about 100 other companies who mostly switched their support to the World Wide Web's P3P project when OPS was folded in.

Separately, the World Wide Web Consortium was working on P3P, its own human- and computer-readable vocabulary for expressing and negotiating privacy preferences, complementary to the data-description standards being developed by Firefly and its partners. Its partner in this effort was the Internet Privacy Working Group (IPWG). The IPWG is a consortium led by Washington's Center for Democracy and Technology, which happens to be run by Jerry Berman, former executive director of the Electronic Frontier Foundation—it's a small world! IPWG's supporters include the usual suspects with a slightly more Washington/ trade-association flavor than TRUSTe's and W3C's own sponsors: America Online, Microsoft, Consumers Union, MCI, Dun & Bradstreet, IBM, AT&T, the Direct Marketing Association, the Electronic Frontier Foundation, TRUSTe, the Coalition for Advertising-Supported Information and Entertainment, the National Consumers League, and the Internet Alliance. Unlike OPS, P3P was designed to be a public standard from the start, so the joint standard is now being enhanced under public scrutiny with input from many of the IPWG and W3C partners. The technical idea behind P3P is to extend the PICS content-labeling protocol to the electronic labeling of privacy/data practices in a way that will allow automatic negotiation between a person's browser or software application and the privacy/data practices of a Web site.

Thus, the combined P3P, launched in mid-1998, is basically a specification for adding software to both browsers and Web sites to allow them to represent user data clearly and to manage a process of "notice and consent" for privacy practices. The availability of P3P, especially if it gets strong support from Firefly's new parent, Microsoft, should loose hundreds of creative programmers on the task of building tools and applications to help people define what data they want to keep private or to share, and to which specific vendors or categories of sites they want to reveal each item.

One gating factor will be the attention that Microsoft pays to this issue, not just in its products but in its advertising. To the extent that Microsoft users (most of the online population) have privacy tools and know how (and why) to use them, data collectors will respond to market demand. There might be defaults for children and perhaps for medical information. Low-end tools might offer three canned options with little flexibility, while higher-end packages could include branching questionnaires, heuristics, and other clever approaches. Users will be able to embed their preferences and restrictions in a browser or software tool that can communicate directly with Web sites and other electronic partners.

Best of all, as a user you can store and manage information in a way you can understand. For example, you could specify (by filling in a simple form):

* Give name, address, vegetarian preference, and credit card information to dailysoup.com;
* Give name and e-mail address to the Electronic Frontier Foundation and the CNET news service because you want alerts from them;
* Give password and pseudonym (no name or e-mail address) to the sweetsorrow discussion group;
* Give nothing to any site not specifically noted.

In the future, as better software is developed, you could also specify sites by categories, such as "companies rated A1" by the hypothetical SafeChild rating service, or various other criteria. P3P does not guarantee security on its own, but it is designed to work with other systems for security and authentication from the sites you visit (not much for your e-mail address, a lot for your credit-card number). Future versions will include more integrated authentication tools.

P3P also allows you to eliminate cookies or replace them (when visiting P3P-observant sites) by creating a temporary or permanent user ID (TUID or PUID), which plays the role of a cookie but is under the user's control. That would allow, for example, a site to recognize a frequent visitor by her PUID, without ever knowing anything else about the person. On the other hand, the user's software can create a new TUID for each site visit, with no record being kept on either side.

If you visit a non-P3P site, your P3P application would alert you that the site might put cookies into your system and collect other data you give it.

More interestingly, P3P will allow you to negotiate, setting conditions. As CDT's Jerry Berman puts it, "You can't just allow people to express their preferences and then they're done. They'll end up missing the sites they might want to see." The task of defining privacy preferences in a way that allows such automatic execution and negotiation will be much like the process of drawing up an insurance policy or a will—confusing to the uninitiated. As with wills, people will be able to use automated tools and forms to express a relatively simple set of preferences; those with complex lives may want to sit down with a privacy expert (probably from an accounting firm, of course) to develop a complex set of preferences. For example:

> I don't want to reveal my age . . . unless I get a senior citizen's discount worth more than 10 percent of the price of an item or $400 in absolute value. (That info cannot then be reused; I don't want to get any catalogs for walking aids, retirement homes, or annuities.)

I don't want to reveal my income . . . unless it's required to see sites offering jewelry and vacations at exclusive places in the Caribbean.

I'd like British Airways and Lufthansa to know how much I fly with American and Delta. Maybe they'd treat me better!

I'd like to be visible to other single women between thirty-five and forty-five in my discussion groups, but not to any men at all.

Overall, P3P will let you control what information gets out to whom while still allowing you the genuine benefits of information exchange—including earning points in an airline club, ordering your special style of support hose by e-mail, receiving customized news, or hearing about advances in turtle ties. With the right application, you can use it to record and manage data about all your Web transactions—including whatever promises merchants make to you about data practices.

P3P is also useful for the other side, the vendors whose Web sites can read and interact with P3P files. P3P will let merchants, vendors, and other Webmasters automate their side of the interaction, expressing their conditions for doing business and their promises about what they'll do with users' data. In the long run, this will lead to happier customers. It will also let merchants send information only to willing recipients and avoid the costs of mailing to people who tear up their catalogs or eventually, I hope, charge for reading their e-mail (⟹ page 142, Chapter 5).

Would users trust such an automated system? That will depend in part on the compliance system behind the scheme. (The user's and the site's choice of auditor or validation scheme could be specified in the label.) For all the same reasons behind TRUSTe, the merchant-side/ Web site users of P3P will have to devise some provisions for attestation—for example, by using TRUSTe. TRUSTe trustmarks are a logo for people to see pointing to information for them to read on a Web site; P3P labels and customer data are computer-readable information and rules that will eventually need the same kind of jurisdiction and enforcement that TRUSTe provides for its logos.

VeriSign: Digital IDs and privacy

One way to help establish trust (but not a replacement for it) is to use technical tools to verify identity and authenticity. Even as people want to protect their privacy, they need to establish their identity and their credentials—and those of their partners. You want to be sure about the true identity or credentials of the person or entity you're dealing with, which can be especially hard in cyberspace. For example, Juan wants to know that the e-mail from Alice really is from *Alice,* and not from some impostor. He wants to know that the Web site he's visiting really is Alice's Restaurant, and that the recipe or the banana bread he's ordering will be the genuine article. He may also want to know more: that Alice will not sell his name to Tupperware or anyone else, that her site really is a TRUSTe licensee, that he can believe her claims that she's using only organic bananas, that she employs only adults, especially if she's located in some other country. U.S. laws may not apply.

On the other hand, Alice may want him to know less: When Juan communicates with her, he may want to check that she truly earned Le Grande Diplome Le Cordon Bleu, but he needn't know her real name to trust her recipes.

VeriSign was created in 1995 as a spin-out from crypto company RSA Data Security to handle just these issues. It creates and manages digital certificates for anyone who wants to issue them, whether it's a company certifying employees, a government registering its citizens, or a vendor recognizing its customers (so that it won't give out account information to unauthorized recipients) and vice versa. Close to 60,000 Web servers now have digital IDs and security that enable secure transmission of information to and from a customer, says VeriSign CEO Stratton Sclavos.

VeriSign also provides a special TRUSTe-enabled Digital ID that lets Web site visitors assure themselves that a proclaimed TRUSTe site truly is one and isn't just making the claim. TRUSTe and VeriSign are also trying to get the browser vendors to add a feature that would automatically inspect for the presence or absence of a privacy policy at a Web site (as certified by VeriSign). Recall that VeriSign was one of several companies (along with Netscape and Firefly) that helped develop the P3P technology for the World Wide Web Consortium, and you'll see how neatly this all hangs together.

Certification is not a one-size-fits-all business, notes Sclavos. "We thought at first that all we had to do was certify someone's authenticity, but it's more complicated than that," he says. "We thought there would be one certificate per identity, but actually there's one certificate per relationship. For example, we certify people for corporate clients as holders of credit cards, employee badges, banking or brokerage accounts, as members of a community of interest or commerce (such as an automotive network exchange), as citizens." There are more than 2 million individuals with almost 3 million digital certificates, he estimates.

Individuals don't necessarily want the same identity everywhere they go. They probably want to keep some information to themselves, and to share only necessary and relevant information with each certificate authority (perhaps using P3P): one set of information for a health-care provider, another for an employer, yet another for the bank.

VeriSign also offers digital certificates that can be anonymous (used today by Netscape's NetCenter). It is exploring services that would allow users to surf anonymously and still divulge information to sites on a selective basis. The customer would have a digital signature (a "Privacy Digital ID") with encrypted information on it. Keys to unlock specific items of information (name, say, but not social security or address or credit-card number) would be available only to merchants or delivery services who meet certain qualifications and receive certification and keys from some trusted third party. You could use this approach to send and receive e-mail, visit sites, and transact business without divulging your identity to that site.

Indeed, physical items could be sent to a third-party service that could resolve addresses using a secure database from VeriSign or other trusted third parties. Thus Amazon.com could sell a book to an un-identified buyer with a credit-card number it never saw. It would ship the book to, say, Federal Express, which could decrypt the address and a name (not necessarily the real name) for shipping, without knowing (other than "books") what was inside or who it was for.

Of course, that means consumers would have to trust VeriSign . . . or *someone*. Do you prefer a single point of possible failure, or distributed risk among many parties you don't know? That's up to you.

Consumerinfo.com

As I've mentioned in many ways, all these consumer-empowerment ideas are not just right, they can even be good business. Another example is Consumerinfo.com, a company that started operations in 1995 but is really coming into its own on the Net. It has just received an infusion of capital from Memberworks, a marketing company that—bless it!—sees an opportunity in offering consumers data about themselves. The company was founded by a group of executives from what was then TRW Credit services and is now Experian. They built Consumerinfo.com as a profit-making venture to do as a business what credit bureaus are required to do by law as a service for a "reasonable fee" (or free once or twice a year if you live in Georgia, Maryland, Massachusetts, or Vermont): Let consumers see their own credit records. But Consumerinfo.com tries to do it with enthusiasm and grace. (Experian tried to do this itself recently, but its security wasn't airtight and it ended up providing information to the wrong people in a debacle that captured press attention. It is now working on a revamped service.)

The company first offered online credit-report ordering as a feature in Quicken Deluxe, but the customer got the report on paper. Since it moved onto the Web in 1997, Consumerinfo.com has had 200,000 online orders for credit reports; about half those customers went on to pay for some additional service. In order to sell the service, Consumerinfo.com allows anyone one free credit report from Experian—with which, naturally enough, it has good relations. Getting the three-fer, with additional reports from Equifax and Trans Union, costs $34.95. You can also get a credit-monitoring membership which gives you

```
*******************TRW CONSUMER CREDIT REPORT*******************
*              consumerinfo.com         *
*                Ref: 100131788         *
***********Dept: CREDIT REPORTS / Queued by: SUPERVISOR***********
DATE: 05-13-1998   TIME: 10:55:09   SUBJECT ID:
DYSON, ESTHER ##########;
CA-104 5TH AV/NEW YORK NY 10011;
PH-212-924-8800;
U-CONSUMERINFO, T-0B, Y-1951, V-06/999/8.00, H-Y;
PAGE 1   DATE 5-13-98   TIME 13:05:44 PCB60   V101   TNJ1
ESTHER DYSON        SS: ##########
*104 5TH AVE FL 20     YOB: 1951
NEW YORK NY 10011-6901
RPTD: 8-95 U 3X
LAST SUB: #######
*375 PARK AVE
NEW YORK NY 10022-6006
RPTD: 7-89 TO 5-93 U
-----------------------------------PROFILE SUMMARY-----------------------------------
                        CNT 01/00/00/00
PUBLIC RECORDS---0   PAST DUE AMT---$0   INQUIRIES---2
SATIS ACCTS---6   INSTALL BAL---N/A   SCH/EST PAY---$212+
INQS/6 MO---0   NOW DEL/DRG---0   R ESTATE BAL---$176,681
R ESTATE PAY---$1,716   TRADELINE---7   WAS DEL/DRG---1
REVOLVING BAL---$15,413   REVOLVING AVAIL---67%   PAID ACCT---0
OLD TRADE---3-76
---------------------------------------------TRADES---------------------------------------------
###     OPEN   AMT-TYP1   AMT-TYP2 ACCTCOND   PYMT STATUS
###   KOB TYP TRM ECOA BALDATE    BALANCE PYMT LEVEL MOS
REV PYMT HISTORY
###     LAST PD   MONTH PAY   PAST DUE   MAXIMUM   BY MONTH
*ATT UNIVERSAL CARD   7-90  $1,500-L  $1,664-H  OPEN   CUR WAS 30
######  BC CRC REV 1   4-22-98  $81  2-97  (94) CCCCCCCCCCCCC
         4-98     $71         CC1CCCCCCCCC
CITIBANK VISA        3-89  $17,400-L        OPEN   CURR ACCT
###### BC CRC REV 1   4-30-98  $7,436  3-89  (99) CCCCCCC-CCCCC
         4-98     $141        CCCCCCCCCCCCC
AMEX        3-76  $18,664-H        OPEN   CURR ACCT
###### N CRC 1   1   4-26-98  $7,896  5-78  (99) CCCCCCCCCCCCCC
                UNK        CCCCCCCCCCCCC
AMEX        10-93  $10,000-L        OPEN   CURR ACCT
###### BC C/C REV 1    4-24-98  $0   10-93  (56) 0000000000000
                000000000000
AMEX        3-76  $531-H            OPEN   CURR. ACCT
###### N CRC REV 1   4-20-98  $0  6-76  (99) NNNNNNNNNNNNNN
                NNNNNN----NN
EMIGRANT MORTGAGE CO   12-85  $108,800-O   OPEN   CURR ACT
###### FS R/C 31Y   1   4-02-98  $95,261  12-85  (99) CCCCCCCCC----
1540###        3-98   $925        CCCCCCCCCCCC
```

EMIGRANT MORTGAGE CO   12-85 $93,000-O   OPEN   CURR ACCT
FS R/C 31Y   1   4-02-98 $81,420   12-85   (99) CCCCCCCCC----
1540###   3-98 $791   CCCCCCCCCCCC
--INQUIRIES--
MONTGOMERY SECURITIES   4-07-97   ####### F1
HOOPER HOLMES INC   1-31-97   ####### FM
END--EXPERIAN
If you feel there are inaccuracies in your Experian credit report, call toll-free
1 (800) 567-5470.   The Experian customer service representative will ask you for
your membership number, and you should respond with: "This is in regard to my
Consumer Review Service report." The representative will then promptly assist you.
Or write to:
Experian National Consumer Assistance Center
P.O. Box 949
Allen, TX 75013-0949
For general questions about your Experian credit report, call ConsumerInfo.Com's
Customer Service Center toll-free at 1 (888) 888-8553.
End of Report Data

> Return to Report Express. For security purposes, you will be unable to view
> or download this report again.
>
> Save your report to disk so you can access it whenever you need to.
>
> Exit this report. For security purposes, you will be unable to view or
> download this report again.

continuing service and notification whenever anyone checks on your
credit, for a price I couldn't easily find on the Web site.

Consumerinfo.com has figured out that it can make a business of
this. Sure, it has to pay the suppliers a small fee for the information,
just as their other subscribers do. But these companies know that they
can avoid the hassle of having to deal with consumers themselves if
they pass the task on to Consumerinfo.com, so they're willing to do so.

I pulled my own report from Consumerinfo.com, following the security procedures—an e-mailed membership number plus a paper-
mailed password—to get the report reproduced on page 265. It's pretty
incomprehensible (but not too embarrassing, fortunately); what makes
it extra valuable is the accompanying "translation" tool the company
provides.

I was surprised that it doesn't include my salary. Somewhere, I
know, there's a lot more interesting information out there, including
my travel patterns and more detail about my spending habits. But

there's no law forcing anyone to give me that—yet. Maybe it won't even require a law: How about it, Consumerinfo.com? Well, says CEO Ed Ojdana, the company is looking at other areas, but he believes that people care more about (and will pay for) services involving information that has the most impact on their lives—that is, whether I get credit, not whether I get travel offers.

The trick here is to change the balance of power between "the authorities" and the rest of us. Many of the services Consumerinfo.com is testing provide information that is "public-record" and easily available to insiders but hard for regular people to get hold of, such as house prices in a neighborhood where you might be looking to buy or sell a house, neighborhood crime levels, or environmental reports. Again, the proper counterpart of personal privacy is public disclosure of what *should be* public.

Other privacy initiatives

While the government was holding conferences and hearings to assess the industry's progress since the July 1997 announcement of the Framework for Global Electronic Commerce, the industry was busy coming up with a variety of approaches to customer data control. Besides the four schemes above, there have been several other notable initiatives: The American Institute of Certified Public Accountants started a program called Webtrust, which certifies commercial sites for a number of qualities including data protection. The Council of Better Business Bureaus and its BBBOnline unit is creating a privacy program to certify and monitor sites' privacy practices. It will do much the same things as TRUSTe, but will probably focus more on small businesses, benefiting from its broad presence and large dispute-resolution staff throughout the United States. On the other hand, TRUSTe has more visibility on the Net and overseas. Competing for licensees and for consumer attention should improve both organizations, although it will of course divide the start-up money available.

The Direct Marketing Association has announced that its privacy "guidelines" will become firm "rules" in July 1999. Separately, for lists maintained by third parties, the DMA already offers MPS and TPS (mail and telephone preference services). Next in line is EMPS, the Electronic Mail Preference Service. In case you were wondering: No, the list will not be posted, and it will in fact be highly secured. Would-be users, says DMA head Robert Wientzen, will bounce their list against the DMA's, which will offer the purging as a service. In other words, a would-be mailer has to have the address in the first place for it to be removed. Some critics complain that the DMA's lists are too inflexible—you can't remove your name selectively—but at least this is a start.

IBM and a group of leading companies, trade associations, and non-profit organizations have formed the Online Privacy Alliance to raise awareness of the issue and help educate consumers. In one way or another, these "regulatory" organizations are taking on some of the functions (or would-be functions) of the Federal Trade Commission and other government organizations. The FTC itself, along with various government organs in Europe and other countries, is watching warily: Will these emerging intermediaries have enough teeth to be effective? Will they meet the requirements of the European Union?

Defining "privacy"

These systems and initiatives encouraging people to take control of their own data are an exciting development. Yet when we say "privacy" we mean lots of things beyond data—everything from the (non)publication of information to control over exactly when one receives a telephone call. Does Juan mind if his information is in a data bank somewhere, unseen by prying eyes? No. But he goes ballistic if he gets called after 7 P.M. Alice, by contrast, gets the willies when she thinks of her transactions being recorded anywhere, but she doesn't really mind the phone calls as long as the callers don't seem to know much about her. One doesn't want to be disturbed; the other is specifically concerned about privacy as an information issue.

Different people have different preferences for their own privacy. And there are already many laws concerning privacy.*

Some people object in principle to the concept of privacy as an assignable right—one that can be sold or bargained away. They'd rather see it as an inalienable right, one the poor can enjoy as fully as the rich. But I believe that people should decide for themselves how to value their data. Since privacy is not an absolute, and since individuals' preferences vary, it seems foolish to insist on an absolute approach.

Moreover, though content is generally displayed the same way for all comers,** rules concerning privacy may apply differently to different customers, at the site's or the customer's option. In the simple model, each Web site may have a blanket policy about data reuse, and customers decide whether or not to interact with it. But a Web site may instead offer a number of options, and customers can negotiate—perhaps paying in anonymous e-cash to see something that would be free to an identified viewer, or providing specific personal information in exchange for a discount or customized service.

Privacy in practice

In practice, privacy protection is more than data or technology. How can we achieve it without making the world into a sterile place where everyone is anonymous? Most customers actually like to be treated as

---

*In the United States, information about individuals' video purchases is protected by law—the result of one unfortunate experience by one legislator that resulted in the law. On the other hand, data linking a person's driver's license number with name, address, age, and other personal data is available from departments of motor vehicles in many states. Much commercial data is more carefully protected, but often more because the possessor wants to sell it than out of respect for the privacy of the individuals concerned.

**Yes, there are instances of clean and dirty versions of games or movies, or different-language versions, or text-only or with-graphics versions. Blind people may rely on captions for graphical content, which also render the content easily searchable—and classifiable. Moreover, sites can deliver content selectively according to their knowledge of individuals, but that slips into those privacy discussions again!

Personal privacy vs. public right to know

In considering rules for privacy, it's important to distinguish between privacy in the context of commercial transactions with consumers whose primary role is to buy something for cash, and privacy for producers or fiduciaries, who promise to *do* something: offer a safe and effective product, fulfill a credit agreement, care for children, or hold a public office. Furthermore, commercial partners have a legitimate interest in the truth of the information people do reveal—no fair lying to the insurance company or claiming a high level of income to get a loan.

Commercial consumer privacy is quite a simple moral issue: Customers should be able to choose what information to reveal and how it may be used, although they may have to give up some privileges to do so. Weighing the trade-offs between privacy and society's right to know in other spheres is a far more difficult, nontechnical question.

Some requests for personal information are not equal-party transactions; they involve coercion (more than just, "You can buy this sweater at a discount if you reveal your favorite color") or a potential breach of trust. For example, you may have to reveal certain information to get insurance coverage . . . and worse, the truth may de facto deny you affordable coverage. Children may be lured into revealing information that their parents would not allow them to. An employer may want to know about your criminal record.

Society also has an interest in disclosure of information ranging from criminal records to safety risks. How bad a risk is a former drug abuser or an abusive spouse? Is the risk only to the company, or to the people who might be in the path of the truck that person is driving or to other employees who might provoke the person's wrath? We also have an interest in full disclosure by politicians and other officials well beyond what we can ask from private individuals.

All these situations cannot be fairly negotiated. Governments do need to provide rules for using such information as appropriate and otherwise keeping it private—securely and consistently.

known individuals by marketers that they in turn know and trust. The rhetoric promises a global village, not a global city. Real privacy—which is respect for people rather than mere absence of data—depends on human judgment and common sense.

Take Four11, a leading Web "white pages" company that was recently acquired by Yahoo!; you can find it at yahoo.foru11.com. Its basic service is collecting and maintaining a database of individuals' names, e-mail addresses, phone numbers, and other data. The telephone data is licensed from Metromail (now part of Experian); the e-mail addresses come primarily from user registrations, public-domain directories on the Net, and Usenet. While visitors are encouraged to register with their own data, you can also ask to be stricken (even if your data shows up again from another source).

All this data is available to anyone who visits Four11 at Yahoo!'s Web site—but only a bit at a time. Aside from its acceptable-use policies (restricting wholesale reuse and general abuse), Four11 avoids hard and fast rules in order to be flexible enough to address new problems as they arise. For example, the company makes it difficult for users to collect names for mass e-mailing or for building any kind of secondary database. It supplies information only one e-mail address at a time, and it monitors user activity for unusual behavior, such as downloading one address after another. It doesn't care who you are; it just cares what you do.

Also, you can't find a name from a phone number or from an e-mail address, or so-called "reverse look-up"; you need to know a person's name before you can get anywhere. However, that wasn't always true. Before the acquisition, Four11 licensed its database to Yahoo! At the time, Yahoo! did allow reverse searching using the Four11 data—quickly creating the Net's most visible, most-used reverse look-up for phone numbers at the time. Former Four11 CEO Mike Santullo said he felt uncomfortable about the reverse look-up service, but both parties noted that it was tremendously popular and did not actually lead to many problems.

Both companies were punctilious about delisting people who asked for their names to be removed. Meanwhile, police departments, suicide prevention centers, and other "good guys" made good use of the service. "Bad guys" didn't seem to be more prevalent than the sometimes annoying people who use caller ID to call you back. But a few months later, in response to perceived pressure, the companies dropped the service. Similar information is still available, but sometimes from companies that may be less careful than Yahoo!

It's a pity that such a potentially valuable service should be abandoned and relegated to nonmainstream providers. The moral of this story—which is not yet over—is that a little self-regulation or fine-grained control over personal data may actually yield a situation where information is more readily available than a situation without controls where all data is simply withheld.

That's the long-term question: How can you make information available selectively? Yahoo! is addressing that in part, although not with reverse look-up for now. People willing to register with the service can get selected additional information about others; presumably, being registered themselves makes them less likely to abuse the information. For example, they are allowed to search the database for people by affiliation, such as "Princeton High School" or "violinist." This information comes from individuals and from the groups themselves; they can specify which information can be made available, and to whom. For example, some groups let only group members query on group-oriented data, so only PHS alumni (as verified by PHS) could find out which other people are PHS alumni.

Yes, it sounds cumbersome and awkward and somewhat arbitrary, but isn't that the way it is in real life? The folks at Four11 have thought about all this a lot, and will refine their approach as they encounter new problems over time, says Santullo. Call it a continuing arms race between the data-providers and the data-snatchers.

Juno: Free e-mail in exchange for your information

Some sites and services make explicit bargains. Juno, for example, offers customers (including my stepmother) free e-mail in exchange for exposing the user to specific advertising based on the user's characteristics. The service has been a success with end-users: About 5 million people have signed up for it, filling in a detailed profile in exchange for free e-mail. They do not have to have Internet access, since Juno offers its own local dial-up throughout the United States, and they do not get Internet access, but they can send and receive e-mail across the Internet. They can also view graphics-filled ads from Juno's advertisers and from Juno itself. The site looks something like a Web site and its ads look like Web banner ads, but the only people who can use it are registered Juno customers.

Although the service is free, it's not quite "the people's e-mail." It still skews Internet-wards, says Juno president Charles Ardai: mostly male (two-thirds) and higher income. You may not need to pay for Internet access, but you still do need a computer with a modem.

The users' identities are not revealed to the advertisers, who simply get a report such as "5,482 men between 18 and 49 who have expressed interest in a new car saw your ad last month; please pay $2,741 within 30 days." Juno may also tell them, for example, that 25 percent of the people who clicked on their ad were female. Note that this means people who actually saw the ad when they logged on to check e-mail; it's more targeted and more intense than a page you might have passed in a magazine.

But how is an advertiser to know this is true? Juno's financials and other numbers, including claims to advertisers, are audited by PricewaterhouseCoopers. "Unlike a Web site, we're pretty simple to audit," notes Ardai. The only people who visit are its own registered and profiled customers, using Juno's proprietary software.

Juno has discovered that it can also sell products itself to its customers—a cookbook to someone who's indicated an interest in cooking, for example. She can send back a purchase order with ease, he notes, and her credit card never goes over the Internet. (That may not be a real issue, but it makes some customers feel more secure.) People who respond to an advertiser's direct offer, of course, lose their anonymity.

Transparency and trust

Mechanisms such as TRUSTe and P3P that give individuals control over use of personal data collected in a formal way by marketers, and companies such as Yahoo!/Four11, Juno, and, potentially, Microsoft who promote their privacy practices, should help to give people an overall sense of security on the Net and clarify the distinction between private and public transactions. When you engage in an explicit transaction, it should be private—with the treatment of the data under your control. When you do anything else, it's public. This sense of boundaries and control is likely to be important both in getting people onto the Net and in making them feel more secure when they get there. In the long run, it's likely that this attitude will spread from the Internet back to other transactions: Consumers will demand the same control over data from transactions generated off the Net. Or people will prefer to do business on the Net, where they know that they can negotiate.

Indeed, I believe that even as people's concern about privacy on the Net lessens, they will become more comfortable about their visibility in the public parts of cyberspace.

What would Deep Blue be like with hormones?

Let's try a thought experiment. Imagine that you have lived your entire life on the Net, isolated from the physical world. You know a lot of people intimately: You've heard their ideas; you've argued with them; you've watched them mature, get angry, trade jokes, do business, make and lose friends. You have made and lost friends yourself. These people are real to you; you want their respect; you ask them for advice. And you are real to them. You and they take your Net presence for granted—all the things you have ever posted, all the data about you, all the Net chatter about you. But you have never seen them.

Now suppose you meet these people in real, physical, terrestrial life. They're fat or thin; blond or dark; young or old; white or African American or Asian; male or female. There's more! Each person has these little peculiarities—a scar, asymmetrical eyebrows, a particular style of dress or pattern of speech, and so on. They are no big deal; they're merely expressions of each person's identity. (Yes, some people do hate their nose, have an obsession with their hair, or even undergo cosmetic surgery, but few people wear a mask.)

None of these features is any big secret, and most are familiar (if not explicitly so) to that person's friends and even acquaintances. With certain people—for example, presidents and movie stars—they are known to the world. Some details are genetically determined; some are shaped by the person; some are an artifact of culture (such as a woman's shaved legs).

But how about you? At first you would probably be very sensitive about your own physical being. You would feel vulnerable and exposed as you joined the physical world. All these people can see how you look, judge your hairstyle, criticize your weight or your taste in shirts. . . . Should you shave? Should you wear your trousers rolled?

But after a while you would probably relax, just as you have already in the real world since being an awkward teenager. People know how you dress and how you look, and most of them now are accustomed to it. Meanwhile, you're accustomed to the face you present to the world. You may be taken aback to see your profile or, worse, the back of your head in a mirror. But on the whole, you're probably relaxed about the physical impression you present because it has come to seem normal.

The same thing is likely to happen with your Net persona.

The new privacy

As people feel more secure in general on the Net, they will become accustomed to seeing their words recorded and replayed. They will no longer feel uncomfortable being on display, since everyone around them is on display too. In the same way, feelings of physical exposure tend to depend on fashion and custom as well as innate sensibility. Thirty years ago the sight of a woman's navel was shocking except at the beach; now it's routine. One hundred years ago, a nanny told my grandmother she was a "shameless hussy" for taking off her shoes at the beach.

Everyone has personal preferences for privacy, but they are influenced by the surrounding culture and by the surrounding economy. It's hard to fulfill a desire for privacy if you're living in a one-room apartment with the rest of your eight-person extended family. If you travel or mingle with people from other cultures, you will notice that Americans expect a lot more "personal space" than most people.

Nowadays, people reveal much more about themselves—for better or worse—than they used to. It's inevitable that they will simply become more comfortable with the fact that more information is known about them on the Net. The challenge is not to keep everything secret, but to limit misuse of such information. That implies trust, and more knowledge of how the information is used. At the same time, we may all become more tolerant if everyone's flaws are more visible.

What will be known?

Right now on the Net, a service called DéjàNews can search all the newsgroups (online discussions) to find out what any person has said in the entire history of the Net. The search engines (Excite, Lycos, AltaVista, Yahoo! and others) can search most of the Web, and Excite also provides access to DéjàNews. And an outfit called, appropriately, Internet Archive is working on keeping archives of the entire World Wide Web over time.

Just think how something you said five years ago might affect your chances of getting a job. Or think how what you're saying now outside your workplace may affect your current job! That's why many communities may decide to keep their records sealed for a certain number of years, or available only to the participants themselves, or to observe whatever limitations the members choose. On the WELL, the most famous Net community of all, several participants chose to delete all their own postings, an act likened to committing suicide by the other members. In most communities that isn't possible.*

---

*It's a long story . . . well described by Katie Hafner in the May 1997 issue of *Wired* magazine; also ⟹ Chapter 9.

Indeed, much of the Net will become more private than it is now. In addition to the one-to-one privacy protections I described earlier, people will have the ability to close themselves off with filtering tools, community boundaries, intranets, and the like. Ultimately, people will spend much of their time within relatively closed spaces, much as they do now in real life. They can stay within a corporate intranet, and venture forth only to find commercial information. But I hope they don't; they'll miss a lot if they do.

Visibility as a desirable norm

Within communities, most people will become accustomed to seeing their own reflections. There will be rules about what is recorded and what is erased after, say, ten days, but more and more will end up being archived. Perhaps we're too narcissistic as a species, but human nature is to save everything. There will be records somewhere of almost everything you've posted, e-mails you've sent, and of course things other people have said about you. Most communities will have registered members but they will be open—to new members, and often to data searches from outside.

Conversely, members will be able to wander outside to anywhere on the Net for public information, send e-mail to anyone (although not everyone will be willing to receive it), and keep in touch with and do business with others worldwide. The challenge is to make sure that something is left outside, in those open spaces. One purpose of this book is to encourage people to make the mainstream of cyberspace nice enough that people will want to live their social lives there. To gain trust, people need to be visible—as they expect others to be. The Net will not have a single culture, but the default needs to be healthy, with people online working actively to maintain clean, well-lighted places.

. . . that is, voluntarily visible

There are commercial, social, and political reasons for us to be voluntarily visible in the potentially murky world online. Disclosure is a foundation for open markets. It's also a foundation for clean politics, whether on the Net or off. And finally, it's a foundation for trust.

People within communities may want to shield themselves from the outside, but they will mostly want transparency and visibility inside. On a much larger scale, so do governments. They want records that are complete and open—except perhaps their own. Although the Electronic Frontier Foundation and many other groups and individuals are fighting vigorously to keep governments and businesses from prying into our private lives without our consent, that urge on the part of governments won't go away. The difference is that communities do it with our consent.

Governments all over the world are cooking up schemes to listen to our conversations and tap our lines. Some governments insist that they will require a court order to do so; others are less punctilious and their promises meaningless.

What can we do in response? In some countries, we have hope of keeping our privacy; in others, it will be more of a challenge. And the more a government feels threatened, usually because it is not liked by those it rules, the more likely it is to spy on its own citizens as well as on foreigners in order to retain power ($\Longrightarrow$ Chapter 10).

Fair play

Our best defense is offense: Spy back!

We need the ability to follow more closely what our governments are doing. So while the Electronic Frontier Foundation, the Center for Democracy and Technology, and other organizations defend our privacy, they are also fighting for more open government. What are governments doing with all the information they collect? Who is looking at it? Who are they talking to? Why aren't they talking to us? Where do government officials receive their outside income? Who pays their bills? How is it biasing their judgment? How are they spending their—our—money? (Could we spend it better ourselves?)

This kind of information will help reverse the imbalance of power. Governments are legitimately concerned about large-scale organized crime rings and terrorists operating in the shadows. But I am also concerned about large-scale *governments* operating in the shadows. Government rule is based on the legitimate concept that we have to decide collectively on some rules and on the allocation of some of our social resources. But we also have a right to oversee how the rules are followed by those in charge and how the resources are used. Surely, even more than investors have a right to disclosure about their investments, we, as involuntary "investors," have a right to disclosure from our government.

This applies to online communities, too. Even though they are voluntary, there's a risk that community managements will become large and bureaucratic just like terrestrial governments and established businesses.

In general, I don't want too many restrictions on what people can say or do, but I do want strong expectations of disclosure from those who hold or want positions of public trust. Ideally, we would not even need laws. There would be no law requiring Steve Forbes or Ross Perot, for example, to disclose their tax returns, but few people would vote for them if they didn't.

Commercial openness and trust

It's a great irony that many of the commercial institutions we trust the most are the most opaque: banks, hospitals, airlines. We routinely put our lives and money in their hands, with few questions asked. A recent Harris poll* said 79 percent of those surveyed trusted hospitals and 77 percent trusted banks to handle confidential data properly, compared with 48 percent for commercial online services, 46 percent for Internet service providers, and 40 percent for online merchants. People also trust the Postal Service. One way or another, we assume we are safe . . . and mostly we are. Banks are regulated and licensed by the government, as are hospitals and airlines. Traditionally, they haven't had to

*"Commerce, Communication and Privacy Online," Louis Harris/Alan F. Westin Survey, Privacy & American Business, © 1997.

give us a lot of information. They file voluminous reports, but most of that information isn't published. At this point, the public pretty much relies on oversight agencies—and precedent—in trusting these institutions.

These long-established, trusted institutions will now be competing with new ones—other financial intermediaries in the case of banks; Federal Express and others in the case of the Postal Service. In the medical field, the competition is less direct, but the advent of health management organizations is dramatically changing the landscape. The new players have a huge disadvantage in that they lack the trust built up—or inherited—by the incumbent players.

Their efforts to earn trust rapidly are having a beneficial secondary effect on the established players: Look how friendly banks are becoming. Look at the pressure on HMOs to disclose their practices, and the Postal Service's new marketing efforts.

The new model for trust

How do you generate trust? Not by saying, "I'm trustworthy," but by revealing information.

Let's look at Federal Express. Before it came along, the Postal Service pretty much had a monopoly; officially it still does on certain kinds of mail. In FedEx's early years (when I was covering it as a securities analyst on Wall Street), it launched a massive advertising campaign just to explain what it was—a hub-and-spokes system that sent everything through Memphis, owned its own planes, and catered to its customers. You can trust us, it promised. Absolutely, positively overnight! You don't need to be big to use Federal Express.

Moreover, Federal Express delivered (with rare exceptions) on its promises.

But the company did even more. It answered the phone; it gave receipts; it knew where your package was when you called. Aside from actually delivering more reliability, this responsiveness to its customers was the edge it had over the Postal Service, where mailing an item was like dropping it into a black hole in the hope that it would reappear again at its destination. People paid a huge premium for this level of interaction and certainty. Federal Express spent a lot to provide it. It had massive computer systems to manage all the data, tracking each package and knowing exactly where to pick it up and drop it off. Its computers were almost as important as its airplanes—and the guy who was then running its computers, Jim Barksdale, is now running Netscape.

FedEx has hundreds of people answering the phone at its call center in Memphis, Tennessee. These people sit in cubicles and answer customer questions, usually by finding information in a huge database that tracks packages, knows customer addresses and ZIP codes, and can calculate rates for any destination. It also manages the special relationships FedEx has with many larger customers—discounts, special shipping arrangements, and the like.

But a couple of years ago, this group of people stopped increasing in number even as package volume continued to mount. Now the customers can do the database querying themselves, without relying on intermediaries in the call center. The customer is in control. She can see exactly where her package went through a series of reports as it was scanned at various collection and shipping stations, and, finally, who signed for it at the end—and exactly when—as shown on page 282. The customer trusts FedEx because she knows exactly what is going on.

But you can also do this wrong—as the Social Security Administration did recently by offering public access to its database. All you had to do was enter your name, your mother's maiden name, and a few more items and you could find out the status of your Social Security account. The problem was, so could anyone else who could find out those few pieces of data. This earnest, laudable effort backfired, ironically, because the Social Security Administration itself was too trusting.

Banks, data banks, and trust

Federal Express handles your packages; other Web vendors take your money and sell you things rather than services. But banks do much

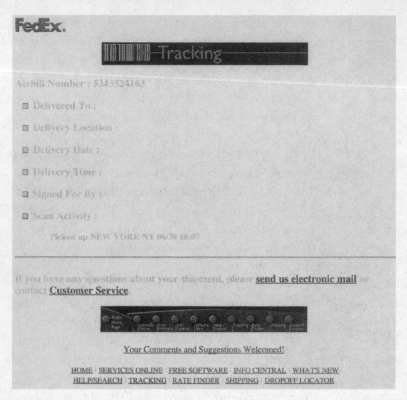

more; they *hold* your money, and they know a lot about you. Building on their special position, banks have the opportunity to play a vital role in the digital age, or to lose it all to newcomers. The battle won't be won or lost by banks as a group, I believe, but by individual institutions—banks and nonbanks—that figure out the opportunity.

There will be some people, maybe you, for whom the confidentiality afforded by systems such as TRUSTe and P3P just isn't enough. You just may not want your name and your data associated anywhere outside your almost direct control. You may be in the public eye and legitimately scared of publicity or you may be paranoid, but there will be services that can give you a higher degree of confidentiality than you can get even by managing your own data. Call them data intermediaries instead of financial intermediaries.

For example, you want to buy a new house and get a mortgage, or you want a new credit card, but you don't want to reveal your financial details to the provider. What you need is a financial intermediary—a bank that will vouch for your creditworthiness without giving up the details on which its assessment is based. (Currently, most banks trade information among themselves, but now you want the bank on your side.) You can maintain your own information privately, but in the end a credit rating is something assigned to you and guaranteed in the outside world; the challenge is to keep the information underlying the rating private. In that case the bank has to take over the financial risk, saying in essence: "We will guarantee your debts, because we know you." For that, the bank must be able to trust you, and it probably wants to know a fair amount about you.

For the benefit of the other side, using a bank as intermediary would also provide some assurance that people will not lie even when they omit information. That is, it's okay not to reveal your income, but it's a little unfair to tell the college development office that you make $70,000 a year, and the Porsche dealer that you're pulling in $120K.

Or you may want to get information about a medical condition without revealing your identity at all. For that, you need a proxy that can manage data on your behalf, selectively revealing facets of your identity matched only to a record in the bank, which would even transfer your e-mail back and forth. It provides anonymity, but it can vouch for you as needed ($\Rightarrow$ Chapter 9). In effect, this third party would manage your online identity, much as VeriSign is proposing ($\Rightarrow$ page 262).

Ultimately, many companies will compete in this market. They will promote their data-safekeeping services and promise special personalized care of the data, competing with specialty companies. The big banks won't allow you much flexibility over how your data is handled, whereas the personal-banker banks, for clients with a lot of money or ones willing to pay special fees, will offer special services.

On its side, the bank or data bank has to select customers it can trust. If they are untrustworthy, it will have to take responsibility for their lies and debts. At some extreme point, these data banks have a legal and social duty beyond their loyalty to their customers, just like regular banks under U.S. law.

Thus, banks are a natural for the role of data intermediaries. Even as auditing firms are the obvious candidate for auditing privacy practices just as they audit financial practices, so are banks the obvious candidate for managing people's data just as they manage their money. The use of banks also establishes an appropriate model: The bank does not own your money; it takes care of it for you. The same with your data.

Chapter 9

Anonymity

We were standing around the barbecue at a spruced-up country inn outside Lisbon, after a long day of discussions about anonymity, censorship, regulation, and the like. I took off my badge and quipped, "I'm anonymous now!"

"Well, I can think of many reasons to be anonymous," leered a bystander, "but I can't discuss them in polite company!"

That's the general attitude to anonymity: You've probably got something to hide, and it's probably disgusting. Good people don't need anonymity.

Well, good people wouldn't need anonymity if

everyone around them were good, too, but there are too many people everywhere willing to take advantage of others' weaknesses, betray their confidences, or otherwise misuse a totally open world. (Of course, in a truly open world blackmail would be impossible.)

Socially, anonymity is a useful mechanism for people to let off steam, explore ideas or fantasies, and hide from social disapproval with a minimum of consequences. Whatever you think of this, it's probably better than the alternative, which is to explore those fantasies or face oppression in real life. It's not that you can't get hurt by emotions engendered online, but you're less likely to. A lot of the anonymous chatter is harmless because no one believes it anyway.

Anonymity may not be desirable in itself, but it is often a rational, best-of-a-bad-situation response to a less than perfect world. Or it may just be an outlet for a kid going through a phase.

My other self

Growing up in the fifties, I didn't know how to be a teenager around my parents, who had emmigrated from Europe after I was born. They were reasonable and flexible, but they would have been nonplussed if I had talked about dating, asked to take driving lessons, started wearing makeup. There was just no concept of "teenager" in my family—only grown-ups and children. I left at the age of fifteen, although for the "respectable" reason of going to college, where I changed identity to become a teenager with a vengeance. It took about ten years for me to feel comfortable at home again.

Had the online world existed, I might have tried out being a teenager online and had less need to leave home—or perhaps the support from outside to stay home and change. I might not even have needed to be anonymous, since my parents probably wouldn't have been in the same circles online, but someone might have forwarded them something I wrote. I might have written something untrue, just because I didn't want to be burdened with my real identity as a slightly dumpy fifteen-year-old with braces and horn-rimmed glasses. I might have wanted to pretend my parents were wicked tyrants—or I simply might have wanted to discuss them in other ways I wouldn't have wanted them to see.

That is one powerful reason for anonymity on the Net: You may be perfectly happy to be open in a specific community—a circle of your teenaged friends, for example—but you might not want to see your words copied out of context, or even read in full by someone outside that community. Think of all the banal or silly or indiscreet conversations you have had over the years at cocktail parties, in movie lines, at kids' soccer games, in locker rooms, among strangers on holiday. . . . Imagine if all that were online and could be searched and retrieved. Haven't you ever told a stranger on a bus or airplane something you might not tell your best friend? Or your mother?

Why else would someone choose to be anonymous? Reasons range broadly:

* discussing personal problems (especially those involving a third party) with others. You could be an abused spouse, a parent with a rebellious teenager, or simply a government lawyer trying to decide if she really wants to stay in that career.
* testing ideas you may not want to be associated with. Are you a politician trying to float a trial balloon? Or perhaps a teenager wondering if there's a case for virginity?
* playing a harmless joke on a friend. This could backfire.
* complaining about anything from messy washrooms to a sexually abusive boss, a corrupt politician, or a tyrannical teacher. Or you could anonymously warn a friend that his job is in trouble, her loud music is annoying the neighborhood, or his kid is skipping school.
* asking dumb questions. One example offered by anonymity service provider Johan Helsingius was that of a C-language programmer who needed answers to some elementary questions and didn't want to reveal his ignorance to his boss.
* trying out a different identity—real or imagined. Many of

these cases have to do with sexual orientation, but they could have to do with age or other aspects of identity. In less innocent cases, people exploit others or pretend to be experts when they're not, and can cause considerable damage. (But this list is about good reasons.)

* rallying support and arousing political consciousness in an oppressive political regime. Often political dissent is crushed because dissidents don't know that others feel the same way. Repressive governments, of course, can also *benefit* from anonymity: It may hide the extent of dissatisfaction and make people afraid to trust one another—which is a downside of anonymity.

* voting—perhaps the most widely recognized and approved form of anonymous behavior. The answer to "Who voted for the opposition?" is properly: No one knows. But their voices will be counted.

Anonymity in practice

Many anonymous communities work perfectly well by their own standards. These include a large variety of newsgroups where people discuss troubling subjects such as addictions, diseases, fantasies, fears, and other potentially uncomfortable topics. Others simply revel in anonymity as part of their culture. For example, there's a strange thing called the Internet Oracle (formerly the Usenet Oracle), where anonymity is accepted and encouraged. People e-mail questions to the Oracle, and other players supply the answers for their own and others' pleasure. That is, you e-mail in a question, and that question is forwarded to another person on the list, who answers it. The organizers cull the best of the questions and answers and post them for all to see. The underlying conceit is that the Oracle embodies the collective wisdom of all the players; he has his own crotchety whims, human frailties, and of course an ever-changing personality. The convention for contributors is anonymity, although it is not required. The system automatically removes people's return e-mail addresses, but the instructions say, "If you do not wish to remain anonymous, you may include a phrase in your answer like 'incarnated as <insert your name and/or address here>.'" Fewer than 1 percent of the contributors identify themselves.

Consider it a giant party game played over the Net. Although it went through a rough spot for a couple of years as a large number of newcomers entered the fray without respect for the Oracle culture, they eventually dropped out and the Oracle retains its spirit of intellectual playfulness. The questions and answers are a mix of pseudomythology, programmer jargon, sophomoric jokes, and truly elegant irony. Entertainment on the Net isn't all virtual reality, video clips, and twitch games.

One of the Oracle's organizers, veteran online user, editor, online columnist, and former English professor David Sewell, surveyed some of the participants about their perceptions of anonymity. He says, "Anonymity provides two crucial advantages: freedom of self-expression, and the shared aesthetic illusion of an Oracle persona. Like college professors who publish murder mysteries or romance novels under pseudonyms for fear of being thought unprofessional, Oracle writers sometimes feel safer when unidentified." In an article published by *First Monday,* an online Internet journal, he quotes some participants and then goes on to explain further one lure of anonymity:

"I think [anonymity is] essential. I wouldn't have the guts to use the Oracle if I knew my name was going with everything I wrote."

"It helps me to give answers which are much more uninhibited. If I knew my identity would be made public I might be a little reluctant to write, since I would not want co-workers to know how much I am involved."

But the second reason for accepting anonymity more resembles that of the medieval author, who, in Hans Robert Jauss's words, wrote "in order to praise and to extend his object, not to express himself or to enhance his personal reputation." The "object" in this case is the collection of a corpus of work by a personality, the Oracle, whose characteristics derive from the collective efforts of contributors. . . . And in fact the Oracle has accreted an identifiable personality. Like a Greek god, he is polymorphous: now a crochety old man, now a super-intelligent computer program, now a deity. A jealous, omniscient, and omnipotent being, he is apt to strike with lightning supplicants who insult him or fail to grovel sufficiently. Nevertheless he is vulnerable to having his plug pulled by his creator Kinzler, his computer's system administrator, or an irate "god@heaven.com." Like Zeus, he has a consort: Lisa evolved from the cliche-geek's fantasy-fulfilling "net.sex.goddess" to the Oracle's companion. It may be that one reason for leaving Oracle submissions unsigned is generic constraint: like Scripture, Oracularities should seem to participants to proceed directly from the voice of God. As E. M. Forster once observed of unsigned newspaper editorials, "anonymous statements have . . . a universal air about them. Absolute truth, the collected wisdom of the universe, seems to be speaking, not the feeble voice of a man." A number of Oracle authors who responded to the questionnaire identified similar reasons for leaving their contributions unsigned:

"I'd put less effort into writing for the Oracle if my identity were public. I prefer the idea of an all-powerful Oracle rather than the various incarnations scenario. . . . Sometimes it would be nice to say, 'I wrote that!' but I prefer to just smile knowingly . . ."

"I don't care who wrote it, but it sort of loses something when I see a signature line. Destroys the myth, so to speak."

"When I read Oracularities . . . I prefer to think of a faceless deity in a cave somewhere, not joe@lharc.netcom.edu. I prefer anonymity."

Anonymous remailers

A wholly different spirit motivates anonymous remailers, which are basically mail-forwarding services that allow people to send e-mail anonymously. Unlike the Oracle or anonymous discussion groups, they are not places or communities in themselves; they are black-box services that allow people to send mail (potentially including spam or harassment) anonymously to anyone or to post in environments where anonymity may not be the norm. At first blush, that might seem a good reason to condemn them wholesale. But the people who run these services tend to be idealists who believe in freedom and free speech, rather than the kind who would abuse these services themselves. And their users have their reasons—including all those listed above.

Obviously, it would be hard for a government to run such a service, since governments are accountable and would have a hard time justifying this activity. Government's role should be limited to allowing such services to exist. For now, at least, the services are not-for-profit—since it's hard to collect bills from anonymous users. That fact also keeps out the more unscrupulous operators, since there's no financial incentive to run such a service and indeed some serious disincentives. In the future, there will be ways to offer such services for fees in anonymous cash, but most users are likely to prefer the free services for reasons that go beyond the financial aspect. A free service just has a stronger feeling of integrity.

In some sense, anonymous remailer operators are self-appointed guarantors of freedom. This is exactly what the world needs: individual citizens standing up publicly and offering others the technical means to exercise their rights—and informally preventing abuses without using the heavy hand of the law.

Anon.penet.fi

One notable example is Johan (Julf) Helsingius of Finland, the country with one of the world's highest proportions of Internet users—almost a million out of 5 million people. Julf started the Finnish commercial arm of the Internet back in 1985, when the Net was still a nonprofit research network. In 1992, operating in the neutral, free-thinking Finnish tradition, he opened an anonymous remailer service called anon. penet.fi, while also running a small consulting company called Penet

Oy to support himself. Finnish law has strong privacy protections, which he assumed would also apply to e-mail, so Finland looked like a good physical location for such a service.

Technically, the service relied on a database of customers with their return e-mail addresses; the messages it sent out were stripped of all identifying characteristics, but they could be traced by someone with access to the information in the database. That also meant that one individual could reply directly to another person's message (either public or private) without knowing where the message came from.

This particular approach is called "weak" anonymity or sometimes a "pseudonym server," since there is in fact a fairly easy way to break the system.* Running such a service is not just a technical matter of setting up an elaborate computer system to remove senders' identities. The provider also has to deal with the social and legal issues that come up when users abuse it. While the messages a remailer sends out are anonymous and usually encrypted, they can generally be traced back to the remailer itself. Depending on the precise operation of the service, the remailer operator may or may not know how to reach the original sender. Spam, at least, is easy to track simply because of its volume. In any case, the operator can block all messages to the complaining party, whether it's an individual receiving unwelcome e-mail or a mailing list, Web site, or newsgroup. (That, of course, stops all communications from the remailer to that party, not just the unwelcome ones.) In this

---

*By contrast, "strong" anonymity requires the sequential use of a number of anonymous remailers, each one stripping off identifying information from the previous sender, until the message is sanitized for final delivery. The message itself is encrypted, along with the addresses, which are decrypted one by one at each remailer. To discover the sender would require the cooperation of all the remailers involved, and would be almost impossible for a single message, although a persistent stream of messages could probably be tracked down. In other words, the recipient of a weakly anonymous message could reply directly to the sender, without ever knowing who he was. Or she could read an anonymous posting and reply directly (and only) to the sender, rather than posting a response publicly. With strong anonymity, there is no way to reply to a private e-mail. And the only way to reply to a posted message is publicly, in the same forum in which the message was posted. Of course, you could copy it and your response elsewhere, too, if you wanted.

way, the community of ISPs and remailers acts as an informal network to stop abusers.

What was anon.penet.fi used for? I asked Julf.

The "usual" range of things, he answered. Political dissidents post anonymously to get information to the outside world—or to others in their own repressive regimes. Well-known examples include dissidents from Bosnia, Indonesia, China, and almost every other country, including the United States. Other posters often had various kinds of personal troubles. Helsingius did not read their messages himself, of course, but he received letters directly from many people thanking him for the service. One in particular he remembers: It was from a man who had trouble finding child care and took a few days off to stay at home with his kids—right at the time his company was working on a big project. He was afraid his boss would find out when he discussed his troubles online. Others, no doubt, used the service to annoy people or to post untrue, scandalous stories.

And another person used it to post—with unfavorable comments—high-level, copyrighted writings of the Church of Scientology, kept secret from all but a few "advanced" members. The poster(s) shielded themselves for good reason: Earlier, three people—a former minister of the Church, the operator of the bulletin board where he posted, and their Internet service provider—were all sued by the Church in a similar situation.*

Often, the remailer operator has to decide on the validity of such complaints, legally and morally. What do you do if a government complains about dissident postings? Or if a company complains about competitive information? It's easier to decide about complaints from

---

*The Church claimed violations of trade secrets and copyrights. Netcom, the ISP, subsequently settled its part in the case by agreeing to take more responsibility for policing its users on copyright violations than ISPs normally do, or want to. The cases against the other two are still pending. The poster, Dennis Erlich, asserts that he is not in violation of the Church's copyrights because his comments and criticism of their works are a fair use and he was exercising his right to free speech. And the bulletin-board operator, Thomas Klemesrud, claims that as a service provider he should not be liable for the content of messages created and posted by his users, because he is a hands-off distributor rather than a publisher.

individuals receiving material than complaints about what the rest of the world gets to see. One decision concerns a person's ability to block stuff out for himself; the other is about the ability to control *others'* speech. Or what if someone claims that anonymous postings are infringing on its copyrights, as the Church of Scientology did? That was the problem that ultimately caused Helsingius to shut down anon. penet.fi.

The situation in Finland was no less sticky than that in the United States. Contrary to Helsingius's expectations, it turned out that Finnish privacy laws—written before the advent of e-mail—don't cover e-mail, on the grounds that anything not specifically included is excluded. Finland, however, is party to worldwide copyright conventions. When confronted with a request from U.S. law enforcement to help identify one of Julf's anonymous clients who was posting the Church's copyrighted material, the Finnish police felt obliged to help and asked Helsingius for the identity of the anonymous poster. Otherwise, they threatened, they would seize his entire database and the computer that contained it. To protect the privacy of his 600,000 other users (sending about 9,000 messages a day), Julf reluctantly surrendered the name. A year later, a similar situation arose, again with the Church of Scientology; this time Julf resisted and ended up in court. Meanwhile, he felt increasingly uncomfortable with his inability to guarantee his users' privacy, and shut the service down in 1996.

Of course, Julf could have blown up his computer—or simply carefully deleted the entire database in an unrecoverable way—and potentially gone to jail for destroying evidence. But he has not given up.* Finland is a libertarian society, and the case provoked an outcry. Now living in Amsterdam with occasional trips to Finland, Julf is working closely with the Finnish government and indeed with the European

---

*Julf would be willing to give up identities in the case of a "real" crime, but who is to determine what is a real crime? Should a tax-exempt church be allowed to use copyright law to protect what amount to trade secrets? Even if Helsingius were comfortable living by Finnish law, would his users be? What about Saudi Arabian law? What if he had to give up the name of a Singaporean posting derogatory information about the Singapore government?

Union to try to come up with new legislation that would recognize individuals' rights to privacy and anonymity—with appropriate exceptions and due process when other laws are broken.

Why anonymity is sometimes not such a great idea after all

Johan Helsingius, the Oracle, and my teenage self all make a good case for anonymity. But why is it not something we want to promote in general?

First, because it can be done to excess and is not always healthy for individuals, though this is a free country and a free Net. Second, because even good people tend to be "less good" when they're not recognized and building (or keeping) a reputation. And finally, because bad people can use anonymity to get away with truly harmful behavior.

Like alcohol, anonymity can be useful in moderation. For some people it's a harmless release and an outlet; others can overuse it and abuse it to avoid everyday responsibilities and challenges. No, you should not just go and live the rest of your life anonymously online, flitting from identity to identity. Nor should you drown yourself in alcohol, lose yourself in gambling, or escape into drugs. The Net can be an addiction like any other, although it is probably easier on your body than most of them.

It may not be nice to say it, but people do not always behave well, and therefore a little social pressure can be a good thing. For example, I consider myself basically "good," but I'm a lot less nice in airport lines (for instance) than in places where I know someone. Haven't you ever lost your patience with a clerk or a waiter and then been embarrassed when you found out someone you knew was watching? Unfortunately, I have! (This is why people usually behave better in tight communities than in big cities, and tourists abroad behave in ways they wouldn't at home. Consider the well-known reprimand: "Would you do this in your mother's home?")

If you want to be scientific rather than moralistic about it, consider a variety of experiments in game and market theory. The basic finding of all of them is that people work together best by telling the truth, on any task from avoiding jail to setting prices for goods. Sometimes people can gain a short-term advantage by lying, but they usually can't benefit in the long run. Over time markets work better and produce better average outcomes, when people (1) tell the truth and (2) can earn a reputation for doing so.

When people operate anonymously, there's no incentive to tell the truth; dishonest people easily betray others for their own gain. Overall, anonymous markets don't work well. The wrong people get put into jail; the market prices are volatile and misallocate goods or investment; investment doesn't take place because no one can count on long-term gains. Overall, everyone is worse off on average, and the crooks do better than the honest people. However, they must always live in fear of encountering even bigger crooks. (This all sounds to me very much like the current situation in much of Russia. It has markets, yes, but it lacks the rules of disclosure and accountability that make them work.)

But the issue isn't just markets: Visibility leads to healthier communities in general. There should be occasions and places where anonymity is practiced but they should be clearly marked. The worst difficulties arise when you get something in between—especially when people pretend to be other, known people rather than anonymous characters, as happened not long ago in one of the first online communities.

The experience at the WELL

The WELL (perhaps too cutely, it stands for Whole Earth 'Lectronic Link) was started in San Francisco by Stewart Brand, also founder of the Whole Earth Catalogue. It attracted an elite crowd of early adopters. Brand had earlier been part of one of the first online services, called EIES (for Electronic Information Exchange System). On it was one small group of scientists and corporate people who were using it for an ongoing conference in the early '80s. That group had a brief but devastating encounter with anonymity. Recalls Stewart (by e-mail, of course): "They were all respected men and women with responsible

Anonymity vs. pseudonymity

First, let's define anonymity and privacy: They overlap, but they are not the same thing. Anonymity is the lack of identity; privacy is control over the use of confidential information about a specific individual. Privacy means keeping information about a particular individual or a communication between individuals or within a group confidential. Privacy is a contract between identified individuals and other holders (not owners) of information about the person or his actions. Ideally, the information can be used only by certain people and for certain purposes, and is kept from the public. An individual can get a measure of privacy, legitimately or otherwise, by maintaining multiple identities.

By contrast, anonymity keeps an individual's identity from disclosure even as he makes statements or actions *in public*. Anonymity gives people privacy, but it is not quite the same thing. An anonymous individual has no identity.

Then there are pseudonyms, where a person takes a name that is not his legal one, and establishes a fake, but persistent, online identity. If Joe Klein had managed to write a second novel without being discovered, he would have had a persistent pseudonym. You could argue that everyone starts out as a pseudonym, and ends up becoming the person represented by that name. . . .

Anonymity allows someone to attract public attention for a statement without reference to the person who said it or to his previous comments—and no accountability for that person. That is, an anonymous person has no reputation; a pseudonymous person may build one or several (or hide a previous one).

Then there's a sort of middle ground: You don't care who the person is, but you do care about his credentials or his vested interests. Is Doctor Alice really a medical doctor, or did her upwardly mobile parents just give her the name "doctor"? Is Fred a user of WonderWidgets, or a salesman in disguise? Is Juan really over twenty-one, as he claims?

Aside from the heavy-duty anonymity servers, there are many newsgroups where *some* people post anonymously or pseudonymously. (Their anonymity is protected more by convention than by technical force, as in the Oracle.) And of course, you often can't tell. If someone called Henry Higgins posts, what does that mean—other than to the people who know Henry Higgins in the flesh? Even then, how are they to know it's the same old Henry?

In almost any real community—as opposed to a place where people can express themselves but there's no shared investment in the "community"—people build up identities and reputations over time. If someone pretends to be nice online even though he's really a nasty old man, is that a fake identity? Or just his true nature expressing itself? Do many of us in fact have true natures that we're ashamed or otherwise deterred from expressing?

positions in the world. Suddenly one of them was behaving like a 'you can't catch me' prankster. The whole discussion swerved to dealing with that. Amusement turned to resentment and then turned to distrust and distaste. The group fell apart online. The bad odor from that experience lasted for a long time."

That experience led Stewart to make personal identities required on the WELL. Besides, many members already knew each other offline; others joined the community online and then met face-to-face. Over a couple of years, the few hundred members formed a tight little community, full of friendship and gossip, petty rivalries and deep affection, a few romances, some shared secrets . . . a normal community. Then a group of members decided to start a subgroup that allowed anonymity, in spite of Brand's skepticism—but he figured the results might be different the second time around. They were not.

Strange things began to happen. First people posted unpleasant truths, attacking one another. In such a tight little community, it was pretty easy to figure out who was saying what—and trying to guess was fun. Then people started pretending to be one another, and it became harder to tell what was going on. Says Stewart in retrospect: "Because the people actually knew each other, they could pretend to be one another more convincingly. They could reveal secrets. It was far worse than a group of strangers could have been."

He continues: "Now, there were several conferences on the WELL where it was permitted, almost encouraged, for people to say absolutely vicious things about each other, and the strong WELL opinion against censorship made those conferences as sacrosanct as any other.

"But anonymous parody was apparently unacceptable where accountable viciousness was okay. Several people asked Cliff Figallo, who ran the WELL at the time and who used to work at EFF, to shut down the Anonymous conference, and he promptly did. Nobody mourned. The experiment lasted at most two weeks with the world's most permissive online community.

"The two experiences add up to a proof for me. They were wholly separate—different systems, different people, different times. Both had fairly high-minded expectations of anonymity online. Both failed horribly. Different pathologies emerged and became decisive in the two occasions. On EIES, one of a close, trusted group turned into an unaccountable demon and never recanted. On the WELL, people pretended to be other people destructively. In both cases, trust was the casualty. It was easy to destroy; hard to rebuild."

Problems with anonymity

Relatively speaking, the WELL was a mild case. Far worse than its tendency to foster bad behavior (and perhaps allow people to work out their hostilities online rather than in real life), the fundamental argument against anonymity is the third one cited on page 302: lack of accountability for serious wrongdoing by seriously bad people. You might not want your neighbors to know you occasionally exercise your right to read pornography—or that you're the one who keeps correct-ing the school principal's grammar. But if you're abusing children and posting the pictures online, then what?

Indeed, the possibility of anonymity is one of the scariest features of the Net—for parents, for law enforcement, for employers hiring new workers, for victims of nasty rumors, scams, and other misdeeds. It's troubling for merchants who want to know who their customers are, for debt collectors, and for others to whom obligations are owed.

On the other hand, anonymity is also a problem for repressive gov-ernments who want to know who is criticizing them, for maniacs who want to track and pester people they're obsessed with, for con artists trolling for new victims, and in general for people who want to know others' secrets. For anyone, anonymity can make it hard to assess the reliability and value of information.

Accountability

If society suspects someone (for whatever reason) of a crime, what right does it have to find out who it is and catch that person? Presum-ably, the same right online as offline. If it can find the person, following due process with appropriate search warrants and the like, society should be able to prosecute him. There is no ISP-client privilege similar to attorney-client privilege. But at the same time, people should not be forced to make it easy—just as the law doesn't force us to live without window shades or to use postcards instead of letters in envelopes.

In this sense, anonymity online is akin to conditions we take for granted in the terrestrial world. If we required each shopper to show an ID each time she entered a store, that would certainly both reduce crime and make it easier to catch criminals, but it is not likely (thank goodness!) that we will do so in the United States. Law-abiding citizens in the United States are not required to carry their documents with them, although they must do so when driving a car, buying a gun, passing a border, or getting on an airplane. All these are infringements on our liberty, but we accept them (or most of us do) because they reduce real risks. But I don't think the risk someone will do something bad is large enough or grave enough to require forcible identification of everyone online.*

That means that anonymity in itself should not be illegal. There are enough good reasons for people to be anonymous that it should be considered part of the normal range of social behavior—at least in some places on the Net (again as in real life). That also means that using an anonymous remailer in itself is not grounds for suspicion.

Crime and anonymity

There's a difference between online crime and online evidence of offline crime.† The first is basically some kind of information crime—for example, posting copyrighted materials. In many countries, posting certain kinds of material—such as pornography, hate speech, and anti-government material as well as libel and slander—is also a crime. Sexual material involving real children is illegal, even if someone is only distributing it and had no contact with the actual children. One problem with these Internet-based crimes is deciding whose laws apply: those where the item is posted or those where it is received.

A single online posting by someone unknown probably won't do much damage, but a persistent criminal can usually at least be blocked if not found. At the very least, the site where such postings appear

---

*On the other hand, as a matter of etiquette, I wish more people would use sig files, those automatic signature lines that say who you are, list a physical address and affiliation, and often include a clever saying or exhortation. So often I get mail from "John" or "drj" or no signature at all, and their e-mail addresses—for example, DJA@msn.com or RCRI@aol.com or snarky@online.ru—don't help much. These people aren't trying to hide their identities; they're just being careless. My own sig file, for what it's worth, includes my physical coordinates, the dates of my next two conferences and the saying, "Always make new mistakes!" My alternate sig file (only some packages support that) is a listing of the cities I'll be in over the next few months. I often use it when I'm trying to schedule a meeting with someone.

†Other crimes include anonymous security breaches and attacks; they are a more serious problem, but not one that could be solved by outlawing anonymity (⟹ Chapter 10).

could delete them; responding to such complaints (within some reasonable constraints) will be the job of any Internet service provider. In other words, the ISP does not need to screen material itself, but it has to respond to the complaints of people who are injured by it. The service provider can either mete out its own justice, ranging from small sanctions to cutting the customer off entirely, or refer him to law-enforcement agencies ($\Rightarrow$ Chapter 6).

Offline crimes

In other cases, the posting itself is not criminal although the acts referred to are: for example, discussions about actual crimes. Then law enforcement may have a legitimate interest in finding the poster, if only to collect evidence.

So, assuming there's a real crime somewhere, what do you do? The fact that anonymity is legal does not mean that police cannot use whatever means they have at their (legal) disposal to overcome it. In technical fact, there is a broad range of anonymity. The commercial online services offer extremely limited anonymity: You can pick a fake name, and of course you can have several accounts, but America Online and CompuServe generally know their customers. After all, they send them monthly bills. There's usually a physical address; there's certainly a credit card or a bank account that can be traced to a physical person.

At the other extreme, people can be almost impossible to trace if they manage to infiltrate someone else's system remotely—which is generally a crime. The commercial services and ISPs (and the remailers) generally do what they can to help law enforcement when they get official requests; the problem (especially outside the United States) is more often overaggressive legal interference by officials still afraid of this new medium.

Even seriously "anonymous" users are usually pretty easy to trace. Fortunately, from the tracker's perspective, most online criminals are persistent. That is, someone keeps sending harassing mail to just a few people or keeps posting copyrighted material to the same few locations. Tracking people is a typical law-enforcement exercise online or offline.

Usually, the criminal eventually does something stupid, online or of-fline. Did he flee the scene of the crime in an automobile? Did he log in from home? Did he stay online so long in one session that he could be traced? (One notorious cracker fell asleep at the keyboard and typed several hours' worth of "ppppp"s; he was eventually caught.) Are there witnesses? Did he confess to a friend or use an accomplice? In most cases, law enforcement is not uniquely dependent on the Net to catch a criminal. There's no real reason to outlaw anonymity just because some criminals happen to use it.

First line of defense

Right now, Internet service providers, and especially the online service providers such as America Online and CompuServe, have a variety of policies, or terms of service, concerning the confidentiality of their customers. They mostly just want to avoid trouble. They would really prefer to cancel people's accounts rather than get involved with the law.*

They won't give out much specific information about an individual to advertisers (probably more for commercial than ethical reasons), but any law-enforcement officer with a warrant can pretty much see what you've been up to for the last few days: What have you sent and re-ceived, what have you looked at, what have you purchased, what have you posted? (A fellow customer usually can't discover someone's iden-tity, although he can ask to have any sender blocked.)

ISPs should disclose to their customers what sort of policies they have in this respect. When there is a problem, they should warn people first, and with luck stop the problem before it reaches a point where law enforcement has to step in. When the police do call, what do the ISPs ask for before giving up the identity of a customer? Do they warn

---

*Unfortunately, they can also get sued when they *do* cancel people's accounts. America Online tried to block mail from aggressive spammers to protect its own customers, and got hit by a restraining order under the guise of freedom of speech and the customers' rights to receive mail they might want to read.

him? In general, they have no real choice, but the rules are still unclear. What do the police have to do? What notice, if any, must the ISP give to a customer? The ISP should make its policies clear and consistent. In addition, it should have some policy about how to respond to complaints from other people—including the recipients of spam or other unwanted e-mail, people or publishers who claim their copyright is being infringed, and so on.

Like it or not, the ISPs will probably find themselves caught between their customers and the law from time to time. In the same way, U.S. banks don't much like reporting large cash transactions to the government, but they do so, in exchange for the privileges they get as banks. In essence, ISPs rather than national governments can be the guarantors of their members' good behavior—which overcomes much of the problem of jurisdiction.

Could strong anonymity become widespread?

There may be cases where anonymity is hard to crack, but they should be relatively few. From a law-enforcement point of view, the tougher problems generally concern not anonymity, or what is published or sent by unknown people, but secrecy—where known people engage in secret communications. That is, anonymity is a problem for crimes committed by the posting itself; secrecy concerns the use of the medium for crimes offline—such as arranging a terrorist attack, organizing a murder, or coordinating a drug cartel ($\Longrightarrow$ Chapter 10).

In the end, we need to *handle* the dark side of anonymity rather than outlaw anonymity as a whole. We're better off living with the current loose-around-the-edges situation that fosters freedom with certain trade-offs. Any attempt to automate the process of granting anonymity would probably render it more or less traceable . . . and would certainly draw attention to its users. If rampant anonymity becomes a problem, there will be time enough to deal with it. In fact, I think the danger is more likely to be in the other direction—too much government surveillance and too little privacy.

What was the real crime?

Part of the problem with the Internet right now is that it keeps getting pointed to as a factor in all kinds of heinous crimes. In the fall of 1996, for example, a bomb in a ketchup bottle exploded in a Hungarian village. The police immediately went to the local Internet service providers and asked for the names and addresses of all their users. They could easily have asked for all the users' e-mail messages and probably would have, but the real culprit was soon discovered. It was a teenage boy with a roomful of chemistry books and bomb-making instructions—but no Internet account.

The police might as reasonably have gone to all the local grocers to find out who bought that particular brand of ketchup.

Similarly, last year Belgium went through a substantial political upset precipitated in part by police negligence in the abuse/ murder of several young girls. Somehow the Internet kept getting mentioned in conversations about these murders, but try as I might I could find no connection. It was about the same time that the *Observer* newspaper in London was running its stories about child porn (and a year after a similar uproar in the United States perpetrated by a later discredited article in *Time* magazine).

And then there was the Heaven's Gate cult in the United States. The members made a fairly good living as Web site designers, but they were hardly the "Internet cult" that some media described. The Net was merely their medium, not their message, which was a confused combination of science fiction, movie lore, and pseudoreligion.

Rather than the Internet, it sometimes seems to me, the scare stories should focus on car manufacturers, since almost all criminals and crazies use cars. Of course, that's a little disingenuous. People understand cars; the Internet is still a scary mystery.

Anonymity vs. accountability

There's a powerful conflict between the need of society for openness and transparency, and the need for individuals to have the right and ability to speak anonymously. Those who make public statements should generally have some obligation to stand up and be counted, but they risk reprisals from those who have power and use it unjustly. The resolution should offer a legal right to privacy and anonymity for private persons, but within a culture that favors openness and transparency. In a truly just society anonymity would be unnecessary for public critics, but it's still a valuable protective device for those who may be unpopular or at risk from more powerful elements—especially in an unjust (whatever that means) society.

Yet for a society to be healthy overall, its members need to be known. In particular, public companies, public officials, and others in positions of trust should have limited rights to privacy and anonymity. Even private companies should by and large disclose their ownership, especially if they sell to governments or other powerful organizations. Moreover, those who want to reveal relevant information about public figures and organizations should be able to do so with a certain amount of legal protection—and a certain amount of legal accountability.

Getting this balance right—especially when it involves dissidents against repressive governments or companies—will be a challenge. How do we protect both the whistle-blowers and the victims of unreliable or vindictive whistle-blowers? There may well be communities where anything goes—and where intrepid reporters venture to find leads. The information within those environments would be considered unreliable; information published outside them would be held to higher legal standards of truth and accountability.

Webs of trust

In contrast to anonymity, pseudonymity is fairly easy to deal with, because it assumes that there is a persistent identity and someone accountable if something goes wrong. What is a pseudonym anyway? The question is whether you can use the name to find the individual.

MESSAGE FROM ESTHER

One of my favorite stories, true or not, concerns Conrad Hilton, founder of the famous hotel chain. He was appearing on a nationwide television show one night, and the host said to him obsequiously, "Mr. Hilton, you're a famous man. Movie stars have slept in your beds; business tycoons have supped at your tables. Mr. Hilton, tonight all of America is watching you. Do you have anything to say to them?"

Mr. Hilton considered for a moment, and then looked straight into the camera: "Yes, I have just one thing to say. Remember, the shower curtain goes *inside* the tub."

I've been hoping for just such an opportunity, but in the meantime, here's what I would say if I could address the whole Internet:

First of all, use a sig file. That stands for "signature file," and it's the clever thing at least some of my correspondents put after their message (see footnote on page 300). Sig files work automatically in most e-mail software; you write them yourself to say who you are and list your affiliation, address, and contact information.

Unfortunately, not even a sig file covers everything. There are a lot of useful tricks to using e-mail that make it a better tool for both sender and receiver. Some are formal etiquette; some are just tricks of the trade.

So the next one is: Use a helpful subject line. Some messages I get have no subject, which is bad enough. But the ones that say "Message for Esther" are even worse. Clearly, someone took a moment to write that. But it's absolutely useless. I *know* it's a message for me; that's why it's in my inbox. And the sender can see from his outbox whom the message was sent to. Yes, some people have e-mail addresses like "rick519@aol.com," so it may be difficult to remember who they are. (Hi, Rick!)

And then there's the message called "Meet May 20"—which is great, except that it's a reply to a reply. It's now about a meeting on May 19 . . . I've almost missed many an appointment that way! Indeed, it's not a sin to rename a conversation thread; experienced (and socially adept) e-mail users often send messages with titles such as this: "Cosy evening at nightclub?; Was: Lunch to go over documents."

Recently I found a several-months-old message from a stranger in my inbox entitled "Greetings." It turned out to be an interesting business opportunity; I apologized and tried to pick up the thread a couple of months late. After several messages back and forth it's still pending . . . The most recent message in the thread ("From" with e-mail address deleted to protect the guilty, but it's one of those unintelligible ones anyway) was this, in its entirety:

Subject: Re: Re: Re: greetings

yes, june 16 on the peninsula is possible. i leaving in two hours for moscow and will be there till evening of june 4. then i am back to Berkeley for a few days and off to do some continuing work for CO-DETEL in domincan republic but back in california on june 13.our meeting at your convenient location, thanks, paul

Forgive me, but I can't remember what I told him about locations, or even (to be honest) why it was I wanted to talk with him. (And no, I don't know what CODETEL is, either.) If he would just copy the previous conversations so I had a little context . . .

True, that would require some judgement, because another annoying habit some people have is to send around strings of messages that date back 12 or 18 messages, complete with sig files, the addresses of everyone who has received a copy each time, and so forth. So yes, provide context but not baggage. The most elegant way to do this is with the delete key, replacing the missing text with the word "SNIP."

Think about what your recipients need to know to answer properly. Imagine that your e-mail is nestled among 70 other e-mails. Will they be able to pick it out? No, exclamation points !! don't work!! Nor does THEIR OWN NAME. The word urgent—if you don't overuse it and you explain why—sometimes works. But you can get a reputation for overusing it.

Once you handle the basics, you can even get clever. In my own office, we now have a convention I'm proud of instituting. We take phone messages in the format of "Name, company, phone number" in the subject line. You can open the message to find out details—e.g. "Fred says never to call him again!" Or, "Wants to know why your article is late." But once you know what's inside, you can return the call without reopening the message.

Furthermore, when possible, we take the e-mail address of the caller. That way I can return the call by e-mail, with a copy to my assistant. I get my own message right back to the caller, and my assistant knows what's going on. If the person calls back because (shame!) he doesn't read his e-mail, my assistant can then relay the answer I wrote. (Sometimes, too, the caller gets to see how his message got mangled on its way to me. On occasion, I delete something before copying the message back to the caller, for example, "He was pushy." Or I change "this guy" to "this gentleman" or simply the person's name.)

Then there's how to use the copy function. To me, this is a large part of what makes e-mail more than just a fax system—along with the ability to copy and paste, edit, and string threads together. As a journalist, I find e-mail incredibly valuable for checking my facts—which is even more important than just collecting them from the Web! You can use the copy function to forward messages to people, college comments, organize a dinner for eight . . . and annoy people no end. It's nice to keep third parties informed of what you're up to using "reply to all," but not beyond their likely level of interest. You can also use copying to bring people into a conversation; (see the e-mail exchange on page 206) for a little of what I mean.

The point of all this is to think more about the purpose of any communication. (Yes, the title of this essay was ironic!) The communication doesn't end when you send the e-mail, but when someone else reads and understands it. It's your job to make the message easy to respond to—that is, if you want a response. If not, by all means be cryptic. It's the e-mail equivalent of calling at midnight to leave a voice message with no phone number. (The people sending marketing messages who don't want a response but rather an order by phone are another matter entirely.)

Well, what can I say now but . . . SNIP!

A person with a true name but great privacy might be just as hard to locate as one with a pseudonym but lots of "tracks." So it turns out that pseudonymity is like anonymity; it comes in a range of strengths. The relevant question is not, Is this really Fred Bloggs? But, Can I find Fred Bloggs if I need to? Or, Is his credit information accurate?

No one should mind much if Fred Bloggs uses a fake name and is accountable for all he does under that name. The problems crop up if he uses that identity to hide from accountability for what he does under another name, including conflicts of interest. For example, no problem if Fred buys stock in WonderWidgets, unless he happens also to be Fred Jones, who works for the company that has secret plans to take over WonderWidgets.

Or suppose Juan misrepresents himself as a Toyota owner in an online forum where he spreads lies about alleged problems with his car, but in fact he works for a competing car company and is spreading lies on its behalf. Or Alice may promote the benefits of WonderWell herbal tea without disclosing that the company is paying her a commission.

These sorts of things go on in the real world as well, but people tend to be more gullible and less likely to know whom they're speaking with online. By the standards of the U.S. Federal Trade Commission and the U.S. Securities and Exchange Commission, what Juan and Alice are doing is illegal, but they are unlikely to end up in court. By contrast, Fred could well be prosecuted if his ruse were discovered.

What can we do about them without dragging in law enforcement, with its attendant costs and bureaucracy? In most cases markets should work, with a little bit of customer savvy.

Just as with other media, people will start to discriminate between reliable and unreliable sources. When you want a reference on a doctor, you don't ask a stranger. You check with someone whose judgment and ethics you trust. You expect them to give you a fair recommendation, rather than a name out of a phone book. Or they may give you the name of a friend with a medical problem similar to yours who knows the ideal doctor.

What neither you nor your friend does, probably, is call the local licensing authority. People rely on networks of trust, not hierarchies. There's no top point, no single center through which all the recommendations flow, but rather a decentralized web.

How are bad doctors or hairdressers or sleazy promoters exposed? Some of them never are. And some who are otherwise capable may have their reputations ruined by a mistake or two. That's what happens in real life.

Such webs of trust are still scarce on the Net; they are harder to build because people can more easily move around. But that is why they are more necessary than in "real life": You are far more likely to encounter and deal with people you don't know. Some of them will be in a commercial context; others will just be people in a variety of local communities. The community managers will have an incentive to do some quality control, and the community members will have a place to complain to.

Many communities may require some sort of identification/certification system based on people's roles rather than their specific identities. It should not be centralized, but it should be strong enough for people to rely on. For example, at a health site you would like some assurance that people describing their experience with various medications are not working for those vendors or getting some other benefit for their comments. Do I need to know the life history of everyone whose comments I listen to? No, and there are a lot of undisclosed part-time salespeople in real life, too. But this is the kind of regulation that a site manager could foster. Separately, moderated discussions could provide some assurance, but who's moderating the discussions?

And now for a message . . .

This all leads to the problem of confusing advertising material with editorial content. The free world had clear conventions for this when media were one-way: Respectable newspapers made it clear what is advertising and what is editorial (and tried to avoid government propaganda altogether).

It gets to be more of a challenge when "publishers" are not just corporations with access to a printing press or a television broadcast operation, but anyone with access to e-mail or a Web site. Over time, readers have learned to distinguish between the *New York Times* and the *National Enquirer;* viewers have learned to distinguish between Charlie Rose and *Hard Copy*. But how are they to distinguish between Juan, who moonlights as a salesman for Miracle HeartTabs, and Alice, a cardiologist with years of clinical experience? Alice has a friendly way of posting that makes her sound approachable but not necessarily expert, whereas "Doctor Juan" fills his postings with impressive medical mumbo jumbo. Should their sig files be regulated by law? In the old days, if you went to visit Juan, you would find an office with a dime-store diploma on the wall, in impressive if counterfeit Latin. If you went to see Alice, you'd see a similar diploma—except that it happens to be real. What's the online equivalent? And what are the enforcement mechanisms?

In the long run, respectable medical schools will probably make lists of their graduates available on the Net, and anyone can check with them to verify someone's alleged credentials. But is the person online really who he claims to be?

Honesty begins at home

All these questions will ultimately drive most users to defined communities or to search for validated labels for many of their activities and interactions online. On the medical site, we don't care about Juan's driving record or his country; we do care whether or not he's a doctor, whether or not he's getting a commission from vendors of the products he discusses, and whether or not he actually received his degree from the place he cites.

Disclosure covers more than just financial issues. One of the most germane—and it applies far more broadly—is conflict of interest. Does the person have an undeclared motive for what he is saying, offering, or proposing? Does this person really have the degree from Oxford that he claims? Was he really an advisor to the chairman of Shell or to the president of Brazil?

What connections does this person have—to a vendor, an institution (is he saying nice things about Harvard because his son is applying for admission?), or even another person (is Alice saying nice things about Juan because Juan is membership chair of an exclusive club Alice wants to join?)? This last example is almost beyond the scope of any kind of formal regulation—yet it's the kind of situation that causes people to lose trust. That's why I think people will ultimately join communities where the members are known for at least part of their lives.

Real-life experience

As I sit here writing this chapter on anonymity, I have just received a strange missive from a stranger, someone calling himself ******. I have no idea who he (?) is, but he knows a fair amount about me. Nothing he couldn't have read somewhere; it's probably not someone I know. But it's familiar enough: He knows the shape of my family, some of my background (Russia), and he's clever enough to make some inside jokes that only I could appreciate. How much do I want to say here? If he's obsessed with me, surely he'll be reading these words, too. As Carly Simon sings: "You're so vain, I bet you think this song is about you." But it isn't, it's about the other one; take that! Whatever, this person hasn't harmed me, asks nothing of me other than to read his quite clever ramblings.

What should I do? His e-mail comes from a commercial service; I could probably track him down if I wanted to. But why should I? To ask him to stop? Time enough to do that if he starts bothering me. First, I could filter and automatically delete everything he sends. If I got seriously unpleasant or threatening mail, I could go to his Internet service provider and ask it to ask him to stop. But the best approach is probably simply to ignore it.

Yet it feels creepy. And I have to compare it with several other anonymous messages, from a single (different) source, that I got after attending a conference last fall. They referred to two other people, one of whom was at the conference and one of whom wasn't. Could the messages have been from one of the people I had met there? Certainly, they spoiled my memory of the previous three days. These particular messages were quite obscene and offensive, but in some sense they were less troubling than the one I just received. This writer didn't seem to know much about me other than my gender; his comments were graphic and disgusting, but they had nothing to do with me personally. And besides, I was one of three well-known (in the Internet community) people he was attacking; the messages seemed to come *from him* rather than *to me*. It's invasion of privacy coupled with anonymity that's so creepy in this other, more recent message.

All these messages are the result of a trade-off I have made. I have become well known, and now strangers can write to me anonymously and disturb me. I could filter them out, taking mail only from people I know, but that would be ridiculous. As time passes, presumably I will become even more visible and get more e-mail, some of it helpful and enlightening, some of it wasteful of time, and some of it no doubt hurtful. That's the trade-off I'm making, and one I'm increasingly aware of. But I do have the choice.

Choice is what I want to preserve. Other people may choose differently. I would like the choice of having a secret e-mail account for my special friends. Perhaps I'd like to join some communities under a false name, if only to avoid the assumptions people will make when they hear my real one. While anonymity gives other people the opportunity to annoy me and others, it also gives me the opportunity to avoid those annoyers.

What will I do when they start posting lies, not just to me but to the world at large? That's when it gets more troubling. I hope I'll have the fortitude to live by what I say here. At the same time, I hope people in general start to get wiser. It's one thing to read a lie about yourself in the *New York Times,* another to read it in the *National Enquirer.* It's one thing when it's said by a friend you know, another when it's said by someone who doesn't even dare to publish his name. Why honor him with attention?

Chapter 10

Security

Imagine if cars were sold without locks. You'd have to buy your own, and ask the dealer to retrofit your car or drill the holes in the car doors yourself. Of course, if the car manufacturers hadn't figured it out, there would be a Midas Muffler–style industry of retrofitters. It was once the same with car radios, but the manufacturers quickly wised up. As for locks, cars got them almost as soon as cars became enclosed and lockable.

Ridiculous as lockless cars might seem, this *is* the situation currently with software. People (including me) routinely send their e-mail "in the clear," as if it were postcards rather than sealed letters. Each

Windows PC now offers a simple password but little more; call it a closed door, not a lock. Many people leave their systems on overnight, freely available to the cleaning staff (or anyone masquerading as cleaning staff). Besides, passwords are hardly the most reliable way to secure a system. Better methods include challenge-and-response, where the system asks a random question from several to which only the user knows the answer. Someone who somehow captured a user's log-on still couldn't log on in the next session without knowing a lot more than a stranger would.

People might encrypt their e-mail and use effective protection measures if it were easy and painless, but it is not. The standard e-mail packages—Microsoft, cc:Mail, Eudora—do not offer encryption; Lotus Notes does, but as a default only between Notes users on the same system. If a customer wants security, he usually has to assemble the technical pieces for himself, and there's only a minimal culture of security among the user base as a whole. Most people have an experience or two with computer viruses, and then they go out and buy an antivirus package. They're also accustomed to having their machines crash once in a while and some learn to make local backups, but they rarely store sensitive or vulnerable data at a secure place off-site. Insurance companies rarely even ask about the computer risks that they cover as part of an overall insurance policy.

This somewhat casual attitude to computer security as a whole coincides with a rather paranoid attitude—but few solutions—to security on the Net. People don't worry enough about security internally because they don't perceive a threat, yet they don't expose themselves to the security risks of the Internet because Net risks are perceived as a problem without a solution. Most people and companies simply treat the Net as an unsafe place; they don't risk much on it. They behave like people who never travel with too much cash in order to limit their potential losses.

Ironically, most "Net" security risks don't actually happen on the Internet; they happen at either end of an Internet connection, where an intruder gets in or some information gets out. The information is used over the Net, but it is vulnerable offline as well. That means that "Net" security risks are not limited to online communications and transactions. It's just that the Net increases the amount of information we use, the amount of business we conduct electronically, and the possibility of strangers getting inside to where the real damage can be done.

The challenge is that people won't do much about computer security until it is a problem—and we'll only succeed if it is *not* a problem. Currently, computer security is not a normal part of daily life, but most people do okay anyway and many of the problems that do exist are not reported. But we do need security for the Net so that we can have a situation closer to how people use credit cards: where you can take financial instruments or information of considerable value with you wherever you go, where you can conduct transactions relatively safely and conveniently, where you can count on people to be who they say they are.

Contradictory perceptions

Meanwhile, most breaches of security aren't publicized; compromised companies feel stupid and don't want to advertise their vulnerability. While computer vendors want to sell security tools and consulting, they aren't particularly eager to advertise about security problems; like the airlines, they'd rather pretend they don't exist. (Companies specifically focused on security, such as antivirus or firewall vendors, are exceptions.) Many surveys estimate the actual losses at hundreds of millions of dollars that are never reported, in everything from liability for lost data, business interruptions, fraud, lost work time, release of damaging information, and other causes. (Direct financial losses are small, but I know of three involving more than $10 million that happened to banks; there are many others that have not been reported.)

So what does make people aware of risks? Mostly unfortunate experiences. When I was growing up in bucolic Princeton, New Jersey, we never locked the door. Once we went away overnight during a summer weekend (before air-conditioning) and when we came back we discovered we had actually left it half open! No big deal: No one had gone

A word from an independent expert . . .

I have included this excerpt from a New York Times *essay by George Kennan, who is ninety-four years old and has nothing to do with cyberspace. But he's one of the world's wisest people, and he has everything to do with human nature and the nature of governments.*

SPY & COUNTERSPY by GEORGE F. KENNAN
New York Times, 18 May 1997

It is my conviction, based on some 70 years of experience, first as a Government official and then in the past 45 years as a historian, that the need by our government for secret intelligence about affairs elsewhere in the world has been vastly overrated. I would say that something upward of 95 percent of what we need to know could be very well be obtained by the careful and competent study of perfectly legitimate sources of information open and available to us in the rich library and archival holdings of this country. Much of the remainder, if it could not be found here (and there is very little of it that could not), could easily be nonsecretively elicited from similar sources abroad.

In Russia, in Stalin's time and partly thereafter, the almost psychotic preoccupation of the Communist regime with secrecy appeared to many, not unnaturally, to place a special premium on efforts to penetrate that curtain by secretive methods of our own. This led, of course, to the creation here of a vast bureaucracy dedicated to this particular purpose; and this latter, after the fashion of all great bureaucratic structures, has endured to this day long after most of the reasons for it have disappeared.

Even in the Soviet time, much of it was superfluous. A lot of what we went to such elaborate and dangerous means to obtain secretly would have been here for the having, given the requisite quiet and scholarly analysis of what already lay before us.

The attempt to elicit information by secret means has another very serious negative effect that is seldom noted. The development of clandestine sources in another country involves, of course, the placing and the exploitation of secret agents in that country. This naturally incites the mounting of a substantial effort of counterintelligence on the part of the respective country's government. This, in turn, causes us to respond with an equally vigorous effort of counterintelligence in order to maintain the integrity of our espionage effort.

This competition in counterintelligence efforts tends to grow into dimensions that wholly overshadow the original effort of positive intelligence procurement that gave rise to it in the first place. It takes on aspects which cause it to be viewed as a game, played in its own rights.

Unfortunately, it is a game requiring such lurid and dramatic character that it dominates the attention both of those who practice it and of those in the press who exploit it. Such is the fascination it exerts that it tends wholly to obscure, even for the general public, the original reasons for it.

It would be interesting to know what proportion of the energies and expenses and bureaucratic involvement of the CIA is addressed to this consuming competition, and whether one ever stacks this up against the value of its almost forgotten original purposes. Do people ever reflect, one wonders, that the best way to protect against the penetration of one's secrets by others is to have the minimum of secrets to conceal?

George F. Kennan is professor emeritus of historical studies at the Institute for Advanced Study in Princeton, New Jersey.

in, and we weren't particularly alarmed. But since then, crime has risen in Princeton as it has all over the United States. Now, when I go to visit my parents in that same house, there's an alarm system and we always use keys.

Does this mean we need to have some well-publicized computer security disasters before manufacturers start offering security as a standard? I hope not.

Complexity of security

One group trying to forestall Net-security disasters even as it raises awareness is the Highlands Forum, a discussion group sponsored by the Defense Department to look at the impact of the Information Age on the future of national security—everything from information warfare to social norms, economics, and the security of the national information infrastructure. The question is not just how to wage war or ensure peace, but "What is it that we are fighting for?" The group, mostly business types and academics as well as military people, meets irregularly at sites such as the Santa Fe Institute and the Naval Academy at Annapolis.

At one recent meeting, we briefed the new chairman of the President's Commission on Critical Infrastructure Protection about security risks on the information infrastructure. One point we made is that the "information infrastructure" is more than just what the government owns or used to control: the telecommunications infrastructure, the power grid, and the Federal Reserve and clearing banks. It includes all kinds of communications media on the ground and in the air; it includes private Internet service providers and their host computers; it includes everyone's PCs and all the software (mostly Microsoft) that runs on them. It includes servers in private companies and the federally managed air-traffic control system. At a stretch, it includes all the people with access to these systems: the financial clerk, the sysop, the software designer, the teenager using his parents' Internet account—and of course the malcontent you fired last week.

The more we all use this infrastructure, the more vulnerable we are when something goes wrong. It used to be that only banks needed computers to function; now most elevators, factories, department stores, and the like would shut down if their computers stopped working. Governments, businesses, hospitals, and insurance companies maintain huge databases of sensitive information about individuals; military operations run and are planned on computers; nationwide and international power grids, financial markets, and telecommunications systems all run on computers. Security threats include both malicious attacks from within or without, and random disasters such as fires burning a building containing computers, power-grid outages due to heavy loads or accidents, and system failures due to software bugs or other mistakes.

On the other hand, security is not something individuals or even companies can handle for themselves. One weak link in the chain affects everyone along it, whether it's a central telephone switch that shuts down or a compromised computer system that lets a cracker use a back door to get from a bank into its clients' data, from an accounting system into the payroll department, from a university into a technical research lab. It's similar in some ways to public health: You have to wash your own hands, but you rely on the guy next to you not to sneeze in your face, the canning factory to sterilize your tinned tuna, the office building to maintain its fire escapes. Some of the components are required by regulation; some are just social obligations most of us observe.

A short primer on encryption

Encryption is basically just a fancy word for code—everything from Morse code, to the signals you may have used with your best friend, to German—which we sometimes used in my family so that strangers couldn't understand us when we were out in public. (How many German-speaking people we inadvertently insulted I'll never know!)

With computers, encryption can be made almost automatic, so that you can encrypt messages you send out with little effort. In the old days, you had to have some way of getting the key to the intended recipient, so that he could use it to decrypt the message. However, using new mathematical techniques, you can send a message to anyone using the recipient's "public key," which security-conscious people now include in their messages. (It's that long string of digits and letters that follows "-----BEGIN PGP SIGNATURE-----" you may see on some e-mail.)

The public key is basically a very long number. To simplify, suppose you converted the letters in your message into a number, which technically it is anyway, a very long one. Then you perform some complex calculations with the two numbers. You send the result, which produces the original message only when combined with the private key corresponding to the public key. So anyone can use the public key to encrypt a message, but only the owner of the corresponding private key can decrypt it. Very clever.

Conversely, if someone gives out his public key and encrypts his message with his private key, anyone can use the public key to verify that the message really came from the designated sender. If you combine the two, you can keep the message secret, *and* guarantee the identity of both sender and receiver. An encoded communication can't be changed without detection by anyone without both keys.

The concepts are very simple, but each message is almost completely safe—as long as you use long enough numbers for the keys. The same technology works not just for keeping secrets, but also for guaranteeing authenticity and integrity: These encrypted messages won't be just love letters or secret documents or compromising materials; they can also represent sums of money and designated recipients that cannot be changed—useful for electronic payments. Without a recipient and with a few other technical additions, such a message can be used for e-cash, redeemed ultimately by a bank. Or the messages can represent orders, commitments, and other documents whose integrity and authenticity must be guaranteed.

Interestingly, encryption is one of very few powerful technologies that do not have a destructive downside. . . . About the worst it can do is protect criminals from detection or keep shady electronic transactions secret.

We need to have similar complementary approaches to protecting the security of the information infrastructure. It can't be done by central forces monitoring everyone under their sway, top-down, like an army. Nor can it be done effectively by regulation, as, for example, environmental regulations. What we need is a public-health approach. That means a security-oriented version of the Centers for Disease Control (which exists—it's called the Internet Engineering Task Force), but we also need an immune system—something that recognizes and overcomes intruders, even when they appear in new guises. Harder still, it should even notice "authorized" people from inside when they turn bad and start to deviate from normal behavior patterns.

Governments and the case against encryption

Like the Highlands Forum, the rest of the U.S. government is concerned about security, but I believe it is taking the wrong tack. Its basic angle now is to slow down the development and use of encryption, despite reports from a variety of scientific and advisory organizations recommending the opposite. It has imposed restrictions on the export of encryption technology that deter producers from developing it at all, since it's complicated to create two versions of each product (one for domestic use and one for export). The government also wants to make the management of duplicate keys into a regulated activity (where a user has to deposit a duplicate key with an authorized third-party escrow agent, a system called "key escrow"), rather than a security practice under the control of users.

The Russian and French governments are likewise concerned about widespread use of encryption and are trying to control it through a variety of restrictions, including not just export controls and key escrow, but also outright restrictions on its use. The European Union is still trying to come up with a coherent policy. Meanwhile, the right to privacy is enshrined in the Japanese constitution, which ironically was written under the guidance of U.S. General Douglas MacArthur after World War II. Many other governments just haven't addressed the issue yet. To a large extent, they're waiting to see what technology leaders such as the United States do.

That's why—as in so many issues concerning the Internet—U.S. policy is so important.

The foundation of the governments' arguments against encryption is that encryption makes it difficult for law enforcement to do its job

---

From "Jonathan J. Prinz" <jjprinz@invenet.com> [New York-based identity branding consultant]

As Hitler refugees, we also grew up in a "European" household and, like you, used German as a code in public places. Conversely, it was always interesting to eavesdrop on German speakers who never imagined the kids on the bus understood a word of what they were saying.

of detecting and tracking criminals when people can send secret communications over the Internet. It used to be that criminals' activities required border crossings and left physical traces. Now, criminals can conduct almost all of their business undetected over the Net. Governments fear terrorists running loose, drug dealers conducting business freely, lowlifes of all kinds plotting crimes and laundering money over the Net . . . while governments are powerless to detect or monitor them. Criminal organizations can operate globally in secret, passing borders and spreading information and cooking up plots out of anyone's sight. Terrorists could conceivably attack a bank or a government facility from the safety of an outlaw foreign country, causing chaos from afar.

Certainly this vision is plausible. Eventually criminals will be using the Net along with the rest of us. These are not spurious threats. The question is whether they represent a new, unique danger that must be stopped, or simply the inevitable use of a powerful new tool by criminals who must be stopped, but not at the expense of our day-to-day freedom.

The case *for* encryption

If banning encryption were effective in fighting crime (which it won't be), it would be worth considering. But in fact, just like locks in cars, widespread use of encryption technology would help prevent crime, by giving individuals, businesses, and governments as well as criminals the means to protect themselves. To transform a much-used saying: "If we outlaw encryption, then only outlaws will use encryption." The drug dealers and terrorists will be able to find unscrupulous programmers to develop powerful encryption for their own purposes, but the rest of society will lose the benefits of encryption for legitimate purposes—including protecting themselves from criminals. The people who might use encryption to hide their misdeeds would abuse its absence to spy on people or misappropriate property or even identities.

Computer security: a matrix

Computer security, broadly defined, depends on two interacting factors: technical systems and social norms. Cutting across another way, there are intentional and unintentional breaches of security. Also, you have to consider what's inside the system and what's outside.

	Technical	Social
Unintentional	Bugs, crashes, viruses, loopholes	Lost passwords, errors, carelessness
Intentional	Code-cracking, Trojan horses, viruses	Disgruntled employees, bad guys

Of course, all these factors interact. Security loopholes require bad guys to take advantage of them; careless employees can cause the inadvertent proliferation of viruses created intentionally by bad guys. Good security measures are still vulnerable to bad actors who are trusted (including government officials, whom you must "trust" by law), and technical security means little when employees are careless with passwords.

In an open society, there are always some criminals who go unpunished by the state. In a totalitarian society, the criminals *are* the state. Having spent considerable time in Russia, I'm more concerned with protecting the weak against the strong than with empowering governments; both governments and individuals can be good or bad, but governments almost always have more power. Moreover, even though some criminals may go uncaught because government authorities weren't able to monitor their conversations, most criminals are caught through their own stupidity, or because some member of a gang decides to confess or to tip off the police anonymously. The larger any criminal group gets, the more "leaky" it gets, too.

In practical terms, this means that governments should allow and even encourage the development and use of strong encryption technology. Encryption is one of the few powerful tools of modern technology that is entirely defensive: It protects information and privacy, and provides the underpinnings for safe electronic commerce, confidentiality, integrity of communications, and the privacy of individuals, to say nothing of the police's own communications. Without it, the Net can never be the safe, secure environment glibly forecast by politicians and computer companies. The government's approach—which amounts to, "you can use encryption if you let us or an authorized third party keep the keys"—limits everyone's ability to keep truly private things private, and also raises the specter of keys in the hands of people you didn't choose.

On a political/commercial basis, encryption technology is a lucrative commercial marketplace in which the United States is rapidly losing its lead to other countries, notably Japan, where the laws are more liberal. Siemens Niedorf, the giant German company, is selling a security system with strong encryption from free-trading Ireland, unrestricted by the constraints that hamper its U.S. competitors. Thus as a practical matter, there is little hope of stopping the development of encryption technology worldwide. There is only the possibility of stopping U.S. citizens and U.S. companies (both vendors and users) from benefiting from it.

Now, however, other parties are beginning to weigh in. The White House is leading the charge with Ira Magaziner's Framework for Global Electronic Commerce ($\Rightarrow$ Chapter 5); this document points out that strong security, including encryption, is vital for electronic commerce to flourish (although it more or less supports the key-escrow plan). That's nice, but hardly surprising. More interestingly, over at the Highlands Forum, at least some of the military (as opposed to law enforcement) are beginning to look at security from a new perspective: Instead of seeing lack of encryption as a way to help catch criminals, they see it as a threat to the overall robustness of the information infrastructure they are ultimately trying to protect.

In Congress, there are different bills promoting each side of the debate. Their provisions keep changing in committee in response to the debate, but they never seem to reach a full vote. Indeed, in 1997, five House committees passed inconsistent versions of the Security and Freedom Through Encryption (SAFE) Act, originally introduced by Representative Bob Goodlatte (R-VA), but the bill has not reached the House floor for a vote. SAFE as introduced would relax current Federal export restrictions on strong encryption, and would prohibit the government from mandating key recovery. Senators John McCain (R-AZ) and Robert Kerrey (D-NE) introduced the Secure Public Networks Act last year, based on Clinton administration proposals. Since it stayed in committee, they are now circulating a revised version. The original bill would require key recovery for all federally funded networks in the U.S., and for all encryption products that the federal government purchases. It would also codify the current 56-bit export limitation, but would allow the Commerce Department greater flexibility to relax those rules.

In May 1998, Senators John Ashcroft (R-MO) and Patrick Leahy (D-VT) introduced the E-Privacy Act, drafted with input from the industry group Americans for Computer Privacy. The bill would allow export of all encryption products that are generally available on the international market, and would prohibit the U.S. government from requiring key recovery or limiting domestic use of encryption. The bill would, however, prohibit encryption of incriminating documents, and would establish a National Electronic Technology center to facilitate decryption of information obtained by law enforcement through authorized wiretaps.

Meanwhile, a court case (*Bernstein v. Department of State*), brought with the help of EFF among other parties, last year upheld the argument that software merits free-speech protection under the First Amendment. That is, the export restrictions cannot prevent authors from posting their encryption software on the Internet. The Justice Department promptly appealed the California district court decision, but the

Bernstein side won, establishing some free-speech protections for encryption. However, a more recent case in another jurisdiction (Ohio), *Junger v. U.S. Secretary of Commerce*, directly and explicitly contradicted the Bernstein ruling and upheld the government's export restrictions.

Sorry you asked? The short version is that the argument continues . . .

How to make it happen

Other than using or banning encryption, what should we be doing about security?

Like perfect health, we cannot hope to achieve perfect Net security; there will always be the technical equivalent of local epidemics, accidents, and the like, but we need to avoid overall social vulnerability on the Net. So much depends on individuals, which is why security needs to be managed bottom-up by everyone, rather than top-down by an omniscient (and locally corruptible or overzealous) government. After all, it was doctors learning about the importance of washing their hands and sterilizing their instruments that made such a difference to public health at the beginning of the twentieth century. We need an equivalent approach to security—along with the equivalent of the notion that officials should publicize and promote hand-washing practices.

The question is how to make this happen. Clearly, making appropriate products available and easy to use is a start. But how to encourage their purchase and use? Advertising with celebrities bragging about the security of their networks probably won't cut it. A more useful approach is probably closer to safe investing than to safe sex.

How do we create an environment where good security is the norm? Any individual has some control over his own security, but he shouldn't have to be a walking fortress. That's a kind of loss of freedom, too—even though it may be "voluntary." People shouldn't have to hide their identities on the Net; they should be able to communicate freely without being assaulted; they should be able to trust most others they encounter.

There is a way this can happen, and with good luck it will. But first it will take a little bit of bad luck—enough to persuade people that they should take measures against computer/online risks.

The costs of security, one way or another

It's 2004, and you're trying to renegotiate the insurance policy for your business, an established online service that sells turtle ties among other things. You've just opened a new data center in Barbados, where skilled employees are still available and taxes are low. The insurance agent, Alice, whips out her handheld device with its wireless Net connection. She presses her fingertip to its surface, then asks for yours. (ID check, of course.) Seconds later, she has downloaded your record to look at: minimal losses over the last few years, except for that unfortunate incident when the ex-employee took your business down for two whole days by deleting several crucial files remotely from his new home in Peru. (After that, you put in a stronger firewall to keep out electronic intruders and started a new policy of updating access privileges.)

Then Alice continues: What kinds of security do you have beyond the firewall? Do you regularly encrypt messages and information? How do you keep your client records secure? Who has access to your intranet? Do you use the latest in biorecognition—fingerprints, eyescans, and the like—to authenticate employees and avoid the well-known security risks of guessable or wandering passwords? Do you have filtering software to keep out viruses and offensive content, and to keep employees from sending out sensitive information? Are your payroll files kept separate from your client records, and are both of them securely encrypted? Are your employees trained to make sure that strangers don't "happen" to sit down at a company computer and fool around? Do you back up your data with a third party that keeps it safe at another site? What about your encryption keys; how do you safeguard them? Who does your programming? Have you had your security practices audited recently? Do you have a privacy policy? Do you want coverage for privacy liabilities?

Well, you've been meaning to get around to all these things, but you've been busy. Besides, the cost . . . The last time you bought insurance, Alice didn't ask you all these pesky questions.

You're right, Alice replies. She tells you that the insurance industry has just gone through a couple of its worst years ever because of computer-security breaches. There was the class action, covered by her firm, against the health maintenance organization that had all its patient records posted on the Internet by an angry high-school student who failed a drug test. There was the phone company that somehow had all its billing records for the month of April 1999 wiped out by an intruder. It recovered the $100 million it was owed, yes, but not from its customers; Alice's insurance company paid. And then there were thousands of less-publicized incidents where small businesses and individuals suffered various kinds of computer/Net-related damages and recovered from their insurance companies. In the past, says Alice, insurance companies were facing a competitive market and couldn't afford to lose business by turning down customers who might lack proper computer security; it took a couple of bad years for the industry to come to its collective senses and start trying to limit the risks it was insuring.

So now you have a choice: You can continue on your merry way and pay outrageously high rates, or you can call in a computer expert or an accounting firm to do a full security audit and follow their recommendations.

Creating a corporate market for security

This is how we can build a robust security environment without top-down laws, regulations that don't keep up with the latest technology, or a draconian system where the government is in charge of everything, including your spare encryption keys.

The idea is quite simple: Instead of regulations, promote the concept of insurance requirements for security risks—and disclosure for those dealing with others who want to go without insurance.

Whereas with data privacy you can have a contract with the party to whom you give your data in a transaction, in security strangers are often vulnerable to the acts of other strangers. The trick is not to make everyone liable and create a highly litigious climate when security *is* breached, but to foster a way of reducing the risks beforehand. That means getting the insurance industry and a cadre of security experts into the act with so-called loss control (reducing losses) as opposed to "risk management" (sharing the burden financially). That is, avoid the losses in the first place instead of redistributing their costs when they occur. The insurance industry has a history of doing this: In the United States, companies have been writing fire insurance since Benjamin Franklin started his private firm for "Insurance for Houses Destroyed by Fire" and pushed local officials and homeowners to concentrate on loss prevention—fire and building codes. Over the years, as fires continued, such codes got stronger and stronger. The insurance industry also instigated the creation of Underwriters Laboratory, which tests everyday products, especially electrical devices, for safety.

As awareness of Net security risks rises, insurance companies are likely to do the same in this area. Already, some leading insurers such as Chubb Corporation are developing experts who can design and validate security systems for a large base of corporate users, and IBM is offering insurers a "boot camp" on Internet security and business risks—figuring that secure electronic commerce can only be good for its business.

There are two more sectors involved. The financial community—investors—will be taking increasing interest in these kinds of risks, much as it is looking at year-2000 risks. Even insured risks will have an impact on stock prices, bond ratings, and judgments by other decentralized "authorities," just as other kinds of liability risks do now. Some security analysts will specialize in the field, and industry specialists will call on them when they are assessing companies—especially ones in relevant areas such as finance, telecommunications, and information systems. Overall, the interest of the financial community will raise the attention paid to security even as insurance companies raise the price of forgoing it. Smaller companies that don't need to raise capital won't be burdened by all this, but they will still have to buy insurance.

And finally, there's you, the public. On the consumer side, you could get a virus from a careless friend—or an unfriendly stranger. Juan could share a password to an online service and then find himself socked with a huge bill—or worse, responsibility for an offensive message sent by someone else. On the business side, the potential risks are far greater. Any of Alice's clients could lose money, compromise information about its customers, see its system shut down, let someone invade its employees' privacy, lose trade secrets, or find itself unable to serve customers. Companies that want to deal with the public will need to assure their customers that they are reliable, both in their services and in how they use their customers' data. Companies will be rated on their security practices not just by investors, but by third parties representing customers' interests, such as privacy watchdog TRUSTe and its likely competitors. After all, TRUSTe validates security *practices* as well as good intentions.

Fostering the technology

In addition to widespread expertise, we also need the tools for experts to use. That means not just encryption technology, but products and systems that incorporate security technology in a way that makes it easy for users. And it also means reliable products.

The market in principle works to ensure product reliability and integrity. Unfortunately, it does not yet actually do so. For a variety of mostly historical reasons, computer users—especially PC users—tolerate glitches that would quickly put any toaster, car, or airline company out of business.

This part of security depends primarily on good product design and implementation. The industry's problem is that almost as soon as anything almost works, the vendor starts "improving" it, in the Silicon Valley syndrome ($\Rightarrow$ page 84, Chapter 3). It gets better features that don't quite work yet—but that can be highlighted in competitive advertising and selling. Large, experienced, failure-intolerant customers often resist such new systems because they know they are untried and unreliable. That's why Bill Gates was right when he called banks dinosaurs (even though he recanted later); they can't afford to be newer.

How the Net fosters product reliability

The challenge is to make the new technology work reliably. Over time that should happen, as customers become more demanding. But there is a way that process can be speeded up, and the Internet information market is helping it to happen by spreading news of unreliable products more quickly than before. Manufacturers themselves are happy to spread the news about reliable products. The most telling example but only one of many was in late 1995, when Intel came out with an unreliable chip. A couple of scientists posted the news that the chip produced errors in certain circumstances. Intel ignored the news—to its later embarrassment. Soon word was out all over the Net, and the company eventually replaced the chip for anyone who asked, gave refunds, and finally apologized for its poor handling of the whole affair.

Now such incidents are commonplace. They no longer create as big a stir, but word of product imperfections is often widely circulated, spurring companies to fix them quickly or avoid them in the first place.

Unfortunately, development is simultaneously being speeded up, so the overall reliability has stayed about the same: poor. (As I wrote this book, one file—the governance chapter—kept crashing MS Word, and I never figured out what was wrong.) Moreover, many of the reliability problems are not a particular vendor's fault; they occur when different systems are hooked together. Sometimes the engineers doing the implementations are inexperienced; often systems that work fine on their own do unexpected things when hooked together. Overall, security systems are cumbersome to use and unstandardized. The trick is to find your spot in the arms race between exciting new technology and dull old reliability.

Innocent carelessness plus bad intentions

But most security risks ultimately involve people—careless people or bad people, and often both combined. People everywhere are trying to get into systems in order to steal valuable data, find out secrets, or even just cause havoc. The first line of defense is passwords, firewalls, and other barriers, but they often don't do much good because they are used carelessly. People pick obvious passwords, such as their own names, their birthdays, a child's name, that can be easily guessed. If you must, use the second (or third, or last letters) in the words of a favorite saying or book title and throw in a number or two; just don't use one that a lot of people know you like. For example, I would *never* use "R2DFLIADA." (But it's better than "Esther" or even "NO-SYDE.") Or people write the password in a notebook or (worst of all) on the computer itself. They lend their passwords to others and don't change them frequently enough. Meanwhile, firewalls tend to be rigid and inflexible, and employees often bypass them. Companies need more specific access controls, which are often complex to administer.

Internal threats

In fact, most security threats come from within—from coworkers, fired workers, trusted customers, consultants, anyone with access. When the Russian parliament held hearings about the Internet, its major security concern was how to keep foreigners out. The U.S. government and many companies, by now, realize that many threats come from within. These internal threats include both intentional mischief by disgruntled employees and others, and carelessness by employees who may be disaffected or simply thoughtless.

The best tack is to limit possible damage by keeping good control of information within the company as well. That is, payroll data should be kept separate from overall accounting data; competitive information and trade secrets should be revealed only to people who need to know that kind of information, and so forth. It's all pretty simple—but so rarely practiced.

Internal security is the toughest area to manage since employees have to be trusted in order to do much that is useful. One way to do it is to detect the bad guys; a better way is to grow your own good guys. That is, companies that trust their employees tend to get trustworthy employees—although they are more vulnerable in the end.

Overall, it comes down to human judgment. The greatest challenge in security is not keeping people out, but determining which people to keep out.

Chapter 11

A design
for living

I began this book by telling you about my own life and how it both formed and reflected my understanding of the world. As you finish reading it, it's your turn to reflect and act on these issues in the context of your own life.

Just as a child can't get an education over the Net, you can't hope to design your life on the Net on the basis of a book. Nonetheless, I hope I have been able to lay out some of the landscape in a way that makes this new world more intelligible and its structure visible.

Many things are familiar on the Net: the same people with the same emotions and motivations, the same frailties. But the Net puts the same people in a new situation. In doing so, it makes everything different: power shifting away from the center toward individuals and small organizations, more fluidity and continuous change, increasingly irrelevant national boundaries. The markets for attention and information are almost as friction-free as those for money.

In each sphere of life on the Net, the opportunities for individuals (and the potential for conflicts between individuals exercising their rights) are enhanced. In work and education and your personal life, you have greater choice—and a greater role not just in choosing but in shaping the organizations and people with whom you deal. You can set your own rules of engagement. In the sphere of intellectual property, you can be not just a consumer but also a creator: an ongoing participant in commercial and noncommercial intellectual processes. You can set your own standards for content, for privacy, for anonymity, for security.

Why you?

As I wrote this book, I kept thinking of Oscar Wilde's ironic comment: "The trouble with Socialism is that it takes so many weekday evenings." In other words, caring about politics and the general welfare is a good idea, but it really cuts into our normal lives.

From: "Jonathan J. Prinz" <jjprinz@invenet.com> [New York-based identity branding consultant]

[Despite] the tremendous potential (and reality) of communications, the internet is largely an individual experience. This is not to say that two (or perhaps more) people can't or aren't communicating, or even that large numbers of people are not exposed to the same information. What's different is that they do so on demand and on their own. This is a very different thing from our experience heretofore where we have been informed by the collective experience beginning with community meetings, church/synagogue services and culminating with global TV—the 1963 March on Washington, JFK or Diana's funerals and, for those who are into it, the super bowl. This has obvious implications for advertising, but also societal issues. I think.

On the Net it's different. Politics and the general welfare are a part of life. The choices you make affect others, because this new world depends on its citizens rather than its history. On the Net, your choices and actions in everyday life will have an impact on the texture of life for the people around you on the Net, an impact potentially far broader than in the terrestrial world. In the terrestrial world, the choices you make in voting or buying products are mostly limited to options offered by established institutions, and the results are summed up centrally. On the Net, you can range more broadly, and your behavior will help create the tone of the communities you live in. Your choices for disclosure and security can foster an atmosphere of trust and openness, as will your demands for the same from others.

Even in the terrestrial world, "government" means more than legislation and funding and administration of programs. Governments can also set a moral tone and influence what we consider proper behavior. Unfortunately, they don't always do it right. But the kind of governance I'm talking about on the Net (through agencies that are truly chosen and managed by citizens) does have a chance of getting it right, if *we* get it right. We have to do it for ourselves. Like businesses of the future, the governing bodies of the Net will focus more on design of rules and their enforcement, and less on administration, regulation, and routine processes.

Realistic idealism

You could read all this and say, "All this idealistic stuff will never happen. People are passive. Lots of them can't even read. Every time I open a newspaper I read about another vicious crime, venal politician, or unscrupulous businessman. The rich are greedy and the poor are lazy."

It's true that every time I read a newspaper, I wonder about my hopes for the new good life on the Net. But in the end, this is not a book of description; it's prescription. It's what you *can* do. . . . That's why I'm addressing this book to individuals, not to governments or businesses (although it is also addressed to individuals in government and business). Whatever sphere you operate in, you have a broader capability than ever before to change it for the good.

As you go out and explore the Net, you have to trust yourself and your own common sense. In a decentralized world, you no longer can or should leave all the decisions up to someone else. Precisely because the Net has and needs fewer broad rules than most environments, it depends more on the good sense and participation of each of its citizens. Broadly speaking, the real world gets its flavor from institutions; the Net gets its flavor from its citizens.

The one thing required of you is to make use of the Net's powers. They are like a Bible on a shelf or an exercise machine in a den—not worth much unless you do something with them. The Net is a tool for some purpose, whether that's getting ahead at work or avoiding work to do something more amusing or fulfilling. You now have more freedom and more responsibilities in everything from how you handle (or change) your job, to how you interact with the government, to how you establish a new friendship.

On the Net, there's a profusion of choices—content, places, shopping environments, discussion groups. Most things are free. Even—especially—the pleasures. You may complain that you're overwhelmed with choices. In the old days, life was simple. Not too many choices, and a structure you could easily complain about because you could never hope to win.

Now you've won, and the world is asking you to make some proposals. You could just leave all this opportunity alone and probably carve out a fairly pleasant life for yourself anyway. The Net will offer you wonderful opportunities as a consumer, and it will make your daily life easier.

But when you have choices, making no choices is itself a choice.

Indeed, the biggest opportunity of the Net is that it allows you to go beyond choosing and start creating. The Net is uniquely malleable: It lets you build communities, find ideas, share information, connect with other people.

Exactly what you do with all this is up to you. You have your own interests and capabilities. My hope is that what you do on the Net will change your offline life, too, by making you less willing to accept things the way they are and more sure of your ability to build a life to suit yourself and your family. The trick is to set your own priorities.

The person to whom I dedicated this book, Marek Car, is an example. Born in Poland under Communism, he forged his own path, becoming a computer expert and a reporter dedicated to the truth, however uncomfortable it might be. He spent several years in Russia as a reporter for the Polish Press Agency, where, among other topics, he reported on the Russian computer scene. He returned to Poland to become high-tech adviser to a formerly local politician whom he had long ago helped to hook up his personal computer. That local politician, Waldemar Pawlak, had become the prime minister of Poland. Marek used his position to start Poland's Internet for Schools program—a visionary effort to connect Poland's schoolchildren to one another and to the world. When Pawlak lost power, Marek joined Poland Online, a commercial effort I'm involved in, as chief editorial officer—convinced as ever that the Net is a medium for society as well as for commerce. He continued to play an active role in the Internet for Schools program. He died early in 1997 in a car crash.

He did much more in his short life than many of us will do in much longer ones.

No, we can't all be heroes. But Marek didn't walk around feeling like a hero. He simply set his own priorities and worked to achieve the goals he had set for himself.

Design rules for living

To put it back in the context of the Net, the point is not that everyone should do the same thing, but that everyone should contribute in his own way, for his own online communities. It's the very diversity of approaches that makes the Net, and life, so exciting and so rich. I would hate for us all to do good the same way. (That's the totalitarian side of the socialism that was to prove such a disappointment to so many well-meaning believers in human perfectibility.)

Nonetheless, there are some underlying principles—design rules, if you will—that do hold true across a broad range of situations. Most of them have very little to do with the Net per se, although they have their own character on the Net. These design rules underlie many of the issues I have covered in the book. Basically, they foster involvement, disclosure, clarity, honesty, respect for yourself and others.

Like most design rules, they're general. The magic is in how you actually apply them. And like most rules, they can and should be broken on certain occasions. In fact, that's the first rule:

Use your own judgment

This rule applies off the Net, too, of course, but many newcomers are tempted to defer to other people in a new environment. You should defer to their knowledge, yes, but you can still make up your mind for yourself. As I've tried to show in many ways, the technology really doesn't change most relations between human beings or what's right and wrong. The Net simply gives you greater ability to find a situation you like or abandon one you don't.

The Net provides an exceptional opportunity for you to find what you want—whether it's a product, a group of friends, or a merchant who respects your privacy. If you're a parent, you can control what your child sees or where she goes to school. If you're looking for work, you can find an employer you like and work you respect. Does your employer respect its customers? If not, move on. Remember that the market doesn't run on money alone. It means you have choice.

Disclose yourself

Let people know who you are and what you stand for. Explain your biases and vested interests. Ask the same of the people and organizations you deal with. Especially on the Net, clarity is helpful. Remember how confusing things can be to someone without context. For example, don't assume that the person you're dealing with knows who you are or what your motivations are. Explain whether you're looking to do business or just trying to be helpful when you answer someone's question. Let people know (politely) if you disagree with them; they may have a good answer to your arguments.

And don't regard secret information as power. Hoarding information and secrets doesn't really make you powerful; it just leaves you vulnerable to exposure.

Trust but verify

It is better to be a sucker than a jerk, but it's best of all to know you can trust the people with whom you are dealing. The Net will provide an increasing number of ways to check the credentials of strangers and organizations. Do your part by being honest when people want to know more about you or come to you for references—but understand that what you say may be quoted.

Ask for and use systems such as TRUSTe and other validation and authentication tools. Make sure you know with whom you are communicating. And as it becomes technically easier, start encrypting your e-mail for your own security and that of your correspondents.

Contribute to the communities you love or build your own

Be an active member of the communities you join. There's nothing more satisfying than creating a community in collaboration with others. If you can't find a community to accomplish something you think should happen, design and build your own. I'm working on such a project, to send free medical information to Russia over the Net and get it translated locally. Most good things start with a single person who saw a need or an opportunity and persuaded some others to join in. Besides, a good community is fun.

Assert your own rights and respect those of others

The golden rule—do unto others as you would have them do unto you—is particularly suited to the Net: It's the ultimate in two-way interaction. Remember that the Net gives other people more choice and more power, too.

Decide for yourself (and your children) what kind of content you want to see and what kinds of e-mail you'll accept. Ask your suppliers and Internet provider for tools to help you do so. And, of course, don't let other people (even me) tell you what to do.

Don't get into silly fights

If you forget this rule, the visibility you will have on the Net is likely to remind you. (Too often, people get into ridiculous flame wars that are embarrassing to all who watch.) In general, it is easier to walk away from conflicts on the Net than it may be in real life. You can refuse to read someone's mail and refuse to let him provoke you once you've left an argument. Just don't let public postings lure you back in.

If something or someone is holding you back or annoying you, you don't need to take on the system as a whole. In many cases, you can bypass the offending person or entity. You don't need to overcome it; maybe you can compete with it.

Ask questions

There's no better way to learn. Being a reporter taught me how much you can find out by asking questions and listening to the answers, even if you thought you already knew the subject. You have to be humble and willing to appear stupid. It's amazing how willing people are to tell you things if only you're ready to listen. I built my career on it. (Just don't ask the same question twice!) The Net is a great place to ask questions, because you are more likely to be able to find someone who knows the answer.

Be a producer

Being a consumer is fine; it helps the economy, and it lets you get the products you want. But don't let the real promise of the Net pass you by: to be a producer without all the overhead that used to accompany producing—factories, printing presses, broadcast stations, government infrastructure. On the Net, you have the choice of all the things that are offered—and the choice to make and offer your own.

For example, you can design your own Web page. For a bigger challenge, you can design a whole community. Look at any of the 210,000 (at last count) online discussions. Most of them were designed by individuals with something on their minds.

Be generous

My aunt Alice (really!) has been important in my life, offering support and counsel and unconditional love. I have never really paid her back; there's no way to. But whenever some young woman asks me for a favor, I think of the real Alice, who lives in Winchester, England. So when someone does you a truly generous favor, don't worry about paying them back (if they want to be paid back, they weren't being generous). Do a favor for someone else. When I help people, it's often in honor of my aunt.

This rule, too, is not Net-specific. But the Net often makes it easier to be generous and do small but important favors—anything from forwarding a résumé from one friend to another, to sending an e-mail of congratulations to a friend, to posting a message asking if anyone could use the old sofa you no longer need.

Of course, true generosity is when it *does* cost you something. Give your time. Give your attention. It's the only thing you have to give that's uniquely yours.

Have a sense of humor

Enough of "In cyberspace no one knows you're a dog" already! The Net is the all-time best medium for the dissemination of jokes, and I find new ones every day. The Net will be a dull and sterile place if we can't also have a little fun. But a sense of humor is more than just laughing at jokes. It means not taking life too seriously. Laugh at problems even as you try to fix them. A perfect world would be boring; an imperfect world offers opportunities for humor.

Always make new mistakes!

This is my all-time favorite rule for living. I like it so much that I use it as my sig file—the little quote that gets inserted along with my address and other coordinates at the end of each of my e-mails. I still have new mistakes to make. The challenge is not to avoid mistakes, but to learn from them. And then to go forward and make new ones and learn again. There's no shame in making new mistakes if you acknowledge them and benefit from them.

Now design your own rules

Please feel free to borrow these rules. Or improve on them for yourself. Good luck!

Acknowledgments

Like the Net, my life is decentralized, and I owe thanks to many people all over the world and all over my life for helping me to produce this book. I could start at one end, with my parents, all three of them, and the five sisters and one brother and numerous nieces and nephews whose lives I hope it will improve. It is from my family that I got the grounding in love and security that makes me want to make the world better for those less fortunate. My parents gave me great freedom, but they also expected me to be responsible for the consequences. That allowed me to recognize the same feature on the Net: huge powers and corresponding responsibility.

Or I could start at the other end, with my editor Janet Goldstein, who helped me turn my manuscript into a book, forcing me to clarify assertions and opinions into a coherent message. (I could say a lot more about how helpful she was, but she would rightly consider it repetitive!) Steve Fenichell helped me, a novice, through the process with the wisdom and assurance of someone who has done all this before. I'd also like to thank Andrew Wylie, the agent who put it all together, helping me to deal with the intellectual process of producing this intellectual product. Through it all, Daphne Kis has run my business, given me sage advice, and made my day-to-day life easy.

In the middle is a never-ending stream of friends and colleagues, many of them named in the book (and others who in a longer version would be). They introduced me to the Net, argued with me about it, wondered about it, and showed me how to do things and to live on it. They include Mitch Kapor, Stewart Brand, and all the other directors of the Electronic Frontier Foundation, Lori Fena, Danny Hillis, John and Ann Doerr (and Mary and Esther Doerr), Kris Olson, Brian Smith, Susan Stucky, Larry Tesler, Colleen Barton, Jerry Kaplan, Vern Raburn, Dottie Hall, Jerry Michalski, Bob and Amy Epstein, John Seely Brown, John Gage, and Jim Barksdale.

For reading various chapters in draft, I especially owe thanks to David Johnson, Shari Steele, Lorrie Faith Cranor, Dave Farber, Saul Klein, Virginia Postrel, Daphne Kis, William Kutik, Nick Donatiello, and Ira Magaziner (who was also the last of many people to advise me to write this book; after that, I decided!). Thanks also to a more recent friend and colleague, EDventure's own Kevin Werbach, who helped me with research on the updates to *Release 2.1*. My new editor, Suzanne Oakes at Broadway, likewise helped me reshape the book for its one-year-later, more-interactive upgrade format.

In Washington, my newest community, I have learned much from Mike Nelson, Sarah Carey, Jerry Berman, David Gergen, Jim Fallows, Jeff Eisenach, Larry Irving, Kay Graham, and many others. Perhaps the most important lesson is that a government is nothing more than another community, and most of its members are struggling to do the right thing (whether or not they all agree on what that is). I have met some exceptions—and mostly I learned something from them, too!

In Russia, I owe much to Anatoly Karachinsky and Nina Grigorieva, Olga Dergunova, Igor Agamirzian, Bob and Ginger Clough (honorary

Russians!), Misha and Masha Krasnov, Boris Nuraliev, Evgeny Veselov, Arkady Borkovsky, Maria Kamennova, Andrei Zotov, Sasha Galitsky, and many others. They have been patient with my naïve astonishment as I learned about life without all the luxuries, conveniences, and rules I took for granted. They have given me faith in human nature that sometimes makes me wonder why we can't do a better job of solving our own problems in the United States. They have also shown me the value of slowing down a little and spending an evening around the kitchen table.

In Europe, I have watched as new societies took shape (and as established ones resisted change). Much of the action has been not in the government per se, but among the builders of the new economic/ information infrastructure. Among those from Central Europe I am proud to count as friends and teachers are Bogdan Wisniewski, Grzeg-orz Lindenberg, Jan Krzysztof Bielecki, Tomek Siclicki, Olaf Gajl, Piotr Sienkiewicz, Marek Goschorski, Andreas Kemi, Peter Szauer, Janos Muth, Gabor Bojar, Eduard Mika, Silviu Hotaran, Julf Helsingius, and Roman Stanek. And then there's Miljenko Horvat, originally from Croatia, who transcends countries!

Other people who have helped me learn in various spheres include Jim Michaels, Jack Rosenthal, John Holland, Fred Adler, Tom Piper, and, of course, Ben Rosen.

And finally I'd like to give thanks to all the Bills I have known, for all that they have taught me.

You all know who you are.

List of URLs

Access Management Engine (AME): www.bascom.com

Alexa: www.alexa.com

AltaVista: altavista.software.digital.com

AltaVista Filtered Search Service: www.altavista.digital.com

Amazon.com: www.amazon.com

America Online Parental Controls: www.aol.com

Apple Computer: www.apple.com

The Atlantic Monthly: www.TheAtlantic.com

Barnes & Noble: www.barnesandnoble.com

BBBOnline: bbbonline.org

Berkeley Software Design, Inc.: www.bsdi.com

Bess (N2H2): www.n2h2.com

Bonus.com, the SuperSite for Kids: www.bonus.com

Bright Light Technologies: www.brightlight.com

Career Mosaic: www.careermosaic.com

Career Path: www.careerpath.com

The Center for Democracy and Technology (CDT): www.cdt.org

CitySearch: www.citysearch.com

Click and Browse Jr.: www.netwavelink.com

CNET (news): www.news.com

The Commercial Internet Exchange: www.cix.org

Compaq: www.compaq.com

CompuServe: www.compuserve.com

Consumerinfo.com: www.consumerinfo.com

Consumer.net (Russell Smith): www.consumer.net

Content Advisor: www.contentadvisor.com

Critical Path: www.criticalpath.net

Csinger, Andrew (corporate site with good links to security topics): www.xcert.com; also, articles at www.interspect.com/articles/index.html

Cyber Patrol: www.cyberpatrol.com

Cyber Promotions: www.cyberpromo.com

CYBERsitter: www.solidoak.com

CYBERSitter: www.cybersitter.com

Cyber Snoop: www.pearlsw.com

Cyberspace Law Institute: www.cli.org

Cygnus Solutions: www.cygnus.com

DéjàNews: www.dejanews.com

Delta: www.delta-air.com

Digital City: www.digitalcity.com

Disney's Daily Blast: www.disney.com

EDventure Holdings: www.edventure.com

EdView—Secure and Smart Channel to the Internet: www.edview.com

The Electronic Frontier Foundation: www.eff.org

Electronic Privacy Information Center: www.epic.org

E-Mail for All (Markle Foundation): www.iaginteractive.com/emfa

ESRB: www.esrb.org

EvaluWEB: www.sserv.com/evaluweb

Experian: www.experian.com

The Federal Communications Commission (FCC): www.fcc.gov

Federal Express: www.fedex.com

The Federal Trade Commission (FTC): www.ftc.gov

First Monday (including articles by David Sewell on the Oracle and by Michael Goldhaber on the Attention Economy): www.firstmonday.dk/issues/issue2_6/sewell/index.html; www.firstmonday.dk/issues/issue2_4/goldhaber/index.html

Forbes **magazine:** www.forbes.com

Four11: www.yahoo.com/four11

Framework for Global Electronic Commerce: www.whitehouse.gov/WH/New/Commerce

GeoCities: www.geocities.com

The Global Business Network (GBN): www.gbn.org

Goldhaber on the Attention Economy: www.firstmonday.dk

Graphisoft: www.graphisoft.com

The Guardian **(UK):** www.guardian.co.uk

GuardiaNet: www.guardianet.net

Harvard Crimson: www.thecrimson.harvard.edu/index.html

Harvard Lampoon: hcs.harvard.edu/~lampoon

I-Gear www.urlabs.com

Harvard University: www.harvard.edu

IBM: www.ibm.com

IBM Web Traffic Express: www.ics.raleigh.ibm.com

Institute for Advanced Study: www.ias.edu

Internet Alliance: www.internetalliance.org

The Internet Archive: www.archive.org

The Internet Filter: www.turnercom.com

The Internet Kids & Family Yellow Pages: www.netmom.com

The Internet Oracle: www.pcnet.com/~stenor/oracle

The Internet Privacy Working Group (IPWG): www.gatetech.edu/ditis/doc/privacy-principles.html

Jennifer Warf's Barbie Website: php.ucs.indiana.edu/~jwarf/dbarbie/html

The Kickstart Project: www.benton.org

Laura Lemay (Cartoon): www.lne.com/lemay/cartoon.jpg

The Learning Company (Cyber Patrol): www.learningco.com

Lotus: www.lotus.com

Markle Foundation: www.markle.org

Mattel's Barbie Website: www.Barbie.com

MCI Mail: www.MCImail.com

Microsoft: www.microsoft.com

N2H2: www.n2h2.com

NetDay: www.NetDay.org

NetFilter: www.netfilter.com

Net Nanny: www.netnanny.com

Net Rated: www.netrated.com

Netscape: www.netscape.com

Net Shepherd: www.netshepherd.com

Net Shepherd World Opinion Rating Service: www.netshepherd.com

Network Abuse Clearinghouse: www.abuse.net

Network Solutions Inc.: netsol.com

New York Times: www.nytimes.com

Onsale: www.onsale.com

Pathfinder: www.pathfinder.com

Peacefire: www.peacefire.org

PlanetView/PlanetWeb: www.planetview.com

Platform for Internet Content Selection (PICS): www.w3.org/ dPICS

Platform for Privacy Preferences Project: www.w3.org/P3

Playboy: www.playboy.com

Poland Online: www.pol.pl

Project 2000 (Owens Graduate School of Management, Vanderbilt University): www.2000.ogsm.vanderbilt.edu

Realtime Blackhole List: maps.vix.com/rbl

Reason Foundation/Magazine: www.reason.org

The Recreational Software Advisory Council (RSAC): www. rsac.org

Release 2.0: www.Release2-0.com

RSACi: www.rsac.org

SafeSurf: www.safesurf.com

The Santa Fe Institute: www.santafe.edu

Scala ECE: www.scala.hu

The Scala Job Bank: www.scala.hu/job-bank

Scholastic Network: www.scholasticnetwork.com

Science Applications International Corporation (SAIC): www. saic.com

Scientific American: www.sciam.com

The Securities and Exchange Commission (SEC): www.sec.gov

Sendmail, Inc.: www.sendmail.com

Sidewalk: www.sidewalk.com

Slate: www.slate.com

SmartFilter: www.smartfilter.com

Smart Valley: www.svi.org

SurfWatch: www.surfwatch.com

Tech for Kids (survey of filtering tools): www.research.att.com/ projects/tech4kids

Ticketmaster: www.ticketmaster.com

TotalNews: totalnews.com

TRUSTe: www.truste.org

Unsolicited commercial e-mail: uce@ftc.gov

VeriSign: www.verisign.com

Wall Street Journal: www.wsj.com

WatchGuard SchoolMate: www.watchguard.com/sm.html

WebChaperone with iCRT: www.webchaperone.com

WebSENSE: www.websense.com

The WELL: www.well.com

The White House (U.S.): www.whitehouse.gov

Wired **magazine:** www.wired.com

Wisewire: www.wisewire.com

The World Wide Web Consortium (W3C): www.w3.org

Yahooligans!: www.yahooligans.com

Index